EVERYMAN, I will go with thee,
and be thy guide,
In thy most need to go by thy side

The Buddha's Philosophy of Man

Early Indian Buddhist Dialogues

Arranged and edited by
Trevor Ling
Professor of Comparative Religion,
University of Manchester

Dent London, Melbourne and Toronto
EVERYMAN'S LIBRARY

Phototypeset in 9/10½ VIP Sabon by
Inforum Ltd, Portsmouth
Printed and bound in Great Britain by
Cox & Wyman Ltd, Reading, for
J.M. Dent & Sons Ltd
Aldine House, 33 Welbeck Street, London W1M 8LX
First published in Everyman Paperback, 1981

British Library Cataloguing in Publication Data

Suttapitaka. *English Selections*. – (Everyman's library)
  Buddhist dialogues.
  1. Hinayana Buddhism
  I. Buddhist dialogues   II. Ling, Trevor
  III. Series
  294.3'823   BQ1192.E53

  ISBN 0–460–01247–9

Contents

Part III The Last Days

Scenes of the Dialogues

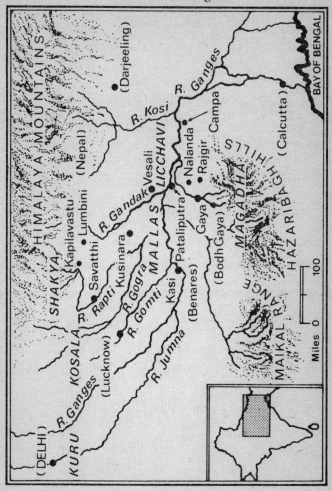

KEY
Kingdoms and republics are in capital letters.
Modern names are in brackets.

For Jeanne

Introduction

The Buddha in His Own Words

Who was the Buddha? No one can say with certainty. For 'Buddha' in the tradition in which the word is found is a generic title. There has been a long series of Buddhas in the past, and there will presumably be a long series of them in the future: such is the Buddhist view. Moreover, the person of the Buddha is of less importance than his message. The doctrine, or *Dhamma*, is the centre of interest for the Buddhist; the teacher is esteemed for the doctrine, which in every age, at a time when it has been forgotten and neglected, he reintroduces. The Dhamma is, so to speak, eternal; the rediscoverer and revealer of the doctrine to humankind in each age bears a strong resemblance to all his predecessors, according to Buddhists. In view of the immensity of the periods of time which are envisaged in this Buddhist philosophy of history it is difficult to know what the evidence might be which would support these claims. The Buddhist answer is one which removes the question from the realm of historical inquiry; such knowledge is of a metaphysical, indeed, gnostic kind: that this *is* the case is revealed by Buddhas.

In the present period of the world's history, it is claimed, the revealer of the Dhamma was a Buddha who lived and taught in northern India in the sixth and fifth centuries BC. The date for the end of his life which is most generally accepted among Indian historians (on the basis of the relations between the Buddha and known figures of Indian history, particularly the rulers of north India) is 486 BC. The Buddhist texts assert that at his passing away into *parinibbana* (complete *nibbana*; or in Sanskrit, *nirvana*) it was fifty-one years since he had gone out, at the age of twenty-nine, from the normal life of a householder to the homeless life of the ascetic wanderer.[1] This gives us the neat figure of eighty as the length of his life; but as A. K. Warder has pointed out, it is possible that this figure is reached by an interpolation in the text made in order to reconcile Buddhist and Brahmanical traditions concerning the life of Bimbisara, the ruler of Magadha, who was also a contemporary of the Buddha.[2]

The latter is known by various other names. One of these is 'Shakyamuni', that is, the sage (*muni*) of the Shakya state, in those days a small republic at the foot of the Himalayas, in what is now Nepal. Another name is 'Gotama',[3] the name of the clan to which he belonged. Another is his personal name, 'Siddhatta' (Sanskrit, *Siddharta*) used in Buddhist tradition mainly for the period of his youth and householder's life. The name 'Siddhatta' indicates that at his birth 'all enterprises succeeded'.[4] In the Pali texts in which his teaching is contained he is generally referred to as 'Bhagavata' (Sanskrit, *Bhagavant*); the most appropriate translation equivalent to this is, in my view, 'Master', since it has the right nuance in the case of one who is presented as a philosopher rather than a divine 'lord', the latter being the significance of the title in such a word as the Indian (Hindu) epic the *Bhagavad-Gita*, the 'Song of the Lord'. Occasionally the Buddha is represented in the texts as referring to himself as the 'Tathagata', a term for which it is virtually impossible to find a satisfactory translation equivalent. Literally it means 'the thus-gone' (*tatha-gata*) or 'the thus-come' (*tatha-agata*). The question of 'thus-ness' receives fuller treatment in the Sanskrit tradition,[5] but this is outside the scope of our present concern, which is with the Pali canon. It is extremely rare in the Pali text to find anyone but the Buddha himself using this title, Tatha-gata, in referring to him.

We are dealing, therefore, with a figure in a tradition, a figure whose historical particularity is somewhat blurred by the tradition itself, and whose primary importance resides in the doctrine which he teaches. The doctrine is what matters, according to Buddhists. If no biographical information whatsoever had been provided concerning 'the Buddha', that is, the one who is understood to have reintroduced this doctrine most recently, it would, presumably, be necessary to invent it: at least, that is the view of some Buddhists.[6] We are not compelled to adopt such a view, however. For the possibility exists that what we have in the 'Buddha-word'[7] is the product of a philosophical *school* in ancient India. This cannot easily be ruled out,[8] and much historical-critical investigation of the texts (of the kind that has been carried out on the Hebrew and Christian biblical texts) would be necessary before this kind of issue could even begin to be resolved. So far, there is little evidence of historical and form-criticism of the Pali texts which could compare in extent and thoroughness with Western theological *Form-geschichte*. For the most part the Pali texts are used in as literalist and fundamentalist a way as, it must be admitted, the biblical texts are in the West by the majority of their readers. The preoccupations of modern students of the Buddhist texts are more likely to be mystical and metaphysical than historical and critical. However, the words of the Indian Pali canonical trad-ition, astronomical in number as they are, do present a reason-ably consistent position, not only in matters metaphysical and psychological but also with regard to ethical and social affairs. Both these aspects of early Buddhism are dealt with in the collection of texts known as the 'Digha Nikaya'. Literally this means the group (*nikaya*) of long (*digha*) discourses or dia-logues. In spite of its importance as a source of the Pali Buddhist tradition the Digha Nikaya is not easy to come by in an English translation,[9] and it is with the discourses of the Digha Nikaya that we shall, therefore, be concerned. Such matters are, of course, dealt with also in the other four collections which, with the Digha Nikaya, go to make up the Sutta section of the Pali canon, but the Digha discourses have a corporate character, both in the sense that they evidently are the product of one school, or have been preserved together by one distinct con-fraternity, and also that in this collection is found within a modest compass (in terms of Buddhist literature) a balance of metaphysical and ethical issues. The Digha Nikaya comes first in order of the five Nikayas of the Pali canon; this order, it is said, is probably also the order of authenticity among the Nikayas.[10]

The Nature of Early Buddhist Thought

Early Buddhist philosophy comes to us in the form of dialogues.

These are of a popular character, superficially, although they are interconnected by the use that is made in one Dialogue of some special term the meaning of which has been expounded in another Dialogue. The more one reads of these Dialogues, therefore, the more familiar one becomes with the range of teaching which they contain, and the less likely to overlook the significance of allusions and references which are not always fully explained in every context.

The dialogue form in which early Buddhist teaching is contained is known as a *Sutta*. This Pali word, from a common Indo-European stock, is related to Latin 'sutura' and the English word 'suture'; the underlying common idea is that of a thread, and of stitching. The Pali Suttas are discourses in which a number of topics are 'threaded' together by some basic element of Buddhist teaching. An example is the *Samanna-phala Sutta*, which brings together various ideas about the rewards, or 'fruit' (*phala*) which were thought to come from the life of the wandering ascetic (*samanna*) in ancient India.

The scene for these discourses is northern India in the latter part of the sixth century BC and the early part of the fifth. At that time considerable social and political changes were taking place: the older small-scale, simple society was giving way to the large-scale, more complex society which was associated with the spread of monarchical government. Questions concerning the nature and meaning of human life perhaps tend to be raised more readily when old ways are disappearing, and when the security of what is familiar and well known is threatened or even shattered by new, unknown and apparently uncontrollable forces. A glimpse of this kind of transition is given us in the opening paragraphs of the *Maha Parinibbana Sutta*, where the plans of the 'all-conquering' raja Ajatasattu are described, to invade and conquer the territory of the Vajjian confederacy, one of the few remaining republican areas of the Ganges plain at that time. Such drastic irruptions into the older, established order of things would have severely undermined the norms of human conduct and the patterns of social relationships. It is in such a context that these early Buddhist Dialogues have to be seen. They are, that is to say, discourses on ethics, values, and attitudes set within the framework of a religious account of the human condition.

To say 'religious', in speaking of early Buddhist philosophy, may raise some eyebrows. Buddhism is sometimes said to be atheistic. That is to say, it is a system of thought and behaviour which does not include *in any essential way* the notion of an almighty god. But the gods are very much a part of the scenery in early Buddhism, as Dr Marasinghe of Sri Lanka has shown convincingly.[11] And Mara the Evil One, the ever-present tempter, the 'killer', is also a familiar figure.[12] To the early Buddhists the gods (*devas*) were inhabitants of the heavens, the leader among them (*devanam indo*) being Sakka, who was regarded by the early Buddhists 'as a god of high character, kindly and just, but not perfect, and not very intelligent'.[13] Certainly Sakka and the other devas are not crucial to the Buddhist prescription for self-understanding and salvation. The goal, the *summum bonum*, the reality to which early Buddhist religious philosophy points is not often mentioned. But although it is mentioned rarely, it is frequently hinted at. In direct terms it is called *nibbana*. It is described in a passage in a text called Udana:

> Monks, there is a not-born, a not-become, a not-made, a not-compounded. Monks, if that unborn, not-become, not-made, not-compounded were not, there would be apparent no escape from this, here, that is born, become, made, compounded.

One kind of misapprehension concerning early Buddhist thought, therefore, would be to say that it is atheistic and materialistic. Avoiding this error some observers have called it 'mystical', and have added (as though it followed naturally), 'a-social'.[14] Now there is some evidence that in the very earliest period of the development of what eventually becomes known as Buddhism the achievement of the Buddhist goal, that is, *bodhi* – 'enlightenment' or 'awakenment' – was thought of as an entirely individualistic, lone enterprise; the condition of bodhi was, it seems, a lone condition, conveyed by no one else and communicated to no one else. In the earliest Pali sources the term *muni* appears to have been used to refer to anyone who was enlightened (*buddha*). The muni was, characteristically, the 'lone wayfarer'. The nature of the Buddhist life as a life *alone* is emphasized in an early text, the *Khaggavisana Sutta*.[15] However, as soon as one practitioner of the homeless life had begun to commend it to others, and once the muni as a solitary figure (who by himself had come to the realization of bodhi) has given place, to some extent at least, to *communication between* such a practitioner and other men, the stage represented by the Digha Nikaya has been reached, with its emphasis on the *didactic* nature of the dialogues between the Shakyamuni and various inquirers who are represented as having sought him out to inquire of him. When that stage has been reached we have to regard early Buddhism as having become *social* in nature. Being a Buddhist then entailed social communication; the Dhamma was henceforth transmitted by teaching, by exhortation, and eventually this took place in the context of fixed residence. Even though the Sangha at the earliest period may or may not have been a bounded community, it was a *community,* and therefore it had a certain social character. Before long it developed beyond that stage, and became a community of *bhikkhus* existing in regular dependence on neighbouring householders, devotees and lay followers. With this development went also a concern with the quality of the life lived by lay people, a concern which the *Sigalavada Sutta* exemplifies.

Yet even nowadays it is sometimes said that Buddhism has no concern with the *social* dimension of life. If this is not explicitly stated it is often implied. This denial of a social dimension to their lives on the part of those who claim to be Buddhist is really rather curious, for the notion of an *un-social Buddhist* is a contradiction in terms. The Buddhist is one who has accepted, in theory at least, that the isolated *individual* is a fiction. What John Donne perceived, that no man is an island entire unto himself, had already been perceived over two thousand years before by the Buddha. This is implied in the two complementary aspects of Buddhist philosophy: (1) analysis of all existing entities, including a so-called 'individual', into constituent physical and mental elements, and (2) the complex relations, actual or potential, between the various elements thus discovered. This is most manifest at the level of consciousness. Consciousness of external objects, cognized by the five senses and the mind, entails also reactions to them. This means that interaction between human persons (understood as present but impermanent aggregates of physical and mental elements) is inescapable. Inescapable, that is, for all except the lone, meditating hermit who gathers from the wilds whatever he eats and drinks and wears. It is significant that what seems to have been the ideal type at some very early stage of Buddhist history, was almost *but not entirely* superseded by the norm of life in the Sangha in the Order of 'Sharesmen', or bhikkhus, in other words, life in a community.

Buddhism is, among other things, an attempt to deal with the human disease of what may be called 'pathological individualism'. Individualism, whether in sixth-century BC India or in twentieth-century Europe, places limits on consciousness, on relations, on love, on understanding, on life itself, and the way of the Buddha is a way of eliminating these limits.

The weakening of the sense of individualism, or the fiction of the self-sufficient 'individual', was assisted by certain positive developments within the Buddhist tradition. These can be broadly summarized as (1) social relations within the Sangha, (2) social relations among lay people, and (3) social relations between the Sangha and lay people. The first is dealt with in the *Patimokkha*, the code of conduct for bhikkhus. The second is dealt with in various places in the Suttas, notably in the *Sigalavada Sutta*. The third can be traced in a multitude of ways, in the Suttas and chronicles and commentarial literature, and in Buddhist history, perhaps most clearly and most notably in the India of Ashoka after the Kalinga war, that is, the Ashoka of the edicts and inscriptions (third century BC). What Ashoka was primarily concerned with as emperor was the social communication and *realization* of dhamma. In *that* context 'dhamma' is not necessarily specifically Buddhist Dhamma, but moral principles generally. What Ashoka sought to achieve, as a ruler who was in sympathy with Buddhist values and aims, was to facilitate the pursuit of those aims and the realization of those values by promoting the right kind of conditions of life for the maximum possible number of his subjects.

Ashoka's various measures were clearly intended to bring into being a certain kind of society. It would be characterized by a social order unlike any which had characterized earlier Indian societies. In that sense what Ashoka aspired to do and in a large measure achieved, was a social revolution, and was probably largely inspired by Buddhist values and the pursuit of Buddhist aims. It is, however, important to emphasize that what Ashoka created was *not* a 'Buddhist State' in the modern sense.

The Digha Nikaya, whatever date may be assigned to the recension of it which forms the basis of the modern text, provides evidence of a period when the nature of Buddhist practice and social interaction justifies one in speaking of Buddhist *ethics,* both for bhikkhus and for householders. It is important to notice that at this stage one is not justified in speaking of Buddhist *politics*. In fact the Suttas of the Digha Nikaya reveal at best a mildly ironical attitude towards political *power,* and often an implied dismissal of the pretensions of political rulers, on the grounds that these are irrelevant to the real issues confronting human beings.

Kingship in the Pali Canon

A summary account of some of the relevant passages is all that is required here in order to bring out the main pattern.

In some places in the canon monarchy appears in a distinctly unfavourable light, notably in the *Maha Parinibbana Sutta*. The Buddha, staying at the royal capital of Magadha (at that time, still Rajagaha) received a message from the 'all-conquering' king, Ajatasattu, asking for his comment on the proposed all-out military campaign against the Vajjian federation which the king was proposing to make. As this was one of the few republican federations which by that time had survived the onslaught of monarchical attack in northern India, the narrative carries the, only slightly concealed, implication, 'What kind of future can there be for republican federations?' and the realistic answer, equally clear to the listener, who knew what the outcome of the campaign had been, would be: 'Virtually none.' Yet the Buddha is represented as commending the Vajjian tradition: he commends it as the model for bhikkhus to follow, in a discussion of the matter with his disciples a little later. But to the king's messenger he declares concerning the Vajjians that they will not be overcome unless they should abandon their well established democratic customs and traditions. The brahman messenger comments that they can only be overcome, then, by 'persuasion', possibly meaning bribery or corruption of some of their members, or by the sowing of seeds of dissension among them. In the subsequent discussion with the bhikkhus the Buddha declares that if they too maintain their traditions of meeting regularly in council, so too their growth rather than their decline may be confidently expected. That is to say, the listener is to understand, the bhikkhus are to become the residual legatees of the republican federations – of which the Buddha's clansmen had formed part before monarchy overtook them, as it had most of the republics of the north Indian plain. A distinction, and indeed an opposition, is thus implied between monarchy and the old republican sanghas; is it possible also that an opposition between monarchy and the new Sangha is hinted at in these words? It is certainly clear which of the two forms of government is regarded more favourably. The significance of this point is enhanced when it is remembered that this episode, with which the *Maha Parinibbana Sutta* opens, is probably among the older portions of the canon and therefore is more likely to reflect an early Buddhist attitude to kingship.

However, in the political conditions which prevailed in northern India at that time, Buddhist compromise with monarchy was virtually inescapable. Even so, the *Agganna Sutta* sets out a view of the origin of the institution of kingship which has a bearing on the Buddhist attitude in the sense of indicating what kind of kingship Buddhists could support; that is, a form of kingship which had originated in a social contract. The Sutta describes how the first ruler of men was *chosen* by the whole people, in order that he should maintain justice and order among them. He was the one 'agreed upon' or '*authorized*' to rule, *Maha Sammata*. This is rather different from the Brahmanical concept of kingship, in which the king had a 'cosmic and divine role', in Heine-Geldern's words, and 'was considered to be either an incarnation of a god or a descendant from a god or both'.[16]

It may be agreed, therefore, that the Buddha preferred a republican form of government but accepted monarchy, as A. K. Warder concludes, 'as a necessary evil in a degenerate period of history' when republican governments were unlikely to be able to withstand the aggressive new force of strongly centralized monarchical power.[17] Nevertheless, there was still a choice between different styles of kingship. It has been argued that the Shakyas themselves had adopted a modified form of republican government, one that was more oligarchical in style, mid-way between republican and monarchical.[18] The references to the Buddha's father as 'raja' found in the *Mahavastu*[19] and other Sanskrit sources are understandable as a later, honorific exaggeration of the nature of Suddhodana's position.

Actual examples of kingship which in the Pali canon appear to be regarded as commendable are, if any, those of Bimbisara, King of Magadha, and Pasenadi, King of Kosala. The nature of the relationship which is portrayed between the Buddha and these two is of a kind which, if it is taken in conjunction with the other references to kingship in the earlier passages of the canon, suggests that this represents the best kind of *modus vivendi* between Sangha and State that can be expected, and that bhikkhus could do no more than encourage and facilitate the establishment of similar close relationships of this sort with contemporary rulers, and should certainly do no less. This appears from the evidence of the edicts and inscriptions to have been the nature of the relationship between Ashoka and the Sangha, rather than the partisan position taken up by Ashoka according to the chronicles; this latter then becomes the model for Sinhalese Buddhist kingship and nationalism.

The Buddha himself is depicted in the canon as one who could have become either a 'Cakkavatti' (Sanskrit, *Cakravartin*) or a Buddha. Another perspective on this relationship which the canon affords is that Buddha and Cakkavatti, as eternal types, are parallel in a number of respects: both are born into the world for the profit and happiness and welfare of the many; both are born as extraordinary human beings; the death of both is regretted by many people; and both are worthy of *stupas*.[20] The strong degree of resemblance between them which is thus established, and what U.N. Ghoshal has called their 'jointly unique role as universal benefactors'[21] throws an additional light on the early Buddhist conception of monarchy. A narrow and unperceptive interpretation of these words might produce the view that they indicate approval of an institutional link between secular government and Sangha. But this is ruled out by the tenor of other references in the canon to the 'rolling of the wheel of Dhamma'. In the Anguttara Nikaya, the Buddha is represented as declaring to his followers: 'Bhikkhus, the king who rolls the wheel of state, a Dhamma-man, a Dhamma-King, rolls indeed no unroyal wheel.' For, as he goes on to make clear in answer to the question 'who is the ruler of the king?' – 'It is Dhamma, O bhikkhu!'[22] The ideal of kingship portrayed here is of the king as subordinate to one power only, that of universal Dhamma. It is clear that it is an *ideal* which is portrayed, and that a Dhamma-raja's rule partakes of a universal quality; for even a plurality of Dhamma-rajas (that is, in various local states), would in fact be exercising an identical rule which would be in effect a universal Dhammarajja. In historical *reality* neighbouring 'Buddhist' kings have not ruled thus in harmony; not infrequently there has been conflict.[23]

The close association which existed between the Buddha and Bimbisara and Pasenadi suggests also that this may have provided the background against which some of the Buddha's ideas concerning good government were formulated. His familiarity with these two monarchs especially, as well as his own early experiences in Kapilavatthu, may well have contributed to or have shaped in certain ways the ideas found in the Kutadanta and other suttas concerning wise government. In the *Kutadanta Sutta* the dilemma of a ruler faced with a serious law and order problem in his realm is considered. The question examined is whether it would be more effective to take harsh, punitive measures, 'by degradation and banishment, and fines and bonds and death', or to adopt another method, that of positive, constructive action which nowadays would be called a development programme, that is, one aimed at increased agricultural production, capital grants for the development of trade, and improved administration. In the case which is being described the latter alternative was followed and proved highly successful. Thus, while the Buddha appears to have preferred republican government, as we have already noted, he appears also to have accepted the fact that in circumstances such as those which had now developed in India, monarchy was unavoidable.

This being the case, his view was that benevolent autocracy was to be commended: such would be wise kingly policy and would redound to the king's good as well as to his people's. A feature of such benevolent autocracy, the Sutta suggests, would be the democratic manner in which policy decisions would be reached, through the king's heeding 'the recommendations of the assemblies of his subjects', as A. K. Warder puts it.[24]

It is noteworthy, however, that the king is not represented as a Buddhist, or even, like Bimbisara and Pasenadi, one who consulted bhikkhus. His chaplain is described as a *brahman*. It has to be remembered, however, that the view of things which emerges from the Suttas as desirable is not a specifically *Buddhist* state, but what today would be called a religiously plural society in which 'brahman' would designate one who was brahman by worth, not by birth; a society in which the *shramana*/brahman distinction had been collapsed and the brahman assimilated to the shramana, identified with him in 'a simple life of meditation and virtuous, tolerant and gentle conduct'.[25] The ideal state is not, if one may put it thus, a denominationally, or institutionally *Buddhist* state, and the ideal man of Dhamma is not the bhikkhu but the reformed brahman.

Buddhism is, thus, primarily philosophical in character. That is to say it is in essence a philosophical system having (like some other philosophical systems) strong psychological concerns, and also (unlike some other systems) an implied concern with social relations. In the Ashokan period, and to a much greater extent afterwards, it took on also the character of a devotional cult, with associated rituals and, later, a mythology which grew more and more elaborate as time went by. This development is defended by some Buddhologists on the grounds that it was necessary in order to secure the allegiance of the common people and to give them some way of expressing their support for Buddhist values. This may or may not seem to be a convincing explanatory account of the transformation (or what Max Weber called the 'ritualization') of Buddhism. In any case, it has little relevance today. What is more, there is evidence of a strongly critical attitude in early Buddhism towards religious rituals, which are regarded as, at best, activities to be tolerated but not endorsed, certainly to be replaced by more profitable Buddhistic activities wherever possible or appropriate, and to be directly challenged in some cases, such as the elaborate and costly performance of royal Brahmanism.[26] On the other hand, the constructive application of the Buddhist understanding of human existence to the conditions of life under which the majority of people lived was regarded as a serious concern, for which support was to be sought from monarchs such as Bimbisara and Ashoka, to whom advice was to be offered concerning ways and means of securing the optimum conditions for the pursuit of Buddhist aims, by ensuring that the maximum number of people lived neither in poverty nor in excessive luxury. A distinguished modern historian of Indian political thought has observed that the most important contribution which Buddhists made to ancient India was their 'total' application of the principles of Dhamma to the various branches of the king's internal and foreign administration. Indeed, one of the major grounds of Buddhist criticism of the costly Brahmanical priestly performance was the waste of economic resources which these entailed; the economic welfare of his people should, they urged, be a primary concern of a wise king.

Social, but not Political

All this may at first seem to justify the uneasiness felt by those Buddhists who fear that down this road lies the way to Buddhist politics. I repeat that it is not so. Thus, while Buddhist theory and practice in ancient India was in certain respects revolutionary in character, in that it entailed a philosophy of social relations and a public as well as a private ethic, the political implementation of this philosophy was not held to be a matter for Buddhists, *qua Buddhists*. There was no explicit political philosophy or political programme which the Buddhist movement itself was committed to put into practice. There is, in fact, in early Buddhism a certain ambiguity towards political power in India. This may perhaps be explained to some extent by the preference which, as I suggested earlier, is sometimes hinted at in the Pali texts for a republican form of government of the kind which had been known in the old tribal republics such as those of the Shakyas, the Vajjis, and so on. What Buddhists were confronted with in India was not a republican form of government but monarchy, and monarchy of a very powerful kind which was associated with many of the developments in social life (such as the increased spirit of individualism) to which Buddhism was opposed. Nevertheless the empirical need for government is recognized; Buddhists were not anarchists. The policy which most commonly seems to have been followed, to the time of Ashoka at least, was that the monarch should be helped, supported and advised by Buddhists, wherever he showed himself open to such cooperation.

The Emergence of Buddhist Ritual

Although Buddhism was primarily philosophical in character, nevertheless in the earliest days it possessed a considerable potential as a religious cult. The *Maha Parinibbana Sutta* ends with an account of the events which followed the Buddha's decease. Such was the respect, indeed veneration, which a religious teacher was afforded in India (and often still is) that the highly formalized rituals of courtesy which characterized any approach to the teacher during his lifetime very easily assumed the character of devotional rituals, addressed to some symbolic representation of the teacher, after his removal from the earthly scene.

To this consideration has to be added the fact that the Buddha himself is regarded, in the tradition, as having found religious shrines attractive places, delightful to visit (as the *Maha Parinibbana Sutta*, Chapter 3, mentions), and conducive to good meditation. Hence we find that in Chapter 5 of the *Maha Parinibbana Sutta* the Buddha is represented as having given instructions that after his decease his remains should be cremated and a memorial mound, or *stupa*, should be erected at the cross-roads, in the same way that the remains of a Universal Monarch, or *Cakkavatti*, were treated, the stupa thereafter becoming a place where people would offer garlands of flowers and would pay their respects, and become 'calm in heart'. The final chapter of the *Maha Parinibbana Sutta* records that this is what happened after the Buddha's decease; the body was cremated and the ashes were divided into eight portions, each portion being received by those who had some special claim to this great honour; over each portion a stupa was built. Two more stupas were built, one over the vessel in which the ashes had been collected, and one over the embers. Thus, according to the tradition, ten Buddhist shrines were instituted very soon after the Parinibbana. In addition to these, three other places became shrines, places where Buddhists might find inspiration: the place of the Buddha's birth at Lumbini, in the foothills; the place of his enlightenment, on the bank of the Neranjara river, in what is now called Bodh-Gaya, in Bihar; and the place of the first proclamation of the Dhamma after his enlightenment, in a park at Sarnath, near Varanasi (Benares). It seems likely that the custom of venerating these places associated with the Buddha would have developed spontaneously, in keeping with the extreme reverence which the Suttas suggest was shown to him in his lifetime. The justification of the custom by means of a saying about such matters attributed to the Buddha would not be without parallel in other religious traditions. What is undeniable is that by the time of the emperor Ashoka, some two centuries after the Parinibbana, the cult of stupas was well established, as archaeological evidence indicates. The wandering religious philosopher had soon become the founder of a new religion, and the recipient of cultic honours.

The Text

When I was invited to undertake this work I had in mind to prepare a selection of Suttas from the Digha Nikaya which are otherwise, as I have said, not easily available in English, and to do so by using the Rhys Davids's translation, with such minor revisions of terminology as seemed necessary or appropriate, having recourse to the Pali text.[27] As soon as I embarked on this task, however, it became clear that the revision would need to be more extensive than I had expected. For one thing I became increasingly impressed by the unsuitability of the English style, which the translators had evidently borrowed from the King James version of the Bible. Such expressions as, 'And then at eventide'; 'Yea, verily, lord, the brahmins do blame and revile us'; 'The manner of the rising up thereof '; 'The night is far spent'; 'Whatsoever a man hath . . .' and so on are not normal, good English usage of the twentieth century. They *sound* archaic, now possibly more than in the 1890s, when the Rhys Davids were doing their work (although the Revised Version of the Bible was by then available to them as an example). And however suitable such language may seem to those of our contemporaries who, nearly a century later, like to hear the Bible (a collection of mainly Hebrew and Greek documents) misrepresented by the use of obsolete English, it is certainly inappropriate in representing the style of speech which the Buddhist Dialogues employed, for the latter was of a kind that would be understood by ordinary people; it was not the high-flown, if beautiful, Sanskrit of the brahmans; indeed the tradition is that the Buddha explicitly forbade his followers to use the language of the brahman class in Buddhist discourse.

Apart from English style, however, it was clear also that there is now more agreement concerning the acceptable translation equivalents of many Pali terms than existed in the 1890s. The revision of the text thus began to assume the proportions of a fairly extensive re-translation. In one case, that of the *Maha Satipatthana Sutta*, I have had to produce what is virtually a fresh translation, for better or for worse. Although I have retained some of the original footnotes (these are indicated by the initials RD in brackets), I have also added a few new footnotes.

The reader may often feel that the text is extremely repetitive. In fact, the version given here is considerably less so than the original. It has to be remembered that for a long period these Dialogues were transmitted orally from one generation of bhikkhus to another (as was most pre-modern Indian literature), and that by this method of constantly repeating long and often complicated passages they were able to engrave the teaching more sharply upon their memories.

In a few cases, where the attempt to translate a term is notoriously difficult, I have retained the original, but these are limited to words such as 'bhikkhu' and 'dhamma', which tend to be retained among Buddhists or students of Buddhism when they are otherwise speaking English. In some cases I have followed Rhys Davids's rendering of 'dhamma' as 'Truth'. One phrase which is archaic in sound I *have* retained: the translation of the Pali words *evam me sutam*, with which each Sutta opens, by the phrase 'Thus have I heard'. It is open to question whether the Pali word 'sutam' is used intentionally in order to suggest the idea that all that follows is of a *shruti* nature, that is to say, belongs to a class of literature which, in Sanskrit, is classified as 'shruti' (divinely heard) and is therefore regarded as more authoritative and more sacred than what is *smriti* (remembered). But even if the intention was not present, this archaic-sounding phrase provides a useful reminder that these discourses are now, and have been for many centuries, regarded by Buddhists as highly *venerable,* if nothing more. When other archaisms have been eliminated the effect is to lay emphasis upon this remaining one, and I have therefore retained it, for, unlike some of the others, it does not obscure the meaning, and on the other hand it does remind us that for the people who preserved these ancient discourses they possessed a value that set them apart from all other discourse. For this reason alone they deserve our attention.

Manchester, 1981 Trevor Ling

1 See below: *Maha Parinibbana Sutta,* Chapter 5, paragraph 27.

2 A. K. Warder, *Indian Buddhism,* 1970, p. 44.

3 'Gautama' in Sanskrit. Generally, however, Pali terms will be used here.

4 Malalasekera, *DPPN* (see Bibliography), II, 1135.

5 In the *Astasahasrika-Prajnaparamita* (The Eight Thousand Perfections of Understanding); for an introductory account see Warder, op. cit., p. 364 ff.; for 'thus-ness' p. 370 ff.

6 It was, for example, the view of the late Edward Conze.

7 *Buddha-vac,* the term sometimes used for referring to all the teachings and sayings of 'the Buddha' contained in the canon.

8 In the terminology used by Edward Conze the Pali canon represents the 'Old Wisdom School', the *Theravada,* which he contrasts with the 'New Wisdom School' of the *Mahayana*, whose

doctrines are contained in Sanskrit Sutras and which, like the Pali canon, is represented also as the 'word' of the Buddha.

9   The standard full translation is that of T. W. and C.A.F. Rhys Davids, in three volumes, *Dialogues of the Buddha,* 1910 (reprinted 1966). A translation of extracts was made by A.A.G. Bennett, *Long Discourses of the Buddha,* Bombay, undated.

10 Warder, op. cit., p. 202 ff.

11 M. M. J. Marasinghe, *Gods in Early Buddhism: A Study in their social and mythological milieu as depicted in the Nikayas of the Pali Canon,* Colombo, 1974.

12 In the present collection, see especially the *Maha Parinibbana Sutta.*

13 Malalasekera, *DPPN,* II, 959.

14 Max Weber, *The Religion of India,* trs. 1958, p. 255.

15 A text, generally agreed to be very early, which forms part of the *Sutta Nipata.* See *Woven Cadences,* trs. E. M. Hare.

16 R. Heine-Geldern, *Conceptions of State and Kingship in Southeast Asia,* 1956, pp. 6, 7.

17 Warder, op. cit., p. 173.

18 See Trevor Ling, *The Buddha,* 1973, pp. 107–11.

19 *Mahavastu,* II, 15ff.

20 *Anguttara,* I, 76 ff.

21 U. N. Ghoshal, *A History of Indian Political Ideas,* 1959, p. 79.

22 *Gradual Sayings,* III, 144 ff.

23 In Burma, Thailand, Laos and Cambodia, for example. See Trevor Ling, *Buddhism, Imperialism and War: Burma and Thailand in Modern History,* 1979, *passim.*

24 Warder, op. cit., p. 173.

25 ibid., p. 180.

26 See, for example, the *Kutadanta Sutta.*

27 The text used is that of the Pali Text Society (see Bibliography).

The Dialogues

The Dialogues which have been selected and are presented here constitute only ten of the thirty-four which go to make up the collection of long discourses known in Pali as the Digha Nikaya or 'Collection of Long (Discourses)'. In each case the participants and the scene of the Dialogue differ: we have Ajatasattu, the raja of Magadha, in the forest outside Rajgir, the capital; a brahman named Sonadanda who lived in Campa, in eastern Bihar; a wandering ascetic philosopher at Savatthi; a brahman named Lohicca; the Buddha's disciples in the land of the Kurus; a brahman named Kutadanta in a village in Magadha; a Buddhist probationer at Savatthi; Buddhist disciples in Magadha; and a young householder in the capital of Magadha. The long Sutta concerning the last days of the Buddha's life with which this selection ends, the *Maha Parinibbana Sutta,* moves on steadily from one scene to another as the Buddha and the disciples make their last journey together; the Buddha's decease, in the little jungle town of Kusinara, is all the time sensed as coming nearer, and as the location of the Parinibbana is approached, the event itself dominates the narrative and enhances the teaching, especially its theme of universal impermanence.

It should be emphasized that the order in which the Suttas are arranged here is not traditional, but has been adopted for editorial convenience. The first five Suttas, forming Part I, present some of the central doctrines, those that are of the essence of the *philosophy* of the Theravada school of Sri Lanka, Burma and Thailand, for whom this Pali literature is authoritative. The next four Suttas, which form Part II, contain teaching which, directly or indirectly, points to certain *social implications* of the Buddhist way as it is here envisaged. The long, final Sutta, which constitutes the whole of Part III, has for its central theme that of *devotion* to the Buddha during his lifetime and to his relics after his Parinibbana; it exemplifies also the element of the miraculous and the supernatural as an inescapable feature of the Buddhist world view found in this literature.

PART I
Personal Being

The Fruits of the Life
of a Wandering Ascetic Philosopher
(*Samanna-phala Sutta*)

We are here introduced to the Buddha, and to one of the most important figures in northern India in the fifth century, Ajatasattu, the ruler of Magadha. His father, Bimbisara, was a friend and supporter of the Buddha. Ajatasattu, however, anxious to seize power for himself, had plotted to kill his father. The latter, hearing of the son's ambitions, abdicated in his favour. Even so, incited by a dissident Buddhist bhikkhu named Devadatta who believed that without Bimbisara's friendship the Buddha's position would be weakened, Ajatasattu was persuaded to continue with his plans to make an end of his father. Eventually he did so by imprisoning Bimbisara and starving him to death. He then helped Devadatta in various attempts to murder the Buddha. These failed, however, and later he felt remorse for his murderous activities. Ajatasattu had become ruler of Magadha eight years before the end of the Buddha's life, when the Buddha would have been about seventy-two. It was at some time during these last eight years that Ajatasattu was persuaded by his physician, Jivaka, to visit the Buddha, to inquire of him about matters on which he had already consulted other religious teachers and philosophers without receiving satisfactory replies. The *Samanna-phala Sutta* sets the scene: a bright, moonlit night, calm and warm, with Ajatasattu and his ministers seated on the upper terrace of his palace enjoying the brilliance of the moonlight. This, we are told, renewed Ajatasattu's desire to converse with some philosopher who might clear his mind of the problems that were still perplexing him. At Jivaka's suggestion, the raja and his ministers set off to visit the Buddha, who was staying in a nearby forest with a company of bhikkhus. The *contrast* between, on the one hand, the pomp surrounding the maharaja as he proceeds out to the forest, and his panic at one point when he thinks the expedition is a trap and he is to be betrayed to his enemies, and on the other the quietness and austerity and serenity of the Buddha and the bhikkhus is very clearly marked in a descriptive passage which is, of course, of Buddhist composition. In general the early Buddhist attitude to monarchy appears, from the evidence of the Pali canonical texts, to have been ambivalent at best, and sometimes unfavourable. Here we are being reminded of the violent means by which monarchs in India (as anywhere else) had very often come to power, and of the violent means they often had to use to maintain themselves in power; the end of the Sutta reveals that Ajatasattu still has his father's death on his conscience.

The nature of much of the middle portion of this Dialogue might be thought to show an excessive concern for the 'trifling matters, the minor details' (paragraph 63) of a Buddhist bhikku's life: we have what seems an endless catalogue of the 'low arts', or various folk-rituals, from which the bhikkhu was expected to abstain. However, this is the text, and these things were considered important to mention in the Buddhist community of the fifth century BC, so that it would constitute a misrepresentation of the character of the text to omit the long section (paragraphs 55 to 66) dealing with these matters in order to hurry on to what is more to the taste of modern readers who are interested in less mundane matters. Nor can it realistically be claimed that palmistry, astrology, sorcery, witchcraft, political prophecy and economic prophecy are very far removed from modern life. Incidentally, there is in this section a wealth of evidence which can be used in reconstructing the ways of life, the recreations and diversions, the important popular concerns of life in the Buddha's India.

The word *samanna* in its root meaning indicates 'generality' or 'equality'. It is used in the Dialogues often in words which are attributed to non-Buddhists, thus suggesting that in the India of the sixth century BC it indicated a general type of wandering ascetic philosopher[1] and is often linked with the term 'brahman', in much the kind of way that in Europe one might speak of 'monks and priests', either because of their similarity, or to indicate an important distinction between them. The title of this Dialogue can be rendered literally, therefore, as 'the fruits of monkhood'. But it is in fact concerned very much with the kind of life lived by the *Buddhist* samanna. All that is said of the samanna here has to be understood as referring to *both* the Buddha and his disciples; the latter are usually referred to in the Dialogues as 'bhikkhus', that is, literally 'sharesmen', those who depended for their food on the 'share' put aside for them daily by some friendly and well disposed householder, after the manner still common in Buddhist countries such as Burma. The word 'bhikkhu' is sometimes also rendered by 'almsman', indicating that he is one who lives by the almsgiving of householders and lay-people generally.

The catalogue of the 'low arts' from which a bhikkhu was expected to abstain (paragraph 55ff.) occurs within a long section which could easily exist separately from the discourse; it consists in a list of the moral precepts to which, it is said, the Buddhist bhikkhu adheres (paragraphs 52 to 61 inclusive). Most of the same list occurs in another of the dialogues (not included here) the *Brahmajala Sutta*, but in that instance the precepts enumerated are attributed to 'Gotama the Samanna'. The fact that the list of precepts is regarded as common to both Gotama (the Buddha) and to those who entered his community, and who are known as bhikkhus, indicates that both the Buddha and the bhikkhus were alike referred to by the term 'samanna', or, as I have rendered it here in three words in English (to get a translation equivalent that includes the complexity of what a samanna was), 'wandering ascetic philosopher'. It should be added that 'philosopher' is here meant in the old sense of 'one who loves *wisdom*', and not merely linguistic disputation, although the Buddhist samannas engaged in plenty of the latter; the Dialogues themselves are evidence of that.

---

1   In the text, wherever I have translated the word *samanna*, I have shortened 'wandering ascetic philosopher' to 'wandering ascetic', or simply 'ascetic'; the reader is asked to bear in mind the fuller rendering.

Thus have I heard:

1. The Master was once staying at Rajgir, in the Mango Grove belonging to Jivaka, the prince's tutor. With him were many members of the Community,[1] about twelve hundred and fifty bhikkhus. At that time Ajatasattu, the raja of Magadha, son of the princess of Videha, was seated on the upper terrace roof of his palace, surrounded by his ministers. It was the full moon night of the month when the white water-lily flowers,[2] and the raja began rhapsodizing to his friends: 'How pleasant is this moonlit night! How lovely, how fair to see, how bright and clear, how auspicious is this moonlit night! Now who is the wandering philosopher or brahman upon whom we could call, who would make our minds also clear and bright?'

2. When he had said this, one of the royal ministers replied: 'Your majesty, there is a certain Purana Kassapa, the head of a community, a man with a following, teacher of a school of thought, well known and highly honoured as the founder of an order, an ascetic for many years, and now come to a great age. It may well be, that if your majesty should visit him, Purana Kassapa would illuminate your mind.' But when this had been said Ajatasattu the raja of Magadha made no reply.

3. Then another royal minister spoke as follows: 'Your majesty, there is a certain Makkhali-Gosalo,[3] the head of a community, a man with a following [etc., as before]. It may well be, that if your majesty should visit him, Makkhali-Gosalo would illuminate your mind.'

[4–7. Again the raja made no reply, nor to four other suggestions from different royal ministers who suggested, in turn, Ajit of the hairy blanket, Pakudh of the marshland road, Sanjay of the Belatthi clan, and Niganth of the Nata clan.]

8. All this time Jivaka the prince's tutor sat in silence not far from Ajatasattu. So the raja said to him, 'You, friend Jivaka, have you nothing to say?'

'Your majesty, there is the Master, the Arahat, the Fully Awakened One; he is staying in our Mango Grove, with many members of the Community, about twelve hundred and fifty bhikkhus. Concerning the Master Gotama this good reputation has got about: 'The Master is an arahat, fully awakened, endowed with wisdom and goodness, well favoured, having supernal knowledge, without an equal as a guide to mortals, a teacher of human and celestial beings, the Awake, the bountiful.' It may well be that if your majesty should visit the Master, he would illuminate your mind.'

'In that case, friend Jivaka, have the elephant-carriages made ready.'

9. 'Just so, your majesty,' answered Jivaka the prince's tutor. He had five hundred she-elephants prepared, and the raja's state elephant, and sent word to the raja, 'Your majesty, the elephants are harnessed; all is ready for whatever is your majesty's intention.' Then the raja had five hundred women ascend the five hundred she-elephants, one on each, and he himself mounted the state elephant, and went forth, with all the majesty of a raja, accompanied by torchbearers, from Rajgir to Jivaka the tutor's Mango Grove.

10. Then, when Ajatasattu, raja of Magadha, son of the princess of Videha was not far from the Mango Grove he was seized by fear, he was terrified and his hair stood on end. Then, agitated and frightened he said to Jivaka: 'You are not trying to trick me, are you, friend Jivaka? You are not deceiving me, are you, friend Jivaka? You are not betraying me to my enemies, are you, friend Jivaka? How indeed can it possibly be that with twelve hundred and fifty members of the bhikkhu community here there should be no voice to be heard, not even a sneeze or a cough?'

'Pray have no fear, great raja! I am playing no trick, your majesty; I am not deceiving you; nor am I handing you over to your enemies. Move on, great raja! Move on! Look, there is the round tent, and there the lights are burning.'

11. So the raja went forward, on his elephant as far as possible, and then on foot, until he came to the door of the great round tent. And waiting at the door he said to Jivaka the tutor, 'But where, Jivaka, is the Master?'

'There he is, great raja. There is the Master, sitting against the middle post, facing the East, sitting in honour among the members of the bhikkhu community.'

12. Then Ajatasattu, raja of Magadha, son of the princess of Videha, approached the Master, and having come to him, stood

respectfully at his side. And surveying the silent assembly, which was calm like a clear lake, he burst out with the cry: 'Oh that my good son, prince Udayi, might have calm, like the calmness of this community!'

'Where your thoughts have gone, is there love?'

'He is very dear to me, sir, my good Udayi, the prince. I wish that he could enjoy such calm as this!'[4]

13. Then the raja bowed to the Master, and holding his palms together in respectful greeting to the Community, he sat down at the side, and said to the Master: 'There is something, sir, I should like to ask you about, if you will kindly permit me to put something to you which I should like you to explain.'

'Ask, great raja, whatever you wish.'

14. There are, sir, a number of crafts, such as elephant drivers, horsemen, charioteers, archers, standard bearers, quartermasters (and many other military occupations), household slaves, cooks, barbers, bath attendants, confectioners, garland-makers, potters, registrators, accountants, and others of the same sort. All these enjoy in this world the fruits of their labours. They maintain themselves, their families and their friends in happiness and comfort. They make donations to wandering ascetics and brahmans, thus promoting their own spiritual welfare, and heavenly happiness as a result. Now, sir, can you make known to me any similar fruit, which can be seen in this very existence, which comes from the life of a wandering ascetic?'

15. 'Can you remember, great raja, whether you have asked this question of any other brahmans or wandering ascetics?'

'Sir, I can remember having asked other brahmans and wandering ascetics this question.'

'Then please tell us how they answered, if it is no trouble to you.'

'Nothing is any trouble, sir, where the Master is concerned, or those who are as the Master is.'

'Then please tell us, great raja.'

16. 'On a certain occasion I went to Purana Kassapa. After we had exchanged the usual friendly and polite greetings and compliments, I sat down at his side and asked him exactly the same question I have just asked you: "There are, sir, a number

of crafts," [and so on].

17. 'When I had put my question Purana Kassapa said to me: "To the one who acts, great raja, or who causes another to act, to the one who slashes, or causes another to slash, who punishes, or causes another to punish, to him who grieves or causes weariness, to him who kills, to him who takes what is not given, who breaks into houses, who commits dacoity, who commits robbery, or adultery, or says what is not true, to him who acts in any of these ways there is no guilt. Were he with an edge as sharp as a razor to make all living things in the world one heap of flesh, no guilt would result. Were he to go along the south bank of the Ganges, striking and slaying, slashing and having men slashed, torturing and having men tortured, there would be no guilt, nor increase of guilt. Nor if he were to go along the north bank of the Ganges giving alms, and ordering alms to be given, offering sacrifices or arranging for them to be offered would there be any merit, nor increase of merit. In generosity, in restraint, in self-control, in speaking the truth there is no merit, nor any increase of merit."

18. In this way, sir, when he was asked to say what was the fruit, in this present existence, of the life of a wandering ascetic, he expounded his doctrine of non-action. It was, sir, just as if when a man is asked to describe a mango he describes a bread-fruit. Then I thought, sir, how could one like me think of disparaging any wandering ascetic or brahman living in my own realm. So I showed neither approval nor scorn for what he had said; although dissatisfied I said no word of approval or disapproval, but rose from my seat and went away.

19. 'On another occasion I went to Makkhali of the cow-pen. [The same sentence as in paragraph 16, regarding greetings, etc., follows.]

20. 'When I had put my question Makkhali of the cow-pen said to me: "There is no cause nor condition responsible for the defilement of beings, great raja; they become defiled without cause or accompanying condition. Similarly there is no cause nor condition responsible for the purification of beings; they are purified without cause or accompanying condition. There are no deeds one generates oneself, and no deeds generated by others; there is no human action, or strength, or energy; there

is no human power and no human effort. All animals, all creatures, all beings, all souls[5] are without force, or strength or energy of their own. They are bent this way or that by their destiny, and by the class to which they belong they experience well-being or suffering.

' "There are fourteen hundred thousand varieties of birth, and another six thousand, and six hundred more. And there are five hundred sorts of karma, and yet five more, and another three, and another one and a half.

' "There are sixty-two modes of conduct, six kinds of distinctions among men, eight stages of a sage's existence, forty nine hundred sorts of occupation, and so on and so on . . . So although the wise should hope: 'By this virtue, or by this performance of duty, or by this penance, or by this act of righteousness I will make my karma to mature', and although the fool should hope, in the same kind of way, gradually to get rid of the effects of his karma that has matured, neither of them can do it. Well-being and suffering, measured out as they are, cannot be altered in the course of transmigration; there can be neither increase nor decrease. Just as when a ball of string is unrolled it will go just as far and no farther than it can unwind; just so, both fools and wise, wandering in transmigration exactly each for their allotted term, shall then, and only then make an end of suffering."

21. 'Thus, sir, did Makkhali of the cow-pen, when he was asked what is the fruit, in this very existence, in the life of a wandering ascetic, explain his theory of purification by the round of rebirth. Again it was like a man describing a breadfruit when he has been asked to describe a mango. So once again . . . although dissatisfied I said no word of approval or disapproval, but rose from my seat and went away.

22–23. 'When one day I asked Ajit of the hairy blanket the same question he replied: "There are no such things, great raja, as alms or sacrifice or offering. There is no fruit or result of good or evil deeds. There is no such thing as this world or the next. There is neither father nor mother, nor beings springing into life without them. There are no wandering ascetics or brahmans in the world who have reached the transcendent, who walk perfectly, and who, having understood and realized by themselves

12

both this world and the next, make their wisdom known to others.

' "A human being is composed of the four elements (earth, water, heat and air). When he dies the earthy in him returns to and is absorbed in the earth, the fluid in him to the water, the heat to the fire, the wind to the air, and his faculties pass into space. The four bearers, the bier making a fifth, carry his dead body away; until they reach the burning-ground men utter eulogies, but there his bones are bleached, and all his offerings end in ashes. It is a doctrine of fools, this talk of almsgiving. It is an empty lie, mere idle talk, when men say there is profit in it. Fools and wise men alike, on the breaking up of the body, are cut off, they are annihilated, for after death they exist no more."

24. 'Thus, sir, Ajit of the hairy blanket, when asked what was the fruit in the life of a wandering ascetic, expounded his theory of annihilation.

25–26. 'Then, another day, when I asked Pakudh of the marshland road the same question, he said: "The following seven things, great raja, are neither made nor caused to be made, they are neither created nor caused to be created, they are barren, so that nothing is produced from them; they are as unmovable as a mountain peak, as a pillar firmly fixed. They do not move, or vary, or interfere with one another, and they have no bearing whatsoever on well-being or suffering. What are these seven? They are the four elements: earth, water, heat and air, together with well-being and suffering, and life as the seventh. So there is neither slayer nor one who causes slaughter, hearer or speaker, knower or explainer. When a person with a sharp sword cuts someone's head in two, no one is depriving another of life; a sword has merely penetrated into the interval between seven elements."

27. 'Thus, sir, Pakudh of the marshland road, when asked what was the immediate fruit in the life of a wandering ascetic, dealt with the question by expounding something else.

28–30. 'When, another day, I asked Niganth of the Nata clan the same question, he said: "A Niganth [man free from bonds], great raja, is restrained with a fourfold restraint: his life is one of restraint with regard to all water; restraint with regard to all evil; he has washed all evil away; and his life is suffused

13

with a sense of evil held at bay. This is his fourfold self-restraint. Since he is thus tied with a fourfold bond he is the Nigantho [free from bonds], he is Gatatto [one whose heart has gone to the summit], his is Yatatto [one whose heart is kept under control], and Thitatto [one whose heart is fixed]."

'Thus, sir, Niganth of the Nata clan, when asked what was the immediate advantage in the life of a wandering ascetic, expounded his theory of the fourfold bond.

31–33. 'When I asked Sanjay of the Belattha clan this question he said: "If you ask me whether there is another world — well, if I thought there were I would say so. But I don't say so. And I don't think it is a matter of this or that. And I don't think it is otherwise. And I don't deny it. And I don't say there neither is nor is not, another world. And if you ask me about the things produced by chance; or whether there is any fruit, any result, of good or bad actions; or whether a man who has won the Truth continues or not, after death — to each or any of these questions I give the same reply."

'Thus, sir, Sanjay of the Belattha clan, when asked what was the immediate fruit in the life of a wandering ascetic, displayed his manner of prevarication. And to him as to all the others I expressed neither approval nor dissatisfaction, but neither accepting nor rejecting what was said I rose from my seat and went away.

34. 'And now, sir, I put the same question to the Master. Can you make known to me any immediate fruit, in this very existence, which comes from the life of a wandering ascetic, such as those following the occupations I mentioned are, each of them, able to show?'

'I can, great raja. And to that end I wish to put a question to you. Please answer in whatever way you please.

35. 'Now what do you think, great raja: suppose among the people of your household there is a slave who works for you, who rises up in the morning before you do, and goes to bed only when you have done so, who is keen to do whatever you wish, anxious to make himself agreeable in what he does and says, a man who anticipates your every need. Now suppose he should think: "This matter of meritorious deeds, this result of merit, is very strange. For here is the raja of Magadha, Ajatasattu, son of

the Videha princess – he is a man, and so am I. But the king lives in the full enjoyment and possession of the five pleasures of sense, virtually a god, it seems to me. And here am I, a slave, working for him, rising before him, and going to bed late, keen to carry out his pleasure, anxious to make myself agreeable in deed and word, and anticipating all his needs. I wish I could be like him, so that I should have the chance to earn merit. So why don't I have my hair and beard shaved off, and put on the yellow robes, and leave my home and become a homeless wanderer?" And suppose, after a time, he does this. Having been admitted into a community he lives a life of restraint in action, speech and thought, is content with the minimum of food and shelter, and delights in solitude. And suppose your people should tell you about him, saying, "If you please, your majesty, do you know that so and so, who used to be your slave, and work for you, [and so on, all as before], has now put on the yellow robes, and has been admitted into a community and lives a life of restraint, content with the minimum of food and shelter, and delights in solitude?" Would you then say, "Let the fellow come back. Let him come and work for me again as my slave."?'

36. 'No, sir. On the contrary, we should greet him with reverence, and stand up out of deference to him, and request *him* to sit down. And we should have robes, and a bowl, and a place to sleep, and medicine, and anything else a wandering ascetic needs all made ready for him, and beg him to accept them. And we should give orders for him to be regularly protected.'

'Well, now, great raja, if that is the case, is there, or is there not, some visible fruit in being a wandering ascetic?'

'Certainly, sir, I agree that there is.'

'Well, this, great raja, is the first kind of fruit, which can be seen in this very existence, which, as I said, results from being a wandering ascetic.'

37–38. 'But can you show me any other fruit, in this existence, which comes from being a wandering ascetic, sir?'

'I can, great raja. And to that end I wish to put another question to you.' [The case is now put, in the same way as before, of a free man who cultivates his land, and being a householder pays taxes and thus increases the king's wealth, but

15

who gives up his small property and his position in his clan, and enters a community. He too receives the same honour, the fruit of being a wandering ascetic.]

39. 'But can you, sir, show me any other fruit in this world from being a wandering ascetic, a fruit better and sweeter than these?'

'I can. Listen, therefore, great raja, and pay careful attention, and I will tell you what it is.

40. 'Suppose there appears in the world a Tathagata,[6] an arahat, a fully awakened one, complete in wisdom and goodness, happy, one who knows all worlds, incomparable as a guide to those who are willing to be led, a teacher for gods and mortals, a revered Master, a Buddha. From his own experience he knows and sees this universe, including the upper worlds of the gods, the Brahmas and the Maras [spirits of evil], and the lower world with its ascetics and brahmans, its princes and peoples – and having understood it he makes his knowledge known to others. He teaches the Truth he knows, beautiful in its origin, beautiful in its progress, beautiful in its fulfilment. He teaches it both in the spirit and in the letter; he makes known the higher life in all its fullness and all its purity.

41. 'A householder, or one of his children, or someone of lesser status, hearing that Truth, trusts the Tathagata [the one who has discovered the Truth], and having such confidence in what he has heard, reasons within himself as follows: ' "The life of a householder is full of hindrances; it is a dusty, defiling path to tread. The homeless wanderer lives an uncluttered life. It is difficult for the householder to live the higher life in all its fullness, in all its purity, in all its perfection. So let me shave off my hair and beard, and put on the yellow robes and leave the household life and become a homeless wanderer."

'Then, before long, forsaking his share of wealth, whether great or small, and forsaking his circle of relatives, whether many or few, he cuts off his hair and beard, puts on the yellow robes and leaves household life for that of the homeless wanderer.

42. 'When he has thus become an ascetic he lives by the rule of life proper to an ascetic. Scrupulous in matters of behaviour and food, realizing the danger which lies in the avoidance of

small faults, he adopts certain principles of good bodily action and speech. He leads a wholesome life, observing fully the moral precepts; he guards the door of his senses; he is alert and self-aware, and rich in contentment.

43. 'And what, great raja, are those principles of good bodily action and speech that he adopts? The bhikkhu, putting away the killing of living things, holds aloof from the destruction of life. He has laid the cudgel and the sword aside, and ashamed of roughness, and full of mercy, he dwells compassionate and kind to all creatures that have life. This is one of his moral precepts. Putting away the taking of what has not been given, the bhikku lives aloof from grasping what is not his own. He takes only what is given, and expecting that gifts will come, he passes his life in honesty and purity of heart. This is another of his moral precepts. Putting away unchastity, the bhikkhu is chaste. He keeps himself from sexual intercourse, from the way of country folk. This is another of his moral precepts.

44. 'Putting away lying words, the bhikkhu holds himself aloof from falsehood. He speaks truth, from the truth he never swerves; faithful and trustworthy, he does not break his word to the world.

'Putting away slander, the bhikkhu holds himself aloof from calumny. What he hears here he repeats not elsewhere to raise a quarrel against the people here; what he hears elsewhere he repeats not here to raise a quarrel against the people there. Thus he lives as a binder together of those who are divided, an encourager of those who are friends, a peacemaker, a lover of peace, impassioned for peace, a speaker of words that make for peace. This is another of his moral precepts.

'Putting away rudeness of speech, the bhikkhu holds himself aloof from harsh language. Whatever word is blameless, pleasant to the ear, lovely, moving, urbane, pleasing to the people, beloved of the people – such are words he speaks.

'Putting away frivolous talk the bhikkhu holds himself aloof from vain conversation. He speaks at the appropriate time, in accordance with the facts, words full of meaning, on religion, on the discipline of the Community. He speaks, and at the right time, words worthy to be remembered, fitly illustrated, clearly divided, to the point. These also are his moral precepts.

45. 'The bhikkhu holds himself aloof from causing injury to seeds, or plants.

'He takes but one meal a day, not eating at night, refraining from food after midday.

'He refrains from being a spectator at shows at fairs, with nautch dances, singing and music.

'He abstains from wearing, adorning or ornamenting himself with garlands, scents and unguents.

'He abstains from the use of large and lofty beds.

'He abstains from accepting silver or gold.

'He abstains from accepting uncooked grain.

'He abstains from accepting raw meat.

'He abstains from accepting women or girls.

'He abstains from accepting bondmen or bondwomen.

'He abstains from accepting sheep or goats.

'He abstains from accepting fowls or swine.

'He abstains from accepting elephants, cattle, horses and mares.

'He abstains from accepting cultivated fields or waste.

'He abstains from acting as a go-between or messenger.

'He abstains from buying and selling.

'He abstains from cheating with scales or coins or measures.

'He abstains from the crooked ways of bribery, cheating and fraud.

'He abstains from maiming, murder, putting in bonds, highway robbery, dacoity and violence.

'These also are his moral precepts.

46. 'Some ascetics and brahmans, while living on food provided by the faithful, continue addicted to the injury of seedlings and growing plants whether propagated from roots, or cuttings, or joints, or buddings, or seeds. The bhikkhu holds aloof from such injury to seedlings and growing plants.

47. 'Some ascetics and brahmans, while living on food provided by the faithful, continue addicted to the use of things stored up; stores, to wit, of foods, drinks, clothing, equipages, bedding, perfumes and curry-stuffs. The bhikkhu holds aloof from such use of things stored up.

48. 'Some ascetics and brahmans, while living on food provided by the faithful, continue addicted to visiting shows; that is

to say: nautch dances, sing-songs, instrumental music, shows at fairs, ballad recitations, handmusic, the chanting of bards, drum-playing, fairy scenes, acrobatic feats by kandalas, combats of elephants, horses, buffaloes, bulls, goats, rams, cocks and quails; bouts at quarterstaff, boxing, wrestling, sham-fights, roll-calls, manoeuvres, reviews. The bhikkhu refrains from visiting such shows.

49. 'Some ascetics and brahmans, while living on food provided by the faithful, continue addicted to games and recreations; that is to say: games on boards with eight, or with ten, rows of squares, the same games played by imagining such boards in the air, keeping going over diagrams drawn on the ground so that one steps only where one ought to go, either removing the pieces or men from a heap with one's nail, or putting them into a heap, in each case without shaking it. He who shakes the heap, loses; throwing dice, hitting a short stick with a long one, dipping the hand with the fingers stretched out in lac, or red dye, or flour-water, and striking the wet hand on the ground or on a wall, calling out, 'What shall it be?' and showing the form required – elephants, horses, [etc.]; games with balls, blowing through toy pipes made of leaves, ploughing with toy ploughs, turning somersaults, playing with toy windmills made of palm-leaves, playing with toy measures made of palm-leaves, playing with toy carts or toy bows, guessing at letters traced in the air, or on a playfellow's back, guessing the playfellow's thoughts, mimicry of deformities. The bhikkhu refrains from such games and recreations.

50. 'Some ascetics and brahmans, while living on food provided by the faithful, continue addicted to the use of high and large couches; that is to say: movable settees, high, and six feet long, divans with animal figures carved on the supports, goats' hair coverlets with very long fleece, patchwork counterpanes of many colours, white blankets, woollen coverlets embroidered with flowers, quilts stuffed with cotton wool, coverlets embroidered with figures of lions, tigers, [etc.]; rugs with fur on both sides, rugs with fur on one side, coverlets embroidered with gems, silk coverlets, carpets large enough for sixteen dancers, elephant, horse and chariot rugs, rugs of antelope skins sewn together, rugs of skins of the plantain antelope, carpets

with awnings above them, sofas with red pillows for the head and feet. The bhikkhu refrains from the use of such things.

51. 'Some ascetics and brahmans, while living on food provided by the faithful, continue addicted to the use of means for adorning and beautifying themselves; that is: rubbing in scented powders on one's body, shampooing it and bathing it; patting the limbs with clubs after the manner of wrestlers; the use of mirrors, eye-ointments, garlands, rouge, cosmetics, bracelets, necklaces, walking-sticks, reed cases for drugs, rapiers, sunshades, embroidered slippers, turbans, diadems, whisks of the yak's tail, and long-fringed white robes. The bhikkhu refrains from such means of adorning and beautifying the person.

52. 'Some ascetics and brahmans, while living on food provided by the faithful, continue addicted to such low conversations as these: tales of kings, of robbers, of ministers of state; tales of war, of terrors, of battles; talk about food and drink, clothes, beds, garlands, perfumes; talk about relationships, vehicles, villages, towns, cities and countries; tales about women and about heroes; gossip at street corners, or places from where water is fetched; ghost stories; speculations about the creation of the land or sea, or about existence and non-existence. The bhikkhu refrains from such low conversation.

53. 'Some ascetics and brahmans, while living on food provided by the faithful, continue addicted to the use of wrangling phrases: such as –

' "You don't understand this doctrine and discipline, I do."

' "How should you know about this doctrine and discipline?"

' "You have fallen into wrong views. It is I who am in the right."

' "I am speaking to the point, you are not."

' "You are putting last what ought to come first, and first what ought to come last."

' "What you've excogitated so long, is all confused."

' "Your challenge has been taken up."

' "You are proved to be wrong."

' "Set to work to clear your views."

' "Disentangle yourself if you can."

' 'The bhikkhu refrains from such wrangling phrases.

54. 'Some ascetics and brahmans, while living on food provided by the faithful, continue addicted to taking messages, going on errands and acting as go-betweens; that is, for kings, ministers of state, kshatriyas, brahmans, or young men, saying: "Go there, come hither, take this with you, bring that from thence." The bhikkhu refrains from such servile duties.

55. 'Some ascetics and brahmans, while living on food provided by the faithful, are tricksters, droners out (of holy words for pay), diviners and exorcists, ever hungering to add gain to gain. The bhikkhu refrains from such deception and patter.

56. 'Some ascetics and brahmans, while living on food provided by the faithful, earn their living by wrong means of livelihood, by low arts, such as these: palmistry – prophesying long life, prosperity (or the reverse), from marks on a child's hands, feet; divining by means of omens and signs; auguries drawn from thunderbolts and other celestial portents; prognostication by interpreting dreams; fortune-telling from marks on the body; auguries from the marks on cloth gnawed by mice; sacrificing to Agni; offering oblations from a spoon; making offerings to gods of husks, of the red powder between the grain and the husk, of husked grain ready for boiling, of ghee and of oil, sacrificing by spewing mustard seeds into the fire out of one's mouth; drawing blood from one's right knee as a sacrifice to the gods; looking at the knuckles, and, after muttering a charm, divining whether a man is well born or lucky or not; determining whether the site, for a proposed house or pleasance, is lucky or not; advising on customary law; laying demons in a cemetery; laying ghosts; knowledge of the charms to be used when lodging in an earth house; snake charming; poison craft, scorpion craft, mouse craft, bird craft, crow craft, foretelling the number of years that a man has yet to live, giving charms to ward off arrows; the animal wheel. The bhikkhu refrains from such low arts.

57. 'Some ascetics and brahmans, while living on food provided by the faithful, earn their living by wrong means of livelihood, by low arts, such as: knowledge of the signs of good and bad qualities in the following things and of the marks in them denoting the health or luck of their owners: gems, staves, garments, swords, arrows, bows, other weapons, women, men,

boys, girls, slaves, slave-girls, elephants, horses, buffaloes, bulls, oxen, goats, sheep, fowls, quails, iguanas, ear-rings,[7] tortoises and other animals. The bhikkhu refrains from such low arts.

58. 'Some ascetics and brahmans, while living on food provided by the faithful, earn their living by wrong means of livelihood, by low arts, such as soothsaying, on such matters as:

'The chiefs will march out.

'The chiefs will march back.

'The home chiefs will attack, and the enemies' retreat.

'The enemies' chiefs will attack, and ours will retreat.

'The home chiefs will gain the victory, and the foreign chiefs suffer defeat.

'The foreign chiefs will gain the victory, and ours will suffer defeat.

'Thus will there be victory on this side and defeat on that.

'The bhikkhu refrains from such low arts.

59. 'Some recluses and brahmans, while living on food provided by the faithful, earn their living by wrong means of livelihood, by such low arts as foretelling. For example, there will be an eclipse of the moon; there will be an eclipse of the sun; there will be an eclipse of a star; there will be aberration of the sun or the moon; the sun or the moon will return to its usual path; there will be aberrations of the stars; the stars will return to their usual course; there will be a fall of meteors; there will be a jungle fire; there will be an earthquake; the god will thunder; there will be rising and setting, clearness and dimness, of the sun or the moon or the stars, or foretelling of each of these fifteen phenomena that they will betoken such and such a result.

60. 'Some ascetics and brahmans, while living on food provided by the faithful, earn their living by wrong means of livelihood, by low arts, such as – foretelling an abundant rainfall; or a deficient rainfall; or a good harvest; or scarcity of food; or tranquillity; or disturbances; a pestilence; or a healthy season; counting on the fingers; counting without using the fingers; summing up large totals; composing ballads, poetizing; casuistry, sophistry. The bhikkhu refrains from such low arts.

61. 'Some recluses and brahmans, while living on food provided by the faithful, earn their living by wrong means of livelihood, by low arts, such as: arranging a lucky day for

marriages in which the bride or bridegroom is sent forth; fixing a lucky time for the conclusion of treaties of peace, or using charms to procure harmony; fixing a lucky time for the outbreak of hostilities or using charms to make discord; fixing a lucky time for the calling in of debts or charms for success in throwing dice; fixing a lucky time for the expenditure of money or charms to bring ill-luck to an opponent throwing dice; using charms to make people lucky; or to make people unlucky; or to procure abortion; incantations to bring on dumbness; or to keep a man's jaws fixed; or to make a man throw up his hands; or to bring on deafness; obtaining oracular answers by means of the magic mirror; or through a girl possessed; or from a god; the worship of the Sun; the worship of the Great Mother; bringing forth flames from one's mouth; invoking Siri, the goddess of Luck. The bhikkhu refrains from such low arts.

62. 'Some ascetics and brahmans, while living on food provided by the faithful, earn their living by wrong means of livelihood, by low arts, such as: vowing gifts to a god if a certain benefit be granted; paying such vows; repeating charms while lodging in an earth house; causing virility; making a man impotent; fixing on lucky sites for dwellings; consecrating sites; ceremonial rinsings of the mouth; ceremonial bathings; offering sacrifices; administering emetics and purgatives; purging people to relieve the head [that is, by giving drugs to make people sneeze]; oiling people's ears [either to make them grow or to heal sores on them]; satisfying people's eyes [soothing them by dropping medicinal oils into them]; administering drugs through the nose; applying collyrium to the eyes; giving medical ointment for the eyes; practising as an oculist; practising as a surgeon; practising as a doctor for children; administering roots and drugs; administering medicines in rotation. The bhikkhu refrains from such low arts. This is another of his moral precepts.

63. 'And then that bhikkhu, great raja, being thus master of the minor moralities, sees no danger from any side; that is, so far as concerns his self-restraint in conduct. Just as a sovereign, duly crowned, whose enemies have been beaten down, sees no danger from any side; that is, so far as enemies are concerned, so is the bhikkhu confident. And endowed with this body of morals, so worthy of honour, he experiences, within himself, a

sense of ease without alloy. Thus is it, great raja, that the bhikkhu becomes righteous.

64. 'And how, great raja, is the bhikkhu guarded as to the doors of his senses?

'When, great raja, he sees an object with his eye he is not entranced in the general appearance or the details of it. He sets himself to restrain that which might give occasion for evil states, covetousness and dejection, to flow in over him so long as he dwells unrestrained as to his sense of sight. He keeps watch upon his faculty of sight, and he attains to mastery over it. Similarly, when he hears a sound with his ear, or smells an odour with his nose, or tastes a flavour with his tongue, or feels a touch with his body, or when he cognizes a phenomenon with his mind he is not entranced in the general appearance or the details of it. He sets himself to restrain that which might give occasion for evil states, covetousness and dejection, to flow in over him so long as he dwells unrestrained as to his mental (representative) faculty. He keeps watch upon his representative faculty, and he attains to mastery over it. And endowed with this self-restraint, so worthy of honour, as regards the senses, he experiences within himself a sense of ease into which no evil state can enter. Thus is it, great raja, that the bhikkhu becomes guarded as to the doors of his senses.

65. 'And how, great raja, is the bhikkhu mindful and self-possessed?

'In this matter the bhikkhu in going forth or in coming back keeps clearly before his mind's eye all that is wrapped up therein: the immediate object of the act itself, its ethical significance, whether or not it is conducive to the high aim set before him, and the real facts underlying the mere phenomenon of the outward act. So also in looking forward, or in looking round; in stretching forth his arm, or in drawing it in again; in eating or drinking, in masticating or swallowing, in obeying the calls of nature, in going or standing or sitting, in sleeping or waking, in speaking or in being still, he keeps himself aware of all it really means. Thus is it that the bhikkhu becomes mindful and self-possessed.

66. 'And how, great raja, is the bhikkhu content? The bhikkhu is satisfied with sufficient robes to cover his body, with

sufficient food to keep him alive. Wherever he may go these he takes with him as he goes – just as a bird with his wings, wherever he may fly. So the bhikkhu lives content.

67. 'Then, having mastered this excellent body of moral precepts, having gained this excellent self-restraint as to the senses, endowed with this excellent mindfulness and self-possession, filled with this excellent content, he chooses some lonely spot where he can rest on his way – in the woods, at the foot of a tree, on a hill side, in a mountain glen, in a rocky cave, in a cemetery or on a heap of straw in the open field. Returning there after his round for alms he seats himself, when his meal is done, cross-legged, keeping his body erect, and his intelligence alert, intent.

68. 'Putting away all hankering after the world, he purifies his mind of desires. Putting away the corrupting wish to injure, he remains with a mind free from ill-temper, and purifies his mind of malevolence. Putting away torpor of heart and mind, keeping his perception bright, and being mindful and self-possessed, he purifies his mind of weakness and of sloth. Putting away flurry and worry, he remains free from fretfulness, and with mind serene, he purifies himself of irritability and vexation of spirit. Putting away wavering, he remains as one who has passed beyond perplexity; and no longer in suspense as to what is good, he purifies his mind of doubt.

69. 'Then just as when a man, after contracting a loan, should start a business, and his business should succeed, and he should not only be able to pay off the old debt he had incurred, but there should be a surplus over to maintain a wife. Then would he realize: "I used to have to carry on my business by getting into debt, but it has gone so well with me that I have paid off what I owed, and have a surplus over to maintain a wife." He would be of good cheer at that, would be glad of heart at that.

70. 'Then just as if a man were a prey to disease, in pain, and very ill, and could not digest his food, and there were no strength left in him; and after a time he were to recover from that disease, and could digest his food, and his strength came back to him; then, when he realized his former and his present state, he would be of good cheer at that, he would be glad of heart at that.

71. 'Then just as if a man were bound in a prison house, and after a time he should be set free from his bonds, safe and sound, and without any confiscation of his goods; when he realized his former and his present state, he would be of good cheer at that, he would be glad of heart at that.

72. 'Then just as if a man were a slave, not his own master, subject to another, unable to go where he wished, and after a time he should be emancipated from that slavery, become his own master, not subject to others, a free man, free to go where he wished; then, on realizing his former and his present state, he would be of good cheer at that, he would be glad of heart at that.

73. 'Then just as if a man, rich and prosperous, were to find himself on a long road, in a desert, where no food was, but much danger; and after a time were to find himself out of the desert, arrived safe, on the borders of his village, in security and peace; then, on realizing his former and his present state, he would be of good cheer at that, he would be glad of heart at that.

74. 'Just so the bhikkhu, so long as these Five Hindrances are not put away within him, looks upon himself as in debt, diseased, in prison, in slavery, lost on a desert road. But when these Five Hindrances have been put away within him, he looks upon himself as freed from debt, rid of disease, out of jail, a free man, and secure;

75. 'And gladness springs up within him on his realizing that, and joy arises to him, gladdened as he is, and so rejoicing all his body becomes at ease, and being at ease he is filled with a sense of peace, and in that peace his heart is stayed.

'Then estranged from desires, aloof from evil dispositions, he enters into and remains in the first stage of meditation – a state of joy and ease born of detachment, reasoning and investigation going on the while.

'His very body does he so pervade, drench, permeate and suffuse with the joy and ease born of detachment, that there is no spot in his whole frame not suffused therewith.

76. 'Just as, great raja, a skilful bathman or his apprentice will scatter perfumed soap powder in a metal basin, and then besprinkling it with water, drop by drop, will so knead it together that the ball of lather, taking up the moisture, is drenched with it, pervaded by it, permeated by it within and

without, and there is no leakage possible.

'This, great raja, is an immediate fruit of the life of an ascetic, visible in this world, higher and sweeter than the last.

77. 'Then further, great raja, the bhikkhu, suppressing all reasoning and investigation, enters into and remains in the second stage of meditation, a state of joy and ease, born of the serenity of concentration, when no reasoning or investigation goes on – a state of elevation of mind, a tranquillization of the heart within.

'And he so pervades, drenches, permeates and suffuses with the joy and ease born of concentration, his whole body that there is no place in his body they do not reach.

78. 'Just as if there were a deep pool, with water welling up into it from a spring beneath, and with no inlet from the east or west, from the north or south, and the heavenly one should not from time to time send down showers of rain upon it. Still the current of cool waters rising up from that spring would pervade, fill, permeate and suffuse the pool with cool waters, and there would be no part of the pool unreached by it.

'This, great raja, is an immediate fruit of the life of an ascetic, visible in this world, and higher and sweeter than the last.

79. 'Then further, great raja, the bhikkhu, holding aloof from joy, becomes equable; and mindful and self-possessed he experiences in his body that ease which the arahats talk of when they say: "The man serene and self-possessed is well at ease," and so he enters into and abides in the third stage of meditation.

'And he so pervades, drenches, permeates and suffuses with that ease that has no joy with it, his whole body that there is no place in his body it does not reach.

80. 'Just as, great raja, when in a lotus tank the several lotus flowers, red or white or blue, born in the water, grown up in the water, not rising up above the surface of the water, drawing up nourishment from the depths of the water, are so pervaded, drenched, permeated and suffused from their very tips down to their roots with its cool moisture that there is no place in the whole plant, whether of the red lotus, or of the white, or of the blue, which it does not reach.

'This is an immediate fruit of the life of an ascetic, visible in this world, and higher and sweeter than the last.

81. 'Then further, great raja, the bhikkhu, by the putting away alike of well-being and of suffering, by the passing away alike of any elation, any dejection, he had previously felt, enters into and abides in the fourth stage of meditation, a state of pure self-possession and equanimity, without suffering and without well-being.

'He sits there so suffusing even his body with that sense of purification, of translucence of heart, that there is no place in his whole body which it does not reach.

82. 'Just as if a man were sitting so wrapped from head to foot in a clean white robe, that there were no place in his whole body not in contact with the clean white robe – just so does the bhikkhu sit there, so suffusing even his body with that sense of purification, of translucence of heart, that there is no place in his whole body which it does not reach.

'This is an immediate fruit of the life of an ascetic, and higher and sweeter than the last.

83. 'With his heart thus serene, made pure, translucent, cultured, devoid of evil, supple, ready to act, firm and imperturbable, he applies and bends down his mind to that insight that comes from knowledge. He grasps the fact: "This body of mine has form, it is built up of the four elements, it springs from father and mother, it is continually renewed by so much boiled rice and juicy foods, its very nature is impermanence, it is subject to erasion, abrasion, dissolution, and disintegration;[8] so also consciousness is bound up with it and depends on it."

84. 'Just as if there were a Veluriya gem, bright, of the purest water, with eight facets, excellently cut, clear, translucent, without a flaw, excellent in every way, and through it string, blue, or orange-coloured, or red, or white, or yellow were threaded. If a man with keen eyesight were to take it into his hand, he would clearly see how the one is bound up with the other.

'This is an immediate fruit of the life of an ascetic, visible in this world, and higher and sweeter than the last.

85. 'With his heart thus serene, made pure, translucent, cultured, devoid of evil, supple, ready to act, firm and imperturbable, he applies and bends down his mind to the calling up of a mental image. He calls up from this body another body, having form, made of mind, having all his own body's limbs and

parts, not deprived of any organ.

86. 'Just as if a man were to pull out a reed from its sheath. He would know: "This is the reed, this the sheath. The reed is one thing, the sheath another. It is from the sheath that the reed has been drawn forth." Similarly were he to take a snake out of its slough, or draw a sword from its scabbard.

'This, great raja, is an immediate fruit of the life of an ascetic, visible in this life, and higher and sweeter than the last.

87. 'With his heart thus serene, made pure, translucent, cultured, devoid of evil, supple, ready to act, firm and imperturbable, he applies and bends down his mind to the modes of marvellous power.⁹ He enjoys the marvellous power in its various modes – being one he becomes many, or having become many becomes one again; he becomes visible or invisible; he goes, feeling no obstruction, to the further side of a wall, or rampart, or hill, as if through air; he penetrates up and down through solid ground, as if through water; he walks on water without breaking through, as if on solid ground; he travels cross-legged in the sky, like birds on the wing; even the moon and the sun, potent and mighty as they are, he touches and feels with his hand; he reaches in the body even up to the heaven of Brahma.

88. 'Just as a clever potter or his apprentice could make, could succeed in getting out of properly prepared clay, absolutely any shape of vessel he wanted to have, or an ivory carver out of ivory, or a goldsmith out of gold.

'This, great raja, is an immediate fruit of the life of an ascetic, and higher and sweeter than the last.

89. 'With his heart thus serene, made pure, translucent, cultured, devoid of evil, supple, ready to act, firm and imperturbable, he applies and bends his mind to supra-normal hearing, by means of which, far surpassing as it does normal hearing, he hears sounds both human and celestial, far and near.

90. 'Just as if a man were on the high road and were to hear the sound of a kettledrum, or a tenor-drum, or the sound of trumpets and side-drums, he would know: "This is the sound of a kettledrum, this is the sound of a tenor-drum, this of trumpets and side-drums."

'This is an immediate fruit of the life of an ascetic, visible in this life, and higher and sweeter than the last.

91. 'With his heart thus serene, he directs and bends his mind to the understanding of the mind. Having understood his own mind, he is able to understand the minds of other beings, of other men. He is thus able to discern: the passionate mind, and the calm mind, the angry mind, and the peaceful mind, the dull mind, and the alert mind, the attentive mind, and the wandering mind, the broad mind, and the narrow mind, the mean mind, and the lofty mind, the steadfast mind, and the wavering mind, the free mind, and the enslaved mind; he recognizes each for what it is.

92. 'Just as a woman or a man, or a lad, young and smart, considering carefully the reflection of his own face in a bright and brilliant mirror or in a vessel of clear water would, if it had a mole on it, know that it had, and if not, would know that, too.

'This is an immediate fruit of the life of an ascetic, visible in this world, and higher and sweeter than the last.

93. 'With his heart thus serene, he directs and bends his mind to the knowledge of the memory of his previous existences. He recalls to mind his various existences in days gone by – one birth, or two or three, or ten or twenty, or a thousand or a hundred thousand births, through many ages of world dissolution, many ages of world evolution.[10] "In such a place such was my name, such my family, such my caste, such my food, such my experience of discomfort or of ease, and such the limits of my life. When I passed away from that state, I took form again in such a place. There I had such and such a name, and family, and caste, and food, and experience of suffering or of well-being, such was the length of my life. When I passed away from that state I took form again here" – thus he calls to mind his former existences in all their circumstances.

94. 'Just as if a man were to go from his own to another village, and from that one to another, and from that one should return home. Then he would know: "From my own village I came to that other one. There I stood in such and such a way, sat, spake, and held my peace. From there I came to another village; and there I stood in such and such a way, sat, spake, and held my peace. Now, from that other village, I have returned back again home."

'This is an immediate fruit of the life of an ascetic, visible in this world, and higher and sweeter than the last.

95. 'With his heart thus serene, he directs and bends his mind to the knowledge of the fall and rise of beings. With the pure supra-normal vision, he sees beings as they pass away from one form of existence and take shape in another; he recognizes the mean and the noble, the well-favoured and the ill-favoured, the happy and the wretched, passing away according to their deeds: "Such and such beings, my brethren, who in act and word and thought, are revilers of the noble ones, holding to wrong views, acquiring for themselves that karma which results from wrong views, they, on the dissolution of the body, after death, are reborn in some unhappy state of suffering or woe. But such and such beings, my brethren, who are well-doers in act, and word, and thought, not revilers of the noble ones, holding to right views, acquiring for themselves that karma that results from right views, they, on the dissolution of the body, after death, are reborn in some happy state in heaven." Thus with the supra-normal vision he sees beings as they pass away from one state of existence, and take form in another; he recognizes the mean and the noble, the well-favoured and the ill-favoured, the happy and the wretched, passing away according to their deeds.

96. 'Just as if there were a house with an upper terrace on it in the midst of a place where four roads meet, and a man standing on it who had keen eyesight, and could watch men entering a house, and coming out of it, and walking here and there along the street, and sitting in the square in the midst. He would know: "Those men are entering a house, and those are leaving it, and those are walking up and down the street, and those are sitting in the square in the midst."

'This is an immediate fruit of the life of an ascetic, visible in this world, and higher and sweeter than the last.

97. 'With his heart thus serene, he directs and bends his mind to the knowledge of the destruction of the Influxes.[11] He knows [as it really is]: "This is suffering." He knows as it really is: "This is the origin of suffering." He knows as it really is: "This is the cessation of suffering." He knows as it really is: "This is the Path that leads to the cessation of suffering." He knows [as they really are]: "These are the Influxes." He knows

31

as it really is: "This is the origin of the Influxes." He knows as it really is: "This is the cessation of the Influxes." He knows as it really is: "This is the Path that leads to the cessation of the Influxes." To him, thus knowing, thus seeing, the heart is set free from the bias for sensuality, is set free from the bias for eternal existence, is set free from the bias for ignorance. In him, thus set free, there arises the knowledge of his emancipation, and he knows: "Rebirth has been destroyed. The higher life has been fulfilled. What had to be done has been accomplished. After this present life there will be no rebirth."

98. 'Just as if in a mountain fastness there were a pool of water, clear, translucent and serene; a man, standing on the bank, with keen eyesight, could perceive the oysters and the shells, the gravel and the pebbles and the shoals of fish, as they move about or lie within it, and he would know: "This pool is clear, transparent, and serene, and there within it are the oysters and the shells, and the sand and gravel, and the shoals of fish are moving about or lying still."

'This, great raja, is an immediate fruit of the life of an ascetic, visible in this world, and higher and sweeter than the last. There is no fruit of the life of an ascetic visible in this world, that is higher and sweeter than this.'

99. When he had said this, Ajatasattu the raja said to the Master: 'Most excellent, lord, most excellent! It is as though someone had set up again what had been thrown down, or had revealed what had been hidden away, or had pointed out the right road to someone who had gone astray, or had brought a light into the darkness so that those who had eyes could see the shape of things – just so has the Truth been made known to me, in many a figure, by the Master. Now I take myself, lord, to the Master as my guide, to the Doctrine and to the Community. May the Master accept me as a disciple, as one who, from this day forth, as long as life lasts has taken them as his guide. Sin had overcome me; I was weak and foolish and wrong; for the sake of power, I put to death my father, that righteous man, that righteous ruler. May the Master accept this from me, that I do acknowledge it as a sin, so that in future I may restrain myself.'

100. 'Indeed, great raja, it was sin that overcame you. But now that you look upon it as sin, and confess it according to

what is right, we accept your confession of it. For that is the practice in the discipline of the noble ones, that whoever looks upon his fault as a fault, and rightly confesses it, attains to self-restraint in future.'

101. When he had said this, Ajatasattu the maharaja said to the Master: 'Now, sir, we have to go. We are busy, and there is much to do.'

'Do, great raja, whatever seems to you best.'

Then Ajatasattu, pleased and delighted with the words of the Master, rose from his seat, and bowed to the Master, and keeping him on the right hand as he passed him, went away.

102. Then the Master, not long after Ajatasattu had gone, spoke to the brethren: 'This maharaja, brethren, was deeply affected, he was touched in heart. If, brethren, he had not put his father to death, that righteous man, and righteous ruler, then would the clear and spotless vision of Truth[12] have arisen in him, even as he sat there.'

Thus spake the Master, and the bhikkhus were delighted at what he had said.

Here ends the Samanna-phala Sutta.

1 In Pali, the *Sangha*, the institutional order of the Buddha's disciples.

2 Mid-October to mid-November (*Kartik*), the fourth month of the ancient Indian calendar.

3 Makkhali of the cow-pen.

4 'Buddhaghosa explains this thought by saying that Ajatasattu feared that his own son might follow his own example and kill him as he had killed his own father [Bimbisara]. His fears were justified, for he was killed by his son Udayibhadda, who reigned for sixteen years.' Malalasekera, *DPPN*, I, 374 ff.

5 All animals, all creatures, all beings, all souls (*sabbe satta, sabbe pana, sabbe bhuta, sabbe jiva*): these four classes are intended to include all life on earth, from humans to plants; the four are frequently referred to in the Jaina-Sutras, also, where (II, 25) they are rendered by Jacobi, 'every sentient being, every insect, every living thing, whether animal or vegetable'. See Rhys Davids, *Dialogues*, I, 71.

6   See Introduction, p.x.

7   This comes in here very oddly. But the old commentator had the same reading, and takes the word in its ordinary sense. (RD)

8   This is a favourite description of the body. The words for erasion, abrasion, are also familiar technical terms of the Indian shampooer. The double meaning must have been clearly present to the Indian hearer, and the words are, therefore, really untranslatable. (RD)

9   *Iddhi*: magical or spiritual power – an important concept in Buddhist thought, being regarded as one of the six kinds of higher powers (*abhinna*). See Nyanatiloka, *Dictionary*.

10 This is based on the Indian theory of the periodic destruction and renovation of the universe, each of which takes countless years to accomplish. (RD)

11 *Asava*: the four 'biases', that is, bias for sensuality, for eternal existence, for having views on things, for ignorance.

12 The *Dhamma-cakkhu*, a technical term for conversion, for entering on the Path that ends in arahatship. It is higher than the supra-normal vision mentioned in paragraph 95 of the text, which sees other people's previous births, and below the Eye of Wisdom which is the wisdom of the arahat.

Characteristics of the True Brahman
(*Sonadanda Sutta*)

The *Sonadanda Sutta*, so named from the brahman around whom this Dialogue centres, has the town of Campa in eastern Bihar as its setting. Campa was the chief town of the Anga territory, probably on account of its strategic importance on the southern bank of the Ganges, where this great river is joined by the river Chandan. About a hundred miles to the east of Rajgir, the scene of the *Samanna-phala Sutta*, it has been described as a cosmopolitan city where teachers of various different religious doctrines were to be found engaging in public discussion. It is said also to have been a place where the Buddha had numerous followers.[1] It is noteworthy that only forty miles or so beyond the site of Campa, eastwards, one reaches the border of Bengal. This tells us something about the probable eastward expansion of Buddhism as well as Brahmanism at a very early period.

It was here that a rich brahman of the town, Sonadanda, went out to visit the Buddha and to hear his discourse. Appropriately, the subject of the Buddha's teaching on this occasion is represented as having dealt with the question of what essentially makes a man a brahman, *other than* birth and social status. As Rhys Davids pointed out, the logical outcome of the Buddha's argument in this Dialogue is incompatible with the brahmans' *hereditary* supremacy in Indian society. Sonadanda 'is gradually led on by the usual Socratic method adopted in so many of the Dialogues, to accept one self-evident truth after another. There is indeed nothing, till we come to that last paragraph, which any intelligent brahman could not, with safety, and with due regard to his own doctrine, fully accept. In other words, the doctrine of brahman supremacy was intellectually indefensible. It was really quite inconsistent with the ethical standard of the times, which the brahmans, in common with the rest of the people, fully accepted.'[2]

At the conclusion of the Dialogue (paragraphs 24 to 25) Sonadanda is represented (in the stylized convention which is frequently used in the Buddhist Suttas) as confessing his admiration for the Buddha's insight and his allegiance to him henceforth as his guide, asking the Buddha to accept him as a disciple. One reservation, however, is recorded on this particular occasion: Sonadanda asks permission to be allowed, when he is in the company of his fellow-brahmans, *not* to rise from his seat and make obeisance on the entry of the Buddha. The commentator Buddhaghosa suggests, as an explanation, that this was because Sonadanda was much older than the Buddha, the latter being young enough to be his grandson. This is not impossible, if the Dialogue had taken place very soon after the Buddha's enlightenment at about the age of forty; but it is possible also, as Malalasekera points out,[3] that Sonadanda's conversion was only partial.

1 Chaudhury, 1969 (see Bibliography), p. 122.
2 Rhys Davids, *Dialogues*, I, 138.
3 *DPPN* (see Bibliography), II, 1297.

Thus have I heard:

1. The Master once, when going on a tour through the Anga country[1] with a great multitude of the brethren, with about five hundred brethren, arrived at Campa.[2] And there at Campa he lodged on the bank of the Gaggara lotus-pool.[3]

Now at that time the brahman Sonadanda was dwelling at Campa, a place teeming with life, having much grassland, and woodland, and water, and corn. A royal domain had been presented to him by Seniya Bimbisara, the raja of Magadha, as a royal possession, with power over it as though he were a raja.

2. Now the brahmans and householders of Campa heard the news: 'Samanna Gotama of the Shakya clan, who went out from a Shakya family to the life of a homeless wanderer, has now arrived, with a great company of the brethren at Campa, and is

staying there on the shore of the Gaggara lotus-pool. Now this venerable Gotama has a high reputation: that he is fully awakened, endowed with wisdom and goodness, well-favoured, having supernal knowledge, without an equal as a guide to mortals, a teacher of human and celestial beings, an Exalted One, a Buddha. He himself thoroughly knows and sees, face to face, as it were, this universe – including the worlds of the celestial beings, the Brahmas, and the Maras, and the world below with its samannas and brahmans, its princes and peoples. Knowing all this, he makes his knowledge known to others. The truth, lovely in its origin, lovely in its progress, lovely in its consummation, he proclaims both in the spirit and in the letter.

The higher life he makes known in all its fullness, and in all its purity. It is good to pay visits to arahats like that.'

Then the brahmans and householders of Campa began to leave the city, clustered in groups, to go to the Gaggara lotus-pool.

3. At that time Sonadanda the brahman had gone to the upper terrace of his house for his mid-day rest. Seeing the people going by, he said to his doorkeeper: 'Why are the people of Campa all going like this towards the Gaggara lotus-pool?'

So the doorkeeper told him the news. And Sonadanda said: 'Then, good doorkeeper, go to the brahmans and householders of Campa, and say to them: "Sonadanda the brahman requests them to wait. He also will go to see Samanna Gotama." '

'Very good, sir,' said the doorkeeper, and he did so.

4. At that time there were about five hundred brahmans from different kingdoms staying at Campa for some business or other. When they heard that Sonadanda intended to visit Samanna Gotama, they went to him and asked whether that was the case.

'That is my intention, gentleman; I propose to call on Samanna Gotama.'

'It would be better if the venerable Sonadanda did not. It is not appropriate for him to do so. If it were the venerable Sonadanda who went to call upon him, then the venerable Sonadanda's reputation would decrease and Samanna Gotama's would increase. This is the first reason, sir, why you should not call upon him, but he upon you.'

5. They pointed out also to Sonadanda the brahman a number of other considerations, as follows:

That Sonadanda was well born on both sides, of pure descent through the mother and through the father back through seven generations, with no slur upon him, and no reproach, in respect of birth.

That he was a scholar who knew the mantras by heart; was a master of the three Vedic samhitas and other scholarly subjects, as well as legends, idioms, grammar, nature-lore, and the theory of the signs on the body of a great man.

That he was handsome, pleasant in appearance, inspiring trust, with great beauty of complexion, fair in colour, fine in presence and stately in manner.

That he was virtuous, very virtuous, most exceedingly virtuous.

That he had a pleasant voice and pleasing delivery, and had the gift of a polite manner; his words were distinct and suitable for making clear the matter in hand.

That he was the teacher of teachers, who instructed three hundred brahmans in the repetition of the mantras, many young brahmans, also having come from various directions and various counties, all wishing to learn the mantras by heart under him.

That he was venerable, old, and well advanced in years, long-lived and of great seniority.

That he was honoured, esteemed, respected, venerated and revered by Seniya Bimbisara, the raja of Magadha, and by Pokkharasadi, the brahman.

That he dwelt at Campa, a place teeming with life, having much grassland, and woodland, and corn, on a royal domain granted him by Seniya Bimbisara, the raja of Magadha, with power over it as if he himself were a raja.

For each of these reasons it was not fitting that he, Sonadanda the brahman, should call upon Samanna Gotama, but rather that Samanna Gotama should call upon him.

6. To this, Sonadanda replied as follows: 'Now, gentleman, listen, and I will tell you why it *is* fitting that I should call upon the venerable Gotama, and not he should call upon me.

'Most assuredly, gentlemen, the venerable Gotama is well

born on both sides, on the mother's; and on the father's; he is of pure descent back through seven generations, with no slur cast upon him, and no reproach in respect of birth.

'Assuredly Samanna Gotama has taken the life of a homeless wanderer, leaving the great clan of his ancestors.

'Samanna Gotama has gone out from home to the life of the homeless wanderer, giving up money and riches, treasure and property.

'Samanna Gotama, while he was still a young man, without a grey hair in his head, in the pride of his early manhood, went out from home to the homeless wanderer's life; though his father and mother were unwilling, and wept so that their cheeks became wet with tears, he nevertheless cut off his hair and beard, and put on the yellow robes, and went out from home life to the life of a homeless wanderer.

'Most assuredly, gentlemen, Samanna Gotama is handsome, pleasant in appearance, inspiring trust, gifted with great beauty of complexion, fair in colour, fine in presence, stately to behold, virtuous with the virtue of the arahats, good and virtuous, thoroughly endowed with goodness and virtue.

'Samanna Gotama has a pleasant voice, and a pleasing delivery, he has the gift of a polite manner, and his words are distinct and well chosen so as to make clear the matter in hand.

'He is the teacher of those who themselves teach many people.

'Assuredly, for Samanna Gotama lust and passion are extinct, and he has finished with fickleness of mind.

'Assuredly, Samanna Gotama believes both in the law of Karma and in the reality of action; he rates goodness of life higher than brahman birth.

'Samanna Gotama went out from a distinguished family, eminent among the kshatriya clans.

'He went out from a family that was prosperous, well-to-do, and rich.

'And most assuredly, gentlemen, people come right across the country from distant lands to ask questions of Samanna Gotama.

'Multitudes of heavenly beings put their trust in Samanna Gotama.

'The high reputation concerning Samanna Gotama which has spread everywhere is that he is an arahat, exalted, fully awakened, endowed with wisdom and righteousness, well favoured, and having supernal knowledge, an exalted one, a Buddha –

'Samanna Gotama has all the thirty-two bodily marks of a great man. He bids all men welcome, he is congenial, conciliatory, not supercilious, accessible to all, and one who makes conversation easy.

'Samanna Gotama is honoured, esteemed, respected, venerated and revered by the four classes of his followers [the brethren and sisters of the Order, laymen and lay women].

'Assuredly many gods and men believe in Samanna Gotama, and in whatsoever village or town Samanna Gotama stays, non-human beings do the humans no harm.

'Samanna Gotama as the head of a community, of a school, as the teacher of a school, is acknowledged to be foremost of all the founders of such groups. Whereas some samannas and brahmans have gained a reputation in trivial ways, not so Samanna Gotama. His reputation comes from perfection in conduct and righteousness.

'The raja of Magadha, Seniya Bimbisara, with his children and his wives, with his people and his courtiers, has put his trust in Samanna Gotama.

'Pasenadi, raja of Kosala, with his children and his wives, with his people and his courtiers, has put his trust in Samanna Gotama.

'Pokkharasadi the brahman, with his children and his wives, with his people and his intimates, has put his trust in Samanna Gotama.

'Samanna Gotama is honoured, esteemed, respected, venerated and revered by all three; by Seniya Bimbisara, raja of Magadha, by Pasenadi, raja of Kosala, and by Pokkharasadi, the brahman –

'And now gentlemen, Samanna Gotama has arrived at Campa, and is staying on the shores of the Gaggara lotus-pool. All samannas and brahmans who come into our borders are our guests. And we should esteem and honour, venerate and revere our guests. That is how he has come to us, and that is how he should be treated, as a guest.

'In view of all these considerations it is not fitting that Samanna Gotama should call upon us, but rather it is fitting that we should call upon him. And so far I know the excellences of Samanna Gotama only in those respects which I have mentioned, but these are not all of them, for his excellence is beyond measure.'

7. When he had said this, the brahmans responded: 'The venerable Sonadanda declares the praises of Samanna Gotama in such terms that were he to be dwelling even a hundred leagues from here, it would be enough to make a man of faith go thither to call upon him, even had he to carry a bag [for the provisions for the journey] on his back. Let us then all go to call on Samanna Gotama together!'

So Sonadanda the brahman went out to Gaggara lotus-pool with a great company of brahmans.

8. Now the following hesitation arose in Sonadanda's mind as he passed through the wood: 'Were I to ask Samanna Gotama a question, and if he were to say: "The question ought not to be asked in that way; this is how it should be asked," the company might thereupon speak of me with disrespect, and say: "What a fool is this Sonadanda the brahman! how inexpert! He is not even able to put a question correctly." And if they did so my reputation would decrease; and with my reputation my income would grow less, for our prosperity depends on our reputation. Again, if Samanna Gotama were to put a question to me, he might not approve of my explanation of the problem. And if they were then to say to me: "The question ought not to be answered in this way," and then set out how the problem was to be explained, the company might as a result speak of me with disrespect, and say: "How foolish is this Sonadanda the brahman! So inexpert! He is not even able to satisfy Samanna Gotama by his explanation of the problem." And if they did so, my reputation would decrease; and with my reputation my income would grow less, for our prosperity depends on our reputation.

'On the other hand if, having come so far, I should turn back without calling on Samanna Gotama, then the company may speak disrespectfully of me, and say: "What a fool is this

Sonadanda the brahman! How inexpert! And what is more, how obstinate with pride he is, afraid even to call on Samanna Gotama. How can he turn back after having come so far?" If they did so, my reputation would decrease; and with my reputation my income would grow less. And our prosperity depends on our reputation.'

9. So Sonadanda the brahman went up to where the Master was. When he arrived, he exchanged greetings and the compliments of politeness and courtesy with the Master, and sat down at his side. Some of the brahmans and householders bowed to the Blessed One and took their seats on one side; some of them exchanged with him the greetings and compliments of politeness and courtesy, and then took their seats at his side; some of them called out their name and family, and then took their seats at the side; and some of them took their seats at the side in silence.

10. Now as Sonadanda sat there he still felt some hesitation, just as before he set out. But now he added, to himself: 'Oh! if only Samanna Gotama would ask me some question on my own subject, on the threefold Veda, then I should certainly be able to gain his approval by my exposition of the problem!'

11. Now the Master became aware in his own mind of the hesitation in the mind of Sonadanda, and he thought: 'This Sonadanda is feeling nervous; I had better question him on his own doctrine.' So he said to him: 'What are the things, brahman, which the brahmans say a man ought to have in order to be a brahman, so that if he says: "I am a brahman," he speaks accurately and is not guilty of falsehood?'

12. Then Sonadanda thought: 'What I so much wished for, and had in my mind and hoped for, that Samanna Gotama should put to me some question on my own subject, on the threefold Veda, that very thing he now does. If only I can satisfy him with my exposition!'

13. So, drawing his body up erect, and looking round on the assembly, he said to the Master: 'The brahmans, Gotama, declare him to be a brahman able to say "I am a brahman" without being guilty of falsehood, who has five things. What are the five? In the first place, sir, a brahman has to be well born on both sides, on the mother's side and on the father's side, of pure

descent back through seven generations, with no slur upon him, and no reproach in respect of birth.

'Then he must be a scholar who knows the mystic verses by heart, one who has mastered the three Vedic samhitas and other scholarly subjects, as well as legends, idioms, grammar, nature-lore, and the theory of the signs on the body of a great man.

'He must be handsome, pleasant in appearance, inspiring trust, with great beauty of complexion, fair in colour, fine in presence, and stately in manner. He must be virtuous, very virtuous, most exceedingly virtuous.

'Then he must be learned and wise, first-class, or nearly so, among those who handle the sacrificial ladle.'[4]

14. 'Of these five things, brahman, is it possible to leave one out, and to declare the man who has the other four to be a brahman, so that he can, without falsehood, claim to be a brahman?'

'Yes, Gotama, that can be done. We could leave out colour. For what does colour matter? If he has the other four – good birth, scholarly training, virtue and wisdom, as just set forth – brahmans would still declare him to be a brahman; and he could rightly, without danger of falsehood, claim to be one.'

15. 'But of these *four* things, brahman, is it possible to leave one out, and to declare the man who has the other three to be a brahman, so that he can rightly, and without falsehood, claim to be a brahman?'

'Yes, Gotama, that could be done. We could leave out the verses. For what do the verses matter? If he has the other three – good birth, virtue and wisdom – brahmans would still declare him to be a brahman; and he could rightly, without danger of falsehood, claim to be one.'

16. 'But of these *three* things, brahman, is it possible to leave one out, and to declare the man who has the other two to be a brahman, so that he can accurately, and without falsehood, claim to be a brahman?'

'Yes, Gotama, that could be done. We could leave out birth. For what does birth matter? If he has the other two – virtue and wisdom – brahmans would still declare him to be a brahman; and he could rightly, without danger of falsehood, claim to be one.'

17. When he had said this, the other brahmans said to Sonadanda: 'No, no! venerable Sonadanda, this is not so!' And to one another they said: 'He depreciates not only our colour, but he depreciates our scholarship and our good birth. The venerable Sonadanda is going right over to the doctrine of Samanna Gotama.'

18. Then the Master said to those brahmans: 'If you, brahmans, think that Sonadanda is unlearned or that he speaks crudely, or that he is unwise, that he is unable to hold his own with me in this matter, let him keep silence, while you discuss with me. But if you think he is learned, eloquent, wise, and able to hold his own, then you please keep silence, and let him discuss with me.'

19. And when the Master had thus spoken, Sonadanda the brahman said to those other brahmans: 'My venerable friends, please do not say that. I do not depreciate our colour, nor our scholarship, nor our good birth.'

20. Now a young brahman named Angaka, sister's son to Sonadanda the brahman, was sitting among them. And Sonadanda said to the brahmans: 'Venerable friends, you see this Angaka, our nephew?'

'Yes, sir, we see him.'

'Well! Angaka is handsome, pleasant in appearance, inspiring trust, with great beauty of complexion, fair in colour, fine in presence, and stately in manner, no one in this assembly is his equal in colour, save only Samanna Gotama.

'And Angaka, sirs, is a scholar who knows the mantras by heart, he has mastered the three Vedic samhitas as well as legends, idioms, grammar, nature-lore and the theory of the signs of the body of a great man — I myself have taught him the verses.

'And Angaka, sirs, is well born on both sides, on the mother's side and on the father's side, of pure descent back through seven generations, with no slur upon him, and no reproach in respect of birth. I myself know his forebears, on the mother's side and on the father's.

'Now, sirs, if Angaka should kill living things, and take what has not been given, and become an adulterer, and tell lies, and drink liquor, what then would his colour be worth? what the verses? what his birth?

'It is in so far as a brahman is virtuous, very virtuous, exceedingly virtuous, in so far as he is learned and wise, and first-class, or nearly so, among those who handle the sacrificial ladle, that brahmans would declare him, endowed as he is with these two qualities, to be a brahman, to be one who could rightly say, "I am a brahman" without falsehood.'

21. 'Then', said the Master, 'of these two things, brahman, is it possible to leave one out, and to declare the man who has the other to be a brahman, to be one who can rightly, and without falsehood, claim to be a brahman?'

'No so, Gotama! For wisdom, Gotama, is purified by morality, and morality is purified by wisdom. Where there is morality, there is wisdom, and where there is wisdom there is morality. To the one who practises morality there is wisdom, to the one who has wisdom there is morality; wisdom and morality are declared to be supreme in the world. Just, Gotama, as one might wash hand with hand, or foot with foot, just so is wisdom purified by morality and morality by wisdom.'

22. 'That is so, brahman. I, too, say the same. But what *is* that uprightness, and what is that wisdom?'

'We only know, Gotama, the general proposition concerning this matter. Will the venerable Gotama please explain the meaning of the phrase?'

'Well then, brahman, listen carefully, and pay attention, and I will say something about it.'

23. 'Very well, sir,' said Sonadanda in reply. And the Master spoke as follows: [What then follow are the words found in the *Samanna-phala Sutta* (see above), paragraphs 40 to 63, on the appearing of a Buddha, his teaching, the conviction of the hearer, his renunciation of worldly life, the statements concerning morality (*sila*) and the confidence of the bhikkhu. This is followed by the words found in the *Samanna-phala Sutta*, paragraphs 75 to 98 inclusive, which should be read at this point.]

'This, brahman, is that wisdom.'

24. When the Master had said this, Sonadanda the brahman replied: 'Most excellent! Gotama, most excellent! It is as though someone had set up again what had been thrown down, or had revealed what had been hidden away, or had pointed out the

right road to someone who had got lost, or had brought a light into the darkness so that those who had eyes could see the shape of things – just so has the truth been made known to me, in many a figure, by the venerable Gotama. So I, even I, take myself to the venerable Gotama as my guide, to the Doctrine and to the Community. May the venerable Gotama accept me as a disciple, as one who, from this day, as long as life lasts, has taken him as his guide. May the venerable Gotama do me the honour of taking his meal with me tomorrow, and also the members of the Community with him.'

The Master signified, by silence, his consent. Sonadanda, seeing that the Master had accepted, got up from his seat and bowed before the Master, and walking round him, keeping his right side toward him, went away. At daybreak he had delicious food, both curry and sweetmeats, made ready, and announced to the Master: 'It is time, Gotama, and the meal is ready.'

25. Then the Master, who had dressed early in the morning, put on his robe, and taking his bowl with him, went with the brethren to Sonadanda's house, and sat down in the place prepared for him. And Sonadanda the brahman himself served the Master and the brethren, with his own hand, with that delicious food, until they could accept no more. When the Master had finished his meal, and had cleansed the bowl and his hands, Sonadanda took a low seat, and sat beside him, and said:

26. 'If, Gotama, after I have entered the assembly, I should rise from my seat to bow down before the venerable Gotama, then the assembly would find fault with me.[5] Now should the assembly find fault with someone, his reputation would grow less; and he who thus lost his reputation, would lose also his income. For our property depends upon our reputation. If, then, when I am seated in the assembly, I stretch forth my joined palms in salutation, let the venerable Gotama accept that from me as a rising up from my seat. And if when I am seated in the assembly I take off my turban, let the venerable Gotama accept that from me as a salutation with my head. So if, when I am in my chariot, I were to get down from the chariot to salute the venerable Gotama, the bystanders would find fault with me. If, then, when mounted on my chariot, I bend down low the stick

which is in my hand, let the venerable Gotama accept that from me as if I had got down. And if, when mounted on my chariot, I should wave my hand, let the venerable Gotama accept that from me as if I had bowed low in salutation!'[6]

27. Then the Master instructed, exhorted, gladdened and delighted Sonadanda the brahman with talk concerning Dhamma, and then rose from his seat and went away.

Here ends the Sonadanda Sutta

1 Identified with the modern districts of Bhagalpur and Monghyr in the state of Bihar.

2 Campa was the capital of the Anga country. From India the name was carried to South-East Asia by colonists, or émigré brahmans.

3 So called after Queen Gaggara, who had had it excavated, says Buddhaghosa. He adds that on its banks was a grove of champaka trees, so well known for the fragrance of their beautiful white flowers. It was under those trees that the wandering mendicants settled.

4 That is, 'officiate at a sacrifice by pouring out of a spoon a libation of butter, or of spirituous Soma, to the fire god'.

5 On the ground, says the commentator Buddhaghosa, that he would be saluting a much younger man, one young enough to be his grandson. If this tradition is correct, it would follow that this Sutta must be describing events very early in the public ministry of the Buddha.

6 It will be seen from this section that Sonadanda is represented as being a convert only to a limited extent. He still keeps on his school of Vedic studies, and is keenly anxious to retain the good opinion of his students, and of other brahmans. And if that part of the Buddha's doctrine put before him in this Sutta is examined, it will be found to be, with perhaps one or two exceptions, quite compatible with the best brahman views. No doubt if every detail were carried to its strict logical conclusion there would be no further need for Vedic studies, except from the historical standpoint. But those details are, on the face of them ethical. They belong to a plane not touched on in the then Vedic studies. They could be accepted by an adherent of the soul theory of life. And the essential doctrines of Buddhism – the Path, the Truths and arahatship – are barely even referred to. (RD)

A Buddha's Qualification for Teaching
(*Lohicca Sutta*)

The scene of this Dialogue, known as the *Lohicca Sutta*, is the land of Kosala. The Kosalas were a people who inhabited the area to the north-west of Magadha (and east of modern Lucknow) in what is now the Indian state of Uttar Pradesh. Kosala was a monarchy ruled over by Pasenadi, who, like Bimbisara, was a friend and supporter of the Buddha. He is said to have been generally a ruler who 'valued the companionship of good and wise men' who frequently visited the Buddha to discuss various matters with him. Although he became a follower of the Buddha quite early in the period of the latter's activity, this in no way inhibited his generosity towards other religious leaders. We are told in this Sutta that he had extended his favour towards a brahman named Lohicca, and settled on him an estate at a place called Salavatika. It is this brahman, Lohicca, who here engages in dialogue with the Buddha on the question of who is a fit person to teach others. It is noteworthy that the later brahman view[1] regarding the exclusive divinely imparted right of the brahman class to possess and transmit sacred learning is not here upheld. The general tenor of the Dialogue is that whatever truth a man discovers for himself it is right and proper for him to teach it to others, of whatever social class, *given that he has thoroughly taught himself,* and has thus acquired the right to teach others.

---

1 See *The Law of Manu* (Manava Sastra), I, 88.

Thus have I heard:

1. The Master, when he was passing through the Kosala country with a great multitude of the members of the Community, about five hundred bhikkhus, arrived at Salavatika (a village surrounded by a row of sal trees). At that time Lohicca the brahman had established himself at Salavatika, a place teeming with life, having grassland, and woodland, and corn. A royal domain had been granted him by Pasenadi the raja of Kosala, as a gift, and he had power over it as though he were a raja.

2. At that time Lohicca the brahman was entertaining the following ill-conceived notion: 'Suppose that a samanna or a brahman should reach some good state [of mind], then he should tell no one else about it. For what can one man do for another? To tell others would be like the man who, having broken through an old bond, entangles himself in a new one. This desire to declare one's discoveries to others is a form of greed. For what can one man do for another?'[1]

3. Then Lohicca the brahman heard the news that Samanna Gotama, one of the Shakya clan who left his home for the life of a homeless wanderer, had now on his tour through the Kosala country, with a great company of the brethren of his community, arrived at Salavatika. This venerable Gotama has a high reputation: he is an arahat, fully awakened, endowed with wisdom and goodness, well favoured, having supernal knowledge, without an equal as a guide to mortals, of human and celestial beings an exalted one, a Buddha. He himself thoroughly knows, and sees as it were face to face, this universe – including the worlds of the celestial beings, the Brahmas, and the Maras; and the world below with its samannas and brahmans, its princes and peoples. Knowing all this, he makes his knowledge known to others. The Truth, lovely in its origin, lovely in its progress, lovely in its consummation, he proclaims both in the spirit and in the letter. The higher life he makes known in all its fullness, and in all its purity. It is good to pay visits to arahats like that.

4. Then Lohicca the brahman said to Bhesika the barber: 'Good Bhesika, please go to where Samanna Gotama is staying,

49

and, on your arrival, ask in my name whether his sickness and indisposition has abated, and about his health and vigour and general comfort, and then ask the venerable Gotama, and with him the brethren of his community, to accept a meal tomorrow from Lohicca the brahman.'

5. 'Very well, sir,' said Bhesika the barber, acknowledging what Lohicca the brahman had said, and did exactly as he had been requested. And the Master consented, by silence, to this invitation.

6. And when Bhesika the barber perceived that the Master had consented, he rose from his seat, and passing the Master with his right hand towards him, returned to Lohicca the brahman, and reported to him as follows: 'Sir, I delivered your message to the Master, and he has consented to come.'

7. The next day Lohicca the brahman made ready at his own dwelling-place delicious food, both curry and sweetmeats, and said to Bhesika the barber: 'Now, good Bhesika, go to where Samanna Gotama is staying, and announce to him: "It is time, Gotama, and the meal is ready." '

'Very good, sir,' said Bhesika the barber, and did as Lohicca the brahman had said. So the Master, who had robed himself in the early morning, went, carrying his bowl with him, accompanied by the brethren of the Community, in the direction of Salavatika.

8. As he went, Bhesika the barber walked step by step behind the Master. And he said to him:[2] 'The following ill-conceived notion has occurred to Lohicca the brahman: "Suppose that a samanna or a brahman should reach some good state [of mind], then he should tell no one else about it. For what can one man do for another? To tell others would be like the man who, having broken through an old bond, entangles himself in a new one. This desire to declare to others is a form of greed." It would be good, sir, if the Master would instruct him about the truth of the matter. For what can one man do for another?'

'Perhaps, Bhesika, perhaps.'

9. And the Master went on to the place where Lohicca the brahman lived, and sat down on the seat prepared for him. Lohicca the brahman himself served the Community, and the Buddha at its head, with delicious food, curry and sweetmeats,

until they could accept no more. And when the Exalted One had finished his meal, and had cleansed the bowl and his hands, Lohicca the brahman brought a low seat and sat down beside him. And to him, thus seated, the Master spoke as follows:

'Is it true, what they say, Lohicca, that the following ill-conceived notion has arisen in your mind: [and he set it forth, as above]?'

'That is so, Gotama.'

10. 'Now what think you, Lohicca? Are you not established at Salavatika?'

'That is so, Gotama.'

'Then suppose, Lohicca, someone were to say: "Lohicca the brahman has his own domain at Salavatika. Let him enjoy all the revenue and all the produce of Salavatika, by himself, allowing nothing to anybody else!" Would the utterer of those words be dangerous to the men who live in dependence upon you, or not?'

'Dangerous, Gotama.'

'And if dangerous, would he be a person who could be said to sympathize with their welfare, or not?'

'He would not be one who sympathized, Gotama.'

'And not sympathizing with their welfare, would his attitude be one of love toward them, or enmity?'

'Enmity, Gotama.'

'But when enmity is present, is the man's doctrine likely to be false, or true?'

'False, Gotama.'

'Now if a man holds false doctrine, Lohicca, I declare that one of two future births will be his lot, either purgatory, or rebirth as an animal.'

11. 'Now what do you think, Lohicca? Is not Pasenadi, raja of Kosala, in possession of Kasi and Kosala?'

'Yes, that is so, Gotama.'

'Then suppose, Lohicca, one were to speak thus: "Pasenadi, raja of Kosala, is in possession of Kasi and Kosala. Let him enjoy all the revenue and all the produce of Kasi and Kosala, allowing nothing to anybody else." Would the utterer of those words be a danger to the men who live in dependence on Pasenadi of Kosala – both you yourself and others – or not?'

'He would be a danger, Gotama.'

'And being a danger, would he be a person who sympathized with their welfare, or not?'

'He would not be a sympathizer, Gotama.'

'And not being a sympathizer with their welfare, would his attitude be one of love toward them, or enmity?'

'Enmity, Gotama.'

'But when enmity is present is the doctrine likely to be false, or true?'

'False, Gotama.'

'Now if a man holds false doctrine, Lohicca, I declare that one of two future births will be his lot, either purgatory, or rebirth as an animal.

12 and 14. 'So then, Lohicca, you admit that anyone who says that you, being in occupation of Salavatika, should therefore yourself enjoy all the revenue and produce thereof, bestowing nothing on anyone else; and anyone who says that Pasenadi, raja of Kosala, being in power over Kasi and Kosala, should therefore himself enjoy all the revenue and produce thereof, bestowing nothing on anyone else – would be a danger to those living in dependence upon the raja; and that those who are thus a danger to others, must be wanting in sympathy for them; and that enmity is present in the heart of the man who is thus wanting in sympathy. And that when enmity is present, the doctrine is false.

13 and 15. 'Then just so, Lohicca, in the case of anyone who says, "Suppose a samanna or a brahman reaches some good state [of mind], then should he tell no one else about it. For what can one man do for another? To tell others would be like the man who, having broken through an old bond, entangles himself in a new one. This desire to declare to others, it is a form of greed"; just so, therefore, anyone who speaks in this way is putting obtstacles in the way of those who, having taken upon themselves the Doctrine and Discipline set forth by the Tathagata,[3] and having attained to great distinction therein – to the fruit of conversion, for instance, or to the fruit of once-returning, or to the fruit of never-returning, or even to arahatship – he would be putting obstacles in the way of those who are bringing to fruition the course of conduct that will lead

to rebirth in states of bliss in heaven.⁴ In putting obstacles in their way he would be out of sympathy for their welfare; being out of sympathy for their welfare would show that enmity was present in his heart; and when enmity is present, the doctrine is false. Now if a man holds false doctrine, Lohicca, I declare that one of two future births will be his lot, either purgatory or rebirth as an animal.⁵

16. 'There are these three sorts of teachers in the world, Lohicca, who are worthy of blame. And whoever blames such teachers would be justified in doing so for his rebuke would be in accord with the facts and the truth. What are the three?

'In the first place, Lohicca, there is the teacher who has not himself attained the aim of becoming a samanna, in pursuit of which he left home and adopted the homeless life. Without having himself attained to it he teaches a doctrine to his hearers, saying: "This is good for you, this will make you happy." Then those hearers of his do not listen to him, they pay no attention to his words, and they are in no way changed by what they hear; they go their own way, regardless of his teaching. Such a teacher is open to the criticism of being like a man who continually makes advances to a woman who keeps repulsing him, or who embraces a woman who keeps turning her face away from him. To go on posing as a teacher of men, when no one heeds, since they do not trust you, that is, in the same way, a matter of greed. For what, then, can one man do for another?

'This, Lohicca, is the first sort of teacher in the world worthy of blame. And whoever blames such a teacher would be justified in doing so, for his rebuke would be in accord with the facts and the truth.

17. 'In the second place, Lohicca, there is a sort of teacher who has not attained his aim of becoming a samanna, in the pursuit of which he left his home and adopted the homeless life. Without having himself attained to it he teaches a doctrine to his hearers, saying: "This is good for you; this will make you happy." His disciples listen to him; they pay attention to his words; they become strengthened by their understanding and they never depart from the teaching of the master, or follow their own way. Such a teacher may be criticized for being like a man who, neglecting his own field, is concerned to weed his

neighbour's field. To go on teaching others when you have not taught yourself, that too, is a matter of greed. For what, then, can one man do for another?

'This, Lohicca, is the second sort of teacher in the world worthy of blame. And whoever blames such a teacher would be justified in doing so, for his rebuke would be in accord with the facts and the truth.

18. 'And again, Lohicca, in the third place, there is a sort of teacher who has himself attained the aim of becoming a samanna, in the pursuit of which he left his home and adopted the homeless life. Having attained it, he teaches the doctrine to his hearers, saying: "This is for your good, this will make you happy." But those hearers of his neither listen to him, nor pay attention to his words, nor are they strengthened through their understanding of his doctrine; they go their own way, apart from the teaching of the master. Such a teacher may indeed be criticized for being like a man who, having broken through an old bond, entangles himself in a new one. To go on teaching when you have not trained yourself to teach, that is a matter of greed. For what, then, can one man do for another?

'This, Lohicca, is the third sort of teacher in the world worthy of blame. And whoever blames such a teacher would be justified, in accord with the facts and the truth. These, Lohicca, are the three sorts of teachers of which I spoke.'

19. And when he had thus spoken, Lohicca the brahman said to the Master: 'But is there, Gotama, any sort of teacher not worthy of blame in the world?'

'Yes, Lohicca, there is a teacher not worthy of blame.'

'And what sort of a teacher, Gotama, is that?'

[The reply the Buddha then makes to Lohicca's question consists in the words found in the *Samanna-phala Sutta* (see above), paragraphs 40 to 84, 96, and 97. The refrain throughout, and the closing paragraph is: 'And whoever the teacher may be, Lohicca, under whom the disciple attains such noble distinction, he is a teacher not open to blame. Whoever blames such a teacher would not be justified in doing so, for his rebuke would not be in accord either with the facts or with the truth.']

78. When the Master had thus spoken, Lohicca the brah-

man said: 'Gotama, it is just as if a man had caught hold of another man, falling over the precipitous edge of purgatory, by the hair of his head, and had lifted him up safe back onto the firm land – just so have I, on the point of falling into purgatory, been lifted back onto the land by the venerable Gotama. Most excellent, Gotama, are your words, most excellent! Just as if a man were to set up what has been thrown down, or were to reveal what has been hidden away, or were to point out the right road to him who has gone astray, or were to bring a light into the darkness so that those who had eyes could see external forms – just even so has the Truth been made known to me, in many a figure, by the venerable Gotama. And I, even I, betake myself to the venerable Gotama as my guide, to the Doctrine and to the Community. May the venerable Gotama accept me as a disciple; as one who, from this day forth as long as life endures, has taken him as his guide!'

Here ends the Lohicca Sutta

1   The implied ground of the argument is the proposition that a man's rise or fall, progress or defeat, in intellectual and religious matters, lies in himself. He must work out his own salvation.

2   It is clear that Bhesika was already a follower of the new teaching.

3   A title of the Buddha.

4   Literally: 'Who are making heavenly embryos ripe for rebirth in heavenly states.'

5   Paragraphs 12, 13 are repeated of the case put about Pasenadi, king of Kosala. In the translation both cases are included at the beginning of paragraph 12.

The Soul Theory
(*Potthapada Sutta*)

The setting for this Dialogue is the Anathapindika Park, on the outskirts of the city of Savatthi. This was the capital of the kingdom of Kosala, and one of the six major cities of northern India at the time of the Buddha. The 'Park' took its name from Anathapindika, a rich banker of Savatthi, who had become a follower of the Buddha after hearing him discourse at the city of Rajgir, capital of Magadha, when Anathapindika was there on business. The latter then invited the Buddha to spend the rainy season in Savatthi, and the Buddha agreed to do so. Anathapindika returned there and decided that a suitable place for the Buddha and his community to stay would be Jeta's Wood. This piece of forest land near the city of Savatthi belonged to a Prince Jeta, who asked an extremely high price for the plot of land, which Anathapindaka nevertheless paid. Impressed by the latter's generosity, Jeta himself contributed to the cost of putting up suitable buildings for a rainy season retreat – dwelling huts, dining halls, storerooms, bathrooms and so on. Included among these was an open-sided shelter (*sala*), where public discussions could take place; almost a sort of debating chamber, but perhaps, more appropriately, a venue for philosophical disputations.

Rhys Davids comments that 'the very fact of the erection of such a place is another proof of the freedom of thought prevalent in the eastern valley of the Ganges in the sixth century BC'. Buddhaghosa says that various teachers used to meet at 'the Shelter' for discussion, including brahmans.

This was the scene for a dialogue between the Buddha and a wealthy man called Potthapada, whose name refers to the autumn month (September – October) in which he was born. According to the commentator Buddhaghosa, this wealthy man was a member of the brahman class. Rhys Davids comments that if this were so, it is notable that he addresses the Buddha not by his clan name, Gotama, as brahmans are usually represented as doing in these Dialogues, but as 'Bhante', a term of respect used by the Buddha's followers.

The second part of this Dialogue (paragraphs 25 to 28) introduces the Buddhist concept of the *avyakata* questions, that is, questions which are, literally, 'indeterminate'. In the Buddhist context this means questions that are morally neutral, so that the attempt to answer them is irrelevant. Such questions are: whether the world is eternal; or is not eternal; whether it is infinite; or is finite, and so on. On such questions the Buddha expresses no opinion.

Thus have I heard:

1. The Master was once staying at Savatthi, in the Anathapindika Park, in Jeta's Wood. At that time Potthapada, a homeless wanderer, was at the shelter which had been put up in Queen Mallika's Park as a place for philosophical disputations. It was surrounded by a row of fruit trees [tindukas], and was known simply as 'the Shelter'. With Potthapada was a crowd of other homeless wanderers, about three hundred.

2. Now the Master, who had dressed in the early morning, went in his robes, and with bowl in hand, into Savatthi for alms. Then he thought: 'It is too early now to enter Savatthi for alms. Let me go to the Shelter, in the Mallika Park, where Potthapada is.'

3. When the Master reached the place, Potthapada was sitting with the crowd of mendicants; there was a lot of loud talking and shouting on all kinds of worldly affairs, with stories of kings, robbers, ministers of state, tales of war, talk about food and drink, about clothes and beds and garlands and perfumes, about their relationships, about vehicles, about villages, towns, cities and countries, about women and heroes; all the gossip of the street-corner and the well, ghost stories, legends about the creation of the land or sea, and speculations about existence and non-existence.

4. Then Potthapada, the mendicant, catching sight of the Master approaching, called the assembly to order, and said: 'Be quiet, venerable sirs! No more noise, please. Here's Samanna Gotama coming. He likes quietness and speaks in praise of quietude. It would be nice if, seeing how quiet our assembly is, he were to come and join us!' When he had said this, they all kept quiet.

5. When the Master came to where Potthapada was, the latter said to him: 'Please come and join us. You are very welcome. It is a long time since the Master made such an exception to your regular routine. Please do take a seat. Here is a place all ready.'

So the Master sat down, and Potthapada brought a low stool, and sat down beside him. Then the Master said to Potthapada, seated as he was: 'What is the subject, Potthapada, you are sitting here together to discuss; and what was the talk among you that has been interrupted?'

6. Potthapada replied: 'Never mind, sir, what subject it was we were sitting here to discuss. There will be no difficulty in the Master hearing about that afterwards. But a long time ago, sir, on several occasions, when various teachers, ascetics and brahmans had met together, and were sitting here in the Shelter, the talk was about the cessation of consciousness. The question was: "How is the cessation of consciousness brought about?"

'Now on that occasion some said: "Ideas come to a man without reason and without cause, and in the same way they pass away. At the time they spring up within him, then he becomes conscious; when they pass away, then he becomes unconscious." This was how some explained the cessation of consciousness.

'Another said: "It cannot be as you say. Consciousness is a man's soul. It is the soul that comes and goes. When the soul comes into a man then he becomes conscious, when the soul goes out of a man he becomes unconscious." This was how others explained the cessation of consciousness.

'At that, another one said: "But it cannot be as you say. For there are certain ascetics and brahmans of great power and influence. It is they who infuse consciousness into a man, and draw it away out of him. When they infuse it into him he becomes conscious, when they draw it away he becomes unconscious." That was how others explained the cessation of consciousness.

'Then I remembered the Master, and I thought: "If the Master, the Happy One were here, he who is so skilled in these things, he would know how cessation of consciousness is brought about. So tell us, now, sir: how is it?'

7. 'Well, Potthapada, those ascetics and brahmans who said that ideas come to a man and pass away without a reason, and without a cause, were wrong from the very commencement. For it is precisely through a reason, and by means of a cause, that ideas come and go. By training some ideas arise. By training, others pass away. Now, what is that training?

[Paragraphs 8 and 9 consist in the words found in paragraphs 40 to 74 inclusive of the *Samanna-phala Sutta* (see above), which should be read at this point.]

10. 'But when he has realized that these Five Hindrances have been put away from within him, gladness springs up within him, and thus gladdened he feels joy so that all his frame becomes at ease; being thus at ease he is filled with a sense of peace, and in that peace his heart is stayed. Then liberated from lust and from evil dispositions, he enters into and remains in the first stage of meditation – a state of joy and well-being born of detachment, analysis, and investigation of the mind. Then that consciousness of lust that he had before, passes away. There then arises within him a subtle, but actual consciousness of the joy and peace which arise out of detachment, and he becomes a person to whom that idea is consciously present.

'Thus is it that one idea, one sort of consciousness, arises through training, and through training another passes away. This is the training I spoke of,' said the Master.

11. 'And again, Potthapada, the bhikkhu, proceeding beyond analysis and investigation, enters into and remains in the second stage – a state of joy and well-being, born of concentration, when no reasoning or investigation goes on, a state of one-pointedness of mind, and inner tranquillity. That subtle, but actual consciousness of the joy and peace arising from detachment, that he just had, passes away. There then arises a subtle, but true consciousness of the joy and peace born of

concentration. So he becomes a person conscious of that.

'Thus also is it that one idea, one sort of consciousness, arises through training, and through training another passes away. This is the training I spoke of,' said the Master.

12. 'And again, Potthapada, the bhikkhu goes beyond the feeling of joy and becomes equable. Mindful and attentive, he experiences in his body that well-being which the arahats refer to when they say: "The man serene and attentive is well at ease." So he enters into and remains in the third stage. That subtle, but yet true consciousness, that he just had, of the joy and peace born of concentration, passes away. There then arises a subtle, but real consciousness of the bliss of equanimity. So he becomes a person conscious of that.

'Thus also is it that one idea, one sort of consciousness, arises through training, and through training another passes away. This is the training I spoke of,' said the Master.

13. 'And again, Potthapada, the bhikkhu, going beyond well-being and suffering, and by the passing away of any joy and any grief he had previously felt, enters into and remains in the fourth stage – a state of pure equanimity and mindfulness without suffering or well-being. That subtle, but yet real consciousness that he just had, of the bliss of equanimity, passes away. Thereupon there arises to him a subtle but real consciousness of the absence of suffering and of the absence of well-being. So he becomes a person conscious of that.

'Thus also is it that one idea, one sort of consciousness, arises through training, and through training another passes away. This is the training I spoke of,' said the Master.

14 'Again, Potthapada, the bhikkhu, by passing beyond consciousness of form, by putting an end to consciousness which comes from sensory reaction, by paying no heed to the idea of manifoldness, thinking: "Space is infinite," reaches up to and remains in the dimension of the infinity of space. Then the consciousness that he previously had, of form, passes away, and there arises in him the blissful consciousness, subtle but yet real, of his being concerned only with the infinity of space. And he becomes a person conscious of that.

'Thus also is it that one idea, one sort of consciousness, arises through training, and through training another passes away. This is the training I spoke of,' said the Master.

15. 'And again, Potthapada, the bhikkhu, by going altogether beyond the consciousness of space as infinite, and thinking: "Consciousness is infinite," reaches up to and remains in the dimension of the infinity of consciousness. Then the subtle, but yet real consciousness, that he just had, of the infinity of space, passes away. And there arises in him a consciousness, subtle but yet real, of everything being within the sphere of the infinity of consciousness. And he becomes a person conscious of that.

'Thus also is it that one idea, one sort of consciousness, arises through training, and through training another passes away. This is the training I spoke of,' said the Master.

16. 'And again, Potthapada, the bhikkhu, by passing quite beyond the dimension of the infinity of consciousness, thinking: "There is nothing that really is," enters and remains in the dimension of the unreality of things. Then that sense of everything being within the sphere of infinite consciousness that he just had, passes away. And there arises in him a consciousness, subtle but yet real, of unreality as the object of his thought. And he becomes a person conscious of that.

'Thus also is it that one idea, one sort of consciousness, arises through training, and through training another passes away. This is the training I spoke of,' said the Master.

17. 'So from the time, Potthapada, that the bhikkhu is thus conscious in a way brought about by himself [from the time of the first stage] he goes on from one stage to the next, and from that to the next until he reaches the summit of consciousness. And when he is on the summit it may occur to him: "To be thinking at all is bad. It would be better not to be thinking. Were I to go on thinking and conceptualizing, then these ideas, these states of consciousness I have reached, would pass away, but others, coarser ones, might arise. So I will neither think nor conceptualize any more." And he does not. And neither thinking any more, nor conceptualizing, the ideas and the states of consciousness he had pass away; and no others, coarser than they, arise. So he reaches cessation of consciousness. Thus is it, Potthapada, that the attainment of the cessation of conscious ideas takes place step by step.

18. 'Now what do you think, Potthapada? Have you ever heard, before this, of this gradual attainment of the cessation of conscious ideas? '

'No, sir, I have not. But I now understand what you say as follows: [he repeats the words of paragraph 17.]'

'That is right, Potthapada.'

19. 'And does the Master teach that there is one summit of consciousness, or that there are several?'

'In my opinion, Potthapada, there is one, and there are also several.'

'But how can the Master teach both that there is one, and that there are also several?'

'As he attains to the cessation [of one idea, one state of consciousness] after another, so does he reach, one after another, to different summits up to the last. So is it, Potthapada, that I put forward both one summit and several.'

20. 'Now is it, sir, the idea, the state of consciousness, that arises first, and afterwards knowledge; or does knowledge arise first, and afterwards the idea, the state of consciousness; or do both arise simultaneously, neither of them before or after the other?'

'It is the idea, Potthapada, the state of consciousness, that arises first, and after that knowledge. And the springing up of knowledge is dependent on the springing up of the idea, of the state of consciousness. And this may be understood from the fact that a man recognizes: "It is from this or that cause that knowledge has arisen." '

21. 'Is then, sir, the consciousness identical with a man's soul, or is consciousness one thing, and the soul another?'

'What now, Potthapada! Are you really going to revert to the idea of the "soul"?'

'What I revert to, sir, is a material soul, having form, built up of the four elements, nourished by solid food.'

'Well, if there were such a soul, Potthapada, then, even so, your consciousness would be one thing, and your soul another. That, Potthapada, can be shown from the following considerations. Granting, Potthapada, a material soul, having form, built up of the four elements, nourished by solid food; still *some* ideas, some states of consciousness, would arise to the man, while *others* would pass away. On this account also, Potthapada, you can see how consciousness must be one thing, and soul another.'

22. 'Then, sir, I revert to the notion of a soul made of mind, with all its major and minor parts complete, not deficient in any organ.'

'And granting, Potthapada, you had such a soul, the same argument would apply.'

23. 'Then, sir, I revert to the notion of a soul without form, and made of consciousness.'

'And granting, Potthapada, you had such a soul, still the same argument would apply.'

24. 'But is it possible, sir, for me to understand whether consciousness is the same thing as a man's soul, or whether consciousness is one thing, and the soul another?'

'It is hard for you, Potthapada, holding, as you do, different views, other things approving themselves to you, and setting different aims before yourself, striving after a different perfection, trained in a different system of doctrine, to understand either of these two: "Consciousness is a man's soul", or "Consciousness is one thing and the soul another".'

25–27. 'Then, sir, if that be so, tell me at least: "Is the world eternal? Is this alone the truth, and any other view mere folly?"'

'That, Potthapada, is an undetermined [*avyakata*] question.'

[Then, in the same terms, Potthapada asked each of the following questions: (2) Is the world not eternal? (3) Is the world finite? (4) Is the world infinite? (5) Is the soul the same as the body? (6) Is the soul one thing, and the body another? (7) Does one who has gained the Truth live again after death? (8) Does he not live again after death? (9) Does he both live again, and not live again, after death? (10) Does he neither live again, nor not live again, after death? – And to each question the Master made the same reply:]

'That too, Potthapada, is an undetermined question.'

28. 'But why has the Exalted One expressed no opinion on this question?'

'This question is not calculated to profit, it is not concerned with the Dhamma, it does not lead to the elements of right conduct, nor to detachment, nor to purification from lusts, nor to cessation of passion, nor to calmness, nor to supra-normal knowledge, nor to the highest wisdom, nor to nibbana. Therefore is it that I express no opinion upon it.'

29. 'Then what does the Master expound?'

'I have expounded, Potthapada, what suffering is; I have expounded what is the origin of suffering; I have expounded what is the cessation of suffering; I have expounded what is the method by which one may reach the cessation of suffering.'

30. 'And why has the Master expounded that?'

'Because the question, Potthapada, is calculated to profit, is concerned with the Dhamma, leads to the beginnings of right conduct, to detachment, to purification from lusts, to cessation of passion, to calmness, to supra-normal knowledge, to the highest wisdom, and to nibbana. That is why, Potthapada, I have expounded it.'

'That is so, Master. That is so, Well-Destined One, may the Master please do what seems fit.' So the Master rose, and went away.

31. Now no sooner had the Master gone away than those mendicants bore down upon Potthapada, the mendicant, from all sides with a torrent of jeering and taunting words, saying: 'So that's how it is! Potthapada approves of anything that this Gotama says, with his: "That is so, Master! That is so, Well-Destined One." Now we, on the other hand, fail to see that this Gotama has put forward any doctrine that is distinct with regard to any one of the ten points raised.' And they went through them all in detail.

But when they had said all this, Potthapada, the mendicant, replied: 'Neither do I see that he puts forward, as certain, any proposition with respect to those points. But Gotama, the ascetic wanderer, propounds a method in accordance with the nature of things, true and fit, based on the Dhamma and the certainty of the Dhamma. How could I refuse to approve, as well said, what has been so well said by Gotama as he propounded those things?'

32. Now after the lapse of two or three days Citta, the son of the elephant trainer, and Potthapada, the mendicant, came to the place where the Master was staying. On their arrival Citta,

the son of the elephant trainer, bowed low to the Master and took his seat on one side. Potthapada, the mendicant, exchanged with the Master the greetings and compliments of courtesy and friendship, and sat down at his side. Then he told the Master how the mendicants had jeered at him, and how he had replied.

33. 'All those mendicants, Potthapada, are blind; they can't see. You, however, are able to see. Some things, Potthapada, I have declared as certain but other things I have declared uncertain. The latter are those ten questions you raised, and for the reasons I mentioned I hold them to be matters of uncertainty. The former are the Four Truths I expounded, and for the reasons given I hold them to be matters of certainty.

34. 'There are some wandering philosophers and brahmans, Potthapada, who hold and teach the following view: "The soul is perfectly happy and healthy after death." So I went to them, and asked them whether that was their view or not. And they acknowledged that it was. I asked them whether, so far as they knew it or perceived it, the human world was perfectly happy, and they answered: "No".

'Then I asked them: "Moreover, can you maintain that you yourselves for a whole night, or for a whole day, or even for half a night or day, have ever been perfectly happy?" And they answered: "No".

'Then I said to them: "Further, do you know a way or a method, by which you can realize a state that is altogether happy?" And still to that question they answered: "No".

'And then I said: "Sirs, have you ever heard the voices of heavenly beings who had realized rebirth in a perfectly happy world, saying: 'There is a right path, a true path, which is within human capacity to follow, a path to the world of unfailing bliss, for we ourselves by following it have come to this world of bliss?' " They still answered: "No".

'Now what do you think of that, Potthapada? If all this is so, does not the talk of those ascetics and brahmans turn out to be nonsense?

35. 'It is like a man who says: "How I long for, how I love the most beautiful woman in the land!"

'And then when people ask him: "Well! good friend! this

most beautiful woman in the land, whom you so love and long for, do you know whether that beautiful woman is a noble lady, or of priestly rank, or of the trader class, or of menial birth?" he answers: "No".

'And when people ask him: "Well, friend, this most beautiful woman in the land, whom you so love and long for, do you know what her name is, or her family name, or whether she is tall, or short, or of medium height; whether she is dark or brunette or blonde, or where she lives, in what village, or town, or city?" and he answers: "No".

'Then people say to him: "So, you love this woman whom you do not know and have not seen?"

'And he answers: "Yes".

'Now what do you think, Potthapada? Would it not be fair to say that that man was talking nonsense?'

36, 37. 'It is exactly the same, Potthapada, with the ascetics and brahmans who talk about the soul being perfectly happy and healthy after death. It is, Potthapada, just as if a man were to put up a staircase in a place where four cross-roads meet, as a way up to the upper storey of a mansion. And people were to say to him: "Well, friend, this mansion, to mount up into which you are making this staircase, do you know whether it is in the East, or in the West, or in the South or in the North? whether it is high, or low, or of medium size?", and he should answer: "No".

'And they should say to him: "But friend, you are making a staircase to go up into a mansion you do not know and have not seen?"

'And he should answer: "Yes".

'Now what do you think of that, Potthapada? Would it not be fair to say that he was talking nonsense?'

'Absolutely, sir.'

38. 'Then surely it is just the same, Potthapada, with those ascetics and brahmans who envisage a soul happy and healthy after death. For they acknowledge that they know no such state in this world now. They acknowledge that they cannot say their own souls have been happy here even for half a day. And they acknowledge that they know no way, no method, of ensuring such a result. Now what do you think, Potthapada. In that case, are not they also talking nonsense?'

'Absolutely, sir.'

39. 'In everyday speech, three aspects of personality are referred to, Potthapada. They are: the "material" self, the "mental" self, and the "subtle" self. The first has shape, it is made up of the four elements, and it is nourished by solid food. The second has no shape, it is made up of mind, has all its parts and faculties complete. The third is without material qualities, and is consciousness only.[1]

40–42. 'Now I teach a doctrine, Potthapada, [with respect to each of these[2]] that leads to the putting-off of that personality; so that, if you live according to that doctrine, the evil dispositions which one has acquired will be put away; the dispositions which tend to purification will increase; and one will continue to experience directly, and by oneself come to realize, the full perfection and grandeur of wisdom.

'Now, Potthapada, you will think: "Evil dispositions may be put away, the dispositions that tend to purification may increase, one may continue to experience directly, and by oneself come to realize, the full perfection and grandeur of wisdom, but one may continue sad." Now that would not be an accurate judgment. When such conditions are fulfilled, then there will be joy, and happiness, and peace, and in continual mindfulness and self-mastery one will dwell at ease.

43–45. 'Outsiders, Potthapada, might question us thus: "What then, sir, *is* that material [or that mental, or that subtle] mode of personality for the putting away of which you teach such a doctrine as will lead one who follows it to get free from the evil dispositions already acquired, to increase in the dispositions that tend to purification, and continue to experience directly, and come to realize, the full perfection and grandeur of wisdom?" To that I should reply [describing it in the words I have now used to you]: "Why, this very personality that you see before you: that is what I mean."

'Now what do you think, Potthapada. Would not this seem to you to make good sense?'

'Indeed, sir, it would.'

46. 'It is, Potthapada, just as if a man were to construct a staircase, to go up into the upper storey of a palace, right at the foot of the palace itself. If people were to say to him: "Well,

friend, that palace, to go up into which you are constructing this staircase, do you know whether it is in the East, or in the West, or in the South, or in the North? Is it high, or low, or of medium size?"

'He would certainly answer: "Why! here is the palace. I am constructing my staircase, to lead up into it, right at the foot of the palace!"'

'What do you think, Potthapada? Would not what he said make good sense?'

'Indeed, sir, it would.'

47. 'Then just so, Potthapada, when I answer in the way that I have done, [paragraphs 42 to 45 are here repeated in full] to the questions I was asked.'

48. Now when he had said this, Citta, the son of the elephant trainer, said to him: 'Sir, at the time a man is in possession of any one of the three modes of personality, are the other two unreal to him then? Is it only the one he has that is real?'

49. 'At the time, Citta, when one of the three modes of personality is operating then it does not come under the category of either of the other two. Personality is identified according to the mode which is operating.

'If people should ask you, Citta: "Did you exist in the past, or not? Will you in the future, or not? Are you existing now, or not?" – How would you answer?'

'I should say that I was existing in the past, and was not non-existent; and that I exist now, and am not non-existent.'

50. 'Then if they replied: "Well that past personality that you had, is that real to you now; so that the future personality, and the present are unreal? The future personality that you will have, is that real to you now, so that the past personality, and the present are unreal? The future personality that you will have, is that real to you now, so that the past personality, and the present are unreal? The personality that you have now, in the present, is that real to you; so that the past personality, and the future personalities are unreal?" – how would you answer?'

'I should say that the past personality that I had was real to me at the time when I had it; and at that time the others were unreal. So also in the other two cases, the one that was operating at the time was real and the other two were unreal.'

51. 'Exactly! Citta. When any one of the three modes of personality is operating then it does not come under the category of either of the other two.

52–53. 'Just, Citta, as from a cow comes milk, and from the milk curds, and from the curds butter, and from the butter ghee, and from the ghee junket; but when it is milk it is not called curds, or butter, or ghee, or junket; and when it is curds it is not called by any of the other names; and so on, so also, Citta, when any one of the three modes of personality is operating, it is not called by the name of the other. For these, Citta, are merely names, expressions, figures of speech, designations in common use in the world. A Tathagata [one who has won the Truth] makes use of such words, but is not led astray by them.'[3]

54. When he had said this, Potthapada, the mendicant, said to the Master: 'Most excellent are the words that you speak, most excellent! It is just as if a man were to set up what has been thrown down, or were to reveal what has been hidden away, or were to point out the right road to someone who had gone astray, or were to bring a light into the darkness so that one could discern the shapes of things exactly: so has the truth been made known to me in many ways by the Master. I take myself to the Master as my guide, to the Doctrine and to the Community. May the Master accept me as a disciple, as one who, from this day forth as long as life endures, has taken him as his guide.'

55. But Citta, the son of the elephant trainer, though he made use of the usual words, concluded with the additional request: 'And may I be permitted to go away from the world under the Master; may I receive admission into his Order.'

56. His request was granted, and he was received into the Order. Immediately from the time of his initiation Citta, the son of the elephant trainer, remained alone and separate, earnest, zealous and resolved. Before long he attained to that supreme goal of the higher life for the sake of which the clansmen go out from the household life to become homeless wanderers. By himself, and while yet in this visible world, he brought himself to the knowledge of that supreme goal and continued to realize, and to experience it directly. He became conscious that rebirth was at an end; that the higher life had been fulfilled; that all that should be done had been accomplished; and that, after this

present life, there would be no further rebirth.

So the venerable Citta, the son of the elephant trainer, became yet another among the arahats.

Here ends the Potthapada Sutta

1   These three forms of personality correspond nearly to the planes, or divisions, into which the worlds are divided in the later Buddhist theory: (1) the eleven *kamavakara* worlds, from purgatory below to the *deva* heavens above, both inclusive; (2) the *rupavakara* worlds, which are the sixteen worlds of the Brahma gods, and are attained to by the practice of the Four Raptures (the Four *Jhanas*); (3) the four *arupavakara* worlds, attained to by the practice of four of the *Vimokkhas* (Nos. 4–7).

It will be noticed that the lowest of these three planes includes all the forms of existence known in the West, from hell beneath to heaven above. And that the others are connected with the pre-Buddhist idea of ecstatic meditation leading to special forms of re-existence.

But it is clear from paragraph 58 below that the opinion here put forward is intended to represent, not any Buddhist theory, but a view commonly entertained in the world, such as Potthapada himself would admit, and indeed has admitted (above, paragraphs 21 to 23). In either case, of course, these modes of existence would be, from the Buddhist point of view, purely temporary. They are the fleeting union of qualities that make up for a time only, an unstable individuality. (RD)

2   The whole paragraph is repeated for each of the three modes of personality.

3   The point is, of course, that just as there is no substratum in the products of the cow, so in man there is no ego, no constant unity, no 'soul' (in the animistic sense of the word). There are a number of qualities that, when united, make up a personality – always changing. When the change has reached a certain point, it is convenient to change the designation, the name, by which the personality is known – just as in the case of the products of the cow. But the abstract term is only a convenient form of expression. There never was any personality, as a separate entity, all the time. (RD)

Concerning the Application of Mindfulness
(*Maha Satipatthana Sutta*)

From the area to the east of Lucknow, the scene of the previous
Dialogue, we now move two hundred miles north-west, to the
land of the Kurus, in the vicinity of modern Delhi. The Kuru
people are said to have had a reputation for deep wisdom, and
for good health; some of them had become disciples of the
Buddha and it is to these bhikkhus that the great discourse on
the Application of Mindfulness is said to have been addressed.
The necessity for 'mindfulness' is frequently emphasized in the
Pali Suttas, and a major discourse on the subject appears in most
of the collections of Suttas.[1]

The teaching of 'mindfulness' rests, in this discourse, on the
'Four Bases' of mindfulness: (1) the physical body and physical
actions; (2) the emotional level, and the ethical implications of
mindfulness concerning the emotions; (3) the intellectual level,
and its ethical implications; and (4) Buddhist Dhamma; in
particular, the doctrines of the Five Hindrances; the Five Com-
ponents of a Human Person (*khandhas*); the Six Spheres of
Sense; the Seven Factors of Enlightenment; and the Four Noble
Truths.

From the context of modern Sri Lanka, Dr Malalasekera
wrote that the mere recital of this Sutta (one of the most important in the Buddhist canon) 'is said to ward off dangers and to
bring happiness'; he adds that 'it is the desire of every Buddhist
that he shall die with the *Satipatthana Sutta* on his lips, or, at
least, with the sound of it in his ears'.[2]

1 The five occurrences of a discourse on this subject are:
   Satipatthana Sutta (Majjhima Nik.); *Satipatthana Samyutta*
   (Samyutta Nik.); various passages in *Angutta Nikaya*; *Sutta
   Vibhanga*, and the present Sutta.

2 Malalasekera, *DPPN*, 1, 564.

Thus have I heard:

1. The Master was once staying among the Kurus. The town of the Kurus is called Kammassadhamma. There the Master addressed the company of bhikkhus. 'Bhikkhus,' he said. 'Venerable sir!' replied the bhikkhus. The Master then addressed them as follows:

'The only way, bhikkhus, to purify living beings and to transcend sorrow and lamentation, to extinguish suffering and dejection, to acquire the right mode of life and to reach the realization of nibbana, is that of the Four Applications of Mindfulness.

'Now what are these four? In our community, bhikkhus, one continually so observes the body, *qua* body, that one remains energetic, conscious and mindful, having disciplined both the desire and the dejection which are common in the world. Similarly one continually so observes the sensations *qua* sensations that one remains energetic, conscious and mindful, having disciplined both the desire and the dejection which are common in the world. And one continually so observes thoughts, *qua* thoughts, and states of mind, *qua* states of mind that one remains energetic, conscious and mindful, having disciplined both the desire and the dejection which are common in the world.

2. 'How, then, bhikkhus, does one continually observe the body? In our community, bhikkhus, one goes into the forest, or to the foot of a tree, or into an empty room, and sits down cross-legged, with body erect, and with mindfulness towards the object of one's thought. Mindful one inhales, and mindful one exhales. Inhaling a long breath one is conscious that it is a long breath that has been inhaled. Exhaling a long breath one is conscious that it is a long breath that has been exhaled. And whether one inhales a short breath or exhales a short breath one is conscious of it in each case. One practises with the thought, "Conscious of my whole body I will inhale", and "Conscious of my whole body I will exhale." Again one practises with the

thought, "Tranquillizing my bodily forces I will inhale", and "Tranquillizing my bodily forces I will exhale."

'Just as a skilful turner, or turner's apprentice, turning his lathe at length, or turning it a little, is conscious that he is doing one or the other, so does one practise inhaling and exhaling.

'So, too, does one continually observe the body, *qua* body, either internally or externally, or both internally and externally. One continually observes that the body is something that comes into being, or that passes away, and one continually observes the coming into being together with the passing away. Again, conscious that "There is the body", mindfulness of this becomes established, enough at least for the purposes of knowledge and of recollectedness. And one remains independent, not grasping at anything in the world. This is how a bhikkhu continually observes the body.

3. 'Moreover, bhikkhus, when one is walking, one is aware of it: "I am walking." Similarly when one is standing, or sitting, or lying down, one is aware of one's posture. However one holds the body, one is aware of it. In this way one continually observes the body, either internally or externally, or both internally and externally. One continually observes how the body is something that grows, or again how the body is something that decays. Again, one continually observes the growth with the decay. So, conscious of the fact that "There is a body", mindfulness of it becomes established, enough at least for the purposes of knowledge and of recollectedness. And one remains independent, not grasping at anything in the world. This is how a bhikkhu continually observes the body.[1]

4. 'Moreover, bhikkhus, whether one departs or returns, whether one looks at something or looks away from it, whether one has drawn in one's limbs or stretched them out, or takes one's robes and bowl, or eats or drinks or chews, or rests, or answers the call of nature, one is aware of the action. Whether going or standing still, sitting, sleeping, watching, talking or keeping silence, one is aware of what is being done.

5. 'Moreover, bhikkhus, one contemplates the body, from the soles of the feet to the crown of the head, as something enclosed in skin and full of various impurities: "Here in this

body are head-hair and body-hair, nails, teeth, skin, flesh, sinews, bones, marrow, kidney, heart, liver, membranes, spleen, lungs, stomach, bowels, intestines, excrement, bile, phlegm, pus, blood, sweat, fat, tears, serum, saliva, mucus and urine.

'It is as if there were a bag tied at both ends, full of various sorts of grain, paddy, beans, vetches, sesamum and rice husked for boiling, and a keen-eyed man were to consider as he poured them out: "That's rice, that's paddy, those are beans", and so forth. Even so does one reflect upon the body, from the soles of the feet to the crown of the head, as something enclosed in skin and full of various impurities.

6. 'Moreover, bhikkhus, one contemplates this body, however it be placed or disposed, with respect to its elements: "There are in this body the four primary elements of earth, water, heat and air." Just as a butcher or his apprentice, when he has slaughtered an ox, displays the carcase in portions where he sits at the cross-roads, even so, bhikkhus, does one contemplate this body with respect to its fundamental elements.

7. 'Moreover, bhikkhus, just as if one had seen a body abandoned in the charnel-field, dead for one or two or three days, swollen, turning black and blue, and decomposed, one applies that perception to one's own body, reflecting, "This body, too, is similarly constituted, is of just the same nature and has to share the same fate."

8. 'Moreover, bhikkhus, just as if one had seen a body abandoned in the charnel-field and pecked by crows, ravens, or vultures, and gnawed by dogs or jackals or various insects, one applies that perception to one's own body, reflecting, "This body, too, is similarly constituted, is of just the same nature and has to share the same fate."

9. 'Moreover, bhikkhus, just as if one had seen a body abandoned in the charnel-field, a chain of bones hanging together by the tendons with flesh and blood still about it, or stripped of flesh but still stained with blood, or cleaned of both flesh and blood, or reduced to bare bones loosed from their tendons, scattered here and there, so that the bones of a hand lie in one direction and the bones of a foot in another, and elsewhere those of a leg, a thigh-bone, the pelvis, the backbone, and the skull, so one applies that perception to one's own body,

reflecting, "This body, too, is similarly constituted, is of just the same nature and has to share the same fate."

10. 'Moreover, bhikkhus, just as if one had seen a body abandoned in the charnel-field, reduced to white bones the colour of a seashell, or to a heap of bones a year old, or to bones rotting to powder, so one applies that perception to one's body, reflecting, "This body, too, is similarly constituted, is of just the same nature and has to share the same fate."

11. 'And now, bhikkhus, how does one continually so observe the sensations, *qua* sensations?

'In our community, bhikkhus, when one is affected by a sensation of pleasure, he is aware of it, reflecting, "I have a pleasurable sensation." So also is one aware when affected by a painful sensation, or by a neutral sensation. One is aware, too, when affected either by a pleasant, or painful, or neutral, sensation concerning material things, or by a pleasant, or painful, or neutral, sensation concerning non-material things.

'Thus one continually so observes sensations, *qua* sensations, internally or externally, or both together. One continually observes how sensations come into being, and again how sensations pass away, and one continually observes their coming into being together with their passing away. Again, with the consciousness, "There is a sensation", mindfulness of this becomes established, enough at least for the purposes of knowledge and recollectedness. And one remains independent, not grasping at anything in the world. This is how a bhikkhu continually observes sensations, *qua* sensations.

12. 'And how, bhikkhus, does one continually observe thought, *qua* thought?

'In our community, bhikkhus, if one's thought is lustful one is aware that it is so. Similarly, if one's thought is free from lust. Or if it is full of hate, or without hate; deluded or without delusion; attentive or inattentive; elevated or not elevated; higher or lower; concentrated or wandering; emancipated or unemancipated; in each case one is aware of the nature of the thought, reflecting: "My thought is lustful", and so on.

'So does one continually observe thought, *qua* thought, internally or externally, or both internally and externally together. One continually observes how thought is something that comes into being, and again, how it is something that passes away; again, one continually observes both its coming into being and its passing away together. With the consciousness, "There is a thought", mindfulness of it becomes established, enough at least for the purposes of knowledge and recollectedness. And one remains independent, not grasping at anything in the world. Thus, bhikkhus, does one continually observe thought, *qua* thought.

13. 'And how, bhikkhus, does one continually observe mental objects, *qua* mental objects?

'In our community, bhikkhus, one continually observes mental objects in the context of the Five Hindrances. How, bhikkhus, does one do this?

'In our community, bhikkhus, when one has a sensuous desire one is aware of it, reflecting, "I have within me a sensuous desire." Again, when one has no sensuous desire one is aware of this, too. And one knows of the uprising of a sensuous desire which has not been felt before, and knows too of the renouncing of that sensuous desire when it has arisen, and knows also that the sensuous desire which has been renounced will not arise in future.

'Exactly the same is true of the arising, severally, of ill-will, stupidity and inertia, distraction and worry, and doubt.

'So one continually observes mental objects, either internally or externally, or both internally and externally together. One continually observes how a mental object is something which comes into being; and again how it is something which passes away. Or one continually observes its coming into being together with its passing away. Again, with the consciousness, "There is such and such an idea", mindfulness of it is established, enough at least for purposes of knowledge and of recollectedness. And one remains independent, not grasping at anything in the world. Thus, bhikkhus, does one continually observe mental objects, *qua* mental objects, in the context of the Five Hindrances.

14. 'Moreover, bhikkhus, one continually observes mental objects, *qua* mental objects, in the context of the Five Factors of Clinging to Existence.[2] How, bhikkhus, does one do this?

'In our community, bhikkhus, one reflects, "Such is *cor-*

poreality; such is its coming to be, such is its passing away." So too with *sensations,* such is their coming to be, and such is their passing away; the same with *perception,* and with *mental formations,* and with *consciousness*, such is their coming to be, and such is their passing away. This, bhikkhus, is how one continues to observe mental objects, *qua* mental objects, in the context of the Five Factors of Clinging to Existence.

15. 'Moreover, bhikkhus, one continually observes mental objects *qua* mental objects in the context of the Twelve Bases[3] of mental processes. And how, bhikkhus, does one do this?

'In our community, bhikkhus, one is aware of the organ of sight, is aware of the objects of sight, and of any connection which arises on account of them both. One is aware of the arising of a connection which has not arisen before, and of the removal of a connection which has not arisen before. One is aware, too, that in the future no connection will arise that has once been removed.

'So, too, with respect to the organ of hearing and to sounds; to the organ of smell and to things smelt; to the organ of taste and to things tasted; to the organ of touch and things touched; and to the organ of the mind and to objects of the mind; one is aware both of the faculty and of the objects sensed, and of any connection between faculty and object which has not arisen before, of the removal of that connection, and of the fact that no such connection which has been removed will arise again in the future. This is how one continually observes mental objects, *qua* mental objects, in the context of the Twelve Bases of mental processes.

16. 'Moreover, bhikkhus, one continually observes mental objects, *qua* mental objects, in the context of the Seven Factors of Enlightenment.[4] How, bhikkhus, does one do this?

'In our community, bhikkhus, one is aware of mindfulness if it is inwardly present as a Factor of Enlightenment. One is aware, too, of its absence. One is aware of how such mindfulness, not hitherto present, arises; and also of how the full development of such mindfulness, once arisen, comes about.

'So, too, with the other inward Factors of Enlightenment: investigation of the Way, vigour, joy, tranquillity, concentration and equanimity. One is aware if they are inwardly present, or absent; and one is aware of how any of these Factors, not hitherto present, arises; and also of how there comes about the full development of such a Factor once it has arisen.

'This is how one continually observes mental objects, *qua* mental objects, in the context of the Seven Factors of Enlightenment.

17. 'Moreover, bhikkhus, one continually observes mental objects, *qua* mental objects, in the context of the Four Noble Truths.[5] How, bhikkhus, does one do this?

'In our community, bhikkhus, when one hears the first truth, "This is suffering", one understands that truth as it really is. When one hears the second truth, "This is how suffering comes to be", one understands that truth as it really is. When one hears the third truth, "This is how suffering ceases", one understands that truth as it really is. And when one hears the fourth truth, "This is the path that leads to the cessation of suffering", one understands that truth as it really is.

18. 'What, then, bhikkhus, is the Noble Truth concerning suffering?

'Birth is suffering, old age is suffering, death is suffering; grief, lamentation, pain, dejection and despair also are suffering; not to get what one desires is suffering; in short, the Five Factors of Clinging to Existence are suffering.

'And what, bhikkhus, is birth? Birth is the product, the outcome, the arising in a new form, the reappearing of the Factors of Clinging, the re-establishing of the bases of mental processes, by a particular individual belonging to a particular class of beings. This is what is known as birth.

'And what, bhikkhus, is old age? It is the decay, the break-up, the grey hair and wrinkled skin, the shortening of the time left, the decline of the faculties of a particular individual belonging to a particular class of beings. This is what is known as old age.

'And what, bhikkhus, is dying? Dying is a falling, a dropping out, a dissolving, a wiping out, a killing and dying; it is the conclusion of the life-span, the dissolution of the Factors of Clinging, the putting down of the body of a particular individual belonging to a particular class of beings. This is what is known as dying.

'Grief is that state of woe, heart-ache and affliction, of inward sorrow and hidden wretchedness of one who is visited by some calamity, of one who is smitten by some kind of ill. Lamentation is the act and state of mourning, lamenting, crying, of one who is visited by some calamity or other, of one who is smitten by some kind of ill. Pain is bodily ill, bodily discomfort, ill that is born of bodily contact, being bodily affected by what is painful. Dejection is mental pain, mental suffering, suffering that is born of mental contact, being mentally affected by what is painful. Despair is the act and state of being dejected, of despondency, of one who is visited by some calamity or other, of one who is smitten by some kind of ill. The suffering of not getting what one desires arises in those who are born into this world and who feel, "If only we had not been born, if only we could have avoided being born!" But this is not to be had by wishing. This is the suffering of not getting what one desires. Similarly in the case of those who grow old, fall ill, who are dying, or grieving, or lamenting, or suffering pain, or dejection or despair, the wish arises, "If only we were not subject to old age, or illness or any of these things! If only we could avoid them!" But this cannot be had by wishing. This also is the suffering of not getting what one desires.

'And what, bhikkhus, are 'in short' the Five Factors of Clinging to Existence? These are the Five Factors known briefly as *corporeality, sensation, perception, mental formations* and *consciousness*. These are, in short, the Five Factors associated with suffering.

'This, bhikkhus, is the Noble Truth concerning *suffering*.

19. 'And what, bhikkhus, is the Noble Truth concerning *the origin of suffering*?

'[The origin is] precisely this craving-that-leads-to-rebirth, accompanied as it is by lustful pleasure which finds its satisfaction now here, now there. In other words, craving for sensuous pleasure, for further life, and for no rebirth.

'Now this *craving*, bhikkhus, where does it rise, and where does it establish itself? In those mundane forms that are dear and pleasant to us, in them craving has its rise and establishes itself.

'In what mundane forms that are dear and pleasant to us? In

things that are dear and pleasant to the eye, to the hearing, to the sense of smell, to taste, to touch and to the mind. In them craving has its rise and in them it establishes itself. Things seen, things heard, things smelt, things tasted, things touched and things imagined: these are the things that are dear and pleasant to us, in which craving has its rise and in which it establishes itself.

'Moreover, *thoughts concerning* things seen, heard, smelt, tasted, touched and imagined: these also are the mundane forms that are dear and pleasant to us, in which craving has its rise and in which its establishes itself.

'And *contacts with* things seen, heard, smelt, tasted, touched and imagined: these also are the mundane forms that are dear and pleasant to us, in which craving has its rise and in which it establishes itself.

'And *sensations* born of contacts with things seen, heard, smelt, tasted, touched and imagined: these also are the mundane forms that are dear and pleasant to us, in which craving has its rise and in which it establishes itself.

'Similarly, *perceptions of* things seen, heard, smelt, tasted, touched and imagined, *intentions* with regard to them, the act of *craving* for them, *reflections* about them, *ponderings* over them: these also are the mundane forms that are dear and pleasant to us, in which craving has its rise and in which it establishes itself.

'This, bhikkhus, is the Noble Truth concerning the origin of suffering.

20. 'And what, bhikkhus, is the Noble Truth concerning the cessation of suffering?

'It is the entire and dispassionate ending of craving, abandoning it, becoming emancipated from it, and free from all attachment to it.

'But where exactly is it, bhikkhus, that craving is given up? Where exactly is it that this vanishing occurs? Precisely in those mundane forms which are dear and pleasant to us: that is where craving is given up, that is where it vanishes. Now, what are the mundane forms that are dear and pleasant to us? Why – the sense of sight, the sense of hearing, the senses of smell, taste, touch and imagination; these are the mundane forms that are dear and pleasant to us, and in these may craving be given up, these are where it vanishes.

'And in the things that are seen, and heard, and smelt, and tasted, and touched, and imagined, which are mundane forms dear and pleasant to us, in these craving is given up, in these it vanishes.

'And in *thoughts concerning* things seen, and heard, and smelt, and tasted, and touched, and imagined, which too are mundane forms dear and pleasant to us, in these craving is given up, in these it vanishes.

'And in *contacts with* things seen, and heard, and smelt, and tasted, and touched, and imagined, which too are mundane forms dear and pleasant to us, in these craving is given up, in these it vanishes.

'And in *sensations* born of contacts with things seen, and heard, and smelt, and tasted, and touched, and imagined; and in *perceptions* of such things, and in *intentions* with regard to such things, and in *the act of craving* for such things, and in *reflections* about them, and ponderings over them, in these mundane forms which are dear and pleasant to us, in these craving is given up, in these it vanishes.

'This, bhikkhus, is the Noble Truth concerning the cessation of suffering.

21. 'And what, bhikkhus, is the Noble Truth concerning the Path that leads to the cessation of suffering?

'Just this, that there is an Eightfold Way, which consists in right vision and right purpose, right speech and right action, right livelihood and right effort, right mindfulness and right concentration.

'And what, bhikkhus, is right vision?

'It is, indeed, knowledge concerning suffering, knowledge concerning the origin of suffering, knowledge concerning the cessation of suffering, and knowledge concerning the Path that leads to the cessation of suffering; this, bhikkus, is called right vision.

'And what, bhikkhus, is right purpose?

'It is to purpose renunciation, to purpose non-violence, and to purpose harmlessness; this, bhikkhus, is called right purpose.

'And what, bhikkhus, is right speech?

'It is to refrain from speaking falsehood, to refrain from speaking maliciously, to refrain from speaking harshly, and to refrain from foolish gossip; this, bhikkhus, is called right speech.

'And what, bhikkhus, is right action?

'It is to refrain from taking life, to refrain from taking what has not been given, and to refrain from wrong behaviour in sexual matters; this, bhikkhus, is called right action.

'And what, bhikkhus, is right livelihood?

'In our community, bhikkhus, a disciple of the Noble Path avoids wrong livelihood[6] and gets his living through right livelihood; this, bhikkhus, is called right livelihood.

'And what, bhikkhus, is right effort?

'In our community, bhikkhus, one makes a firm resolve, one strives, one makes an effort, one stretches and exerts the mind so that evil and unwholesome mental states which have not yet arisen may not arise. And one makes a firm resolve, one strives, one makes an effort, one stretches and exerts the mind so that evil and unwholesome mental states which have arisen may be done away. And one makes a firm resolve, one strives, one makes an effort, one stretches and exerts the mind so that wholesome mental states which have not yet arisen may arise. And one makes a firm resolve, one strives, one makes an effort, one stretches and exerts the mind so that wholesome mental states which have arisen may persist, may not become confused, may increase, and abound, and develop, and come to perfection; this, bhikkhus, is what is called right effort.

'And what, bhikkhus, is right mindfulness?

'In our community, bhikkhus, one continually so observes the body, *qua* body, that one remains energetic, conscious, and mindful, having disciplined both the desire and the dejection which are common in the world. Similarly, one continually so observes the sensations, thoughts, and states of mind, that one remains energetic, conscious, and mindful, having disciplined both the desire and the dejection which are common in the world; this, bhikkhus, is what is called right mindfulness.

'And what, bhikkhus, is right concentration?

'In our community, bhikkhus, having separated oneself from sensuous appetites and unwholesome ideas, one enters into and dwells in the first stage of meditation, which is born of seclusion, and is accompanied with delight and happiness, and in which there is thought and deliberation. Then, allaying thought and deliberation, one enters into and dwells in the second stage of meditation, which leads to inner serenity and one-pointedness, accompanied with delight and happiness, and born of concentration, unaccompanied by thought and deliberation. Then, indifferent to joy and dispassion, one continues mindful and conscious, and experiences in one's body that well-being which the pure describe: "One who has equanimity and is mindful continues in well-being." Thus one enters into and dwells in the third stage of meditation. Then, putting away both well-being and suffering, and having extinguished former feelings of elation and of dejection, one enters into the fourth stage of meditation, where is no well-being or suffering, and where is utter purity of equanimity and mindfulness. This, bhikkhus, is what is called right concentration.

'This, bhikkhus, is the Noble Truth concerning the Path that leads to the cessation of suffering.

'So does one continually observe mental objects, *qua* mental objects, internally, or externally, or both internally and externally together. One continually observes how mental objects are things that come into being, and again, how they are things that pass away; again, one continually observes their coming into being and their passing away together. With the consciousness, "There are mental objects", mindfulness of them thereby becomes established, enough at least for the purposes of knowledge and recollectedness. And one remains independent, not grasping at anything in the world. Thus, bhikkhus, does one continually observe mental objects, *qua* mental objects, in the context of the Four Noble Truths.

22. 'Bhikkhus, whoever so practises these Four Applications of Mindfulness for seven years, in him one or other of two kinds of fruit may be expected: either in this present life *highest knowledge,* or else, if there is a remainder of the Factors of Clinging to Existence, the state of the non-returner.[7] Let alone seven years, bhikkhus, whoever so practises these Four Applications for six years, or for five only, or for four only, or for three only, or for two or one, in him one or other of two kinds of fruit may be expected: either in this present life *highest knowledge,* or else, if there is a remainder of the Factors of Clinging to

Existence, the state of the non-returner. Or let alone one year, bhikkhus, whoever so practises these Four Applications of Mindfulness for six months, or for five months, or for four only, or three, or two, or for one month only, or half a month only, in him one or other of two kinds of fruit may be expected: either in this present life *highest knowledge,* or else, if there is a remainder of the Factors of Clinging to Existence, the state of the non-returner. Or let alone half a month, bhikkhus, whoever so practices these Four Applications of Mindfulness for seven days in him one of two kinds of fruit may be expected, either in this present life *highest knowledge* or else, if there is a remainder of the Factors of Clinging to Existence, the state of the non-returner. It is on this account that it was said, at the beginning, "The only way, bhikkhus, to purify living beings, and to transcend sorrow and lamentation, to extinguish suffering and dejection, to acquire the right mode of life and to reach the realization of nibbana, is that of the Four Applications of Mindfulness." ' Thus spoke the Master; the bhikkhus were delighted, rejoicing at what the Master had said.

Here ends the Maha Satipatthana Sutta

1   The words, 'In this way one continually observes the body . . . not grasping at anything in the world. This is how a bhikkhu continually observes the body', are repeated in the original, after each paragraph from 4 to 10 also.

2   Pali: *pancas upadanakkhanda,* the five *khandas*.

3   Pali: *cha ajjhattika-bahira ayatana,* the six personal bases and the six external bases of mental processes, that is, the five physical faculties (eye, ear, nose, tongue, body, plus the mind-base as the sixth) and the six kinds of objects, visible, audible, etc. See Index and Glossary.

4   Pali: *satta-bojjhanga.* The Seven Factors are: *sati* (mindfulness); *Dhamma-vicaya* (investigation of the Way); *viriya* (vigour); *piti* (joy); *passaddhi* (tranquillity); *samadhi* (concentration); *upekkha* (equanimity).

5   Pali: *catu ariya-sacca.* These are set out and expounded in the four following paragraphs (18 to 21).

6 In the Majjhima Nikaya, III, 75, 'wrong livelihood' is described as 'deceitful speech, fortune-telling, trickery and greediness for gain upon gain'.

7 One of the recognized four final stages of attainment: (1) the stream-enterer, (2) the once-returner, (3) the non-returner, (4) the arahat.

PART II

Social Being

The Wrong Sacrifice and the Right
(*Kutadanta Sutta*)

On the road between the capital of Magadha, Rajgir, and
Nalanda there was a royal park, known as the Ambalatthika.
This means, literally, the mango-plant. According to the commentator Buddhaghosa it was a shady park which owed its
name originally to a mango sapling which was at the gateway.[1]
There was another park, very similar to this (presumably)
famous one, which therefore, according to Buddhaghosa, was
given the same name. This second Ambalatthika was near the
village of Khanumata, also in the kingdom of Magadha, and it
was here, we are told, that the Buddha once stayed, and was
engaged in dialogue by a brahman named Kutadanta. We are
told also that the ruler of Magadha, Bimbisara, had presented
this brahman with a large and well-endowed estate, over all of
which the brahman ruled as though he were himself a raja.
These details might lead the reader to suppose that the narrative
concerning Kutadanta the brahman has an historical found-
ation in an encounter between the Buddha and a person of this
name in the village of Khanumata.

Certain details of the story raise doubts, however. We are
told that the brahman, 'Sharp-tooth' (*Kuta-danta*), decided to
ask 'Samanna Gotama' the correct procedure for offering a
great sacrifice. The name itself arouses suspicion as being the
kind that a Buddhist satirical storyteller would be likely to
conjure up, but much more suspect is the idea that a brahman *of
this sort*, bent upon carrying out an important royal sacrificial
ceremony, would be likely to go to that well-known samanna,
Gotama, for advice on how to perform it successfully. The
modern parallel would be that of a Roman priest consulting the
leader of the local humanist society on the proper procedure for
the celebration of Mass (and perhaps even that is less outlandish
an idea nowadays than the situation envisaged in this Dialogue).

We are then told that in reply to the brahman's request for such liturgical advice the Buddha told him the story of a powerful raja of old, 'Wide-realm', and of the sacrifice which *he* once offered to ensure the stability and welfare of his realm. The description of that great sacrifice, presided over by the raja's brahman-chaplain, is such that it exactly reverses the normal mode of Vedic Brahmanical sacrifice and replaces what in the Buddhist view were the objectionable features of Brahmanism by procedures and practices which would gain Buddhist approval. The story of Wide-realm and his chaplain is clearly a piece of Buddhist satire, characterized, as Rhys Davids pointed out, by its piquant 'contrast between the mock seriousness of the extravagant, even impossible details, and the real serious earnestness of the ethical tone'.[2] And as Rhys Davids also commented, the unreality of the situation envisaged in this tale was just as evident to its first teller and his hearers as it is to us now. 'They knew quite well that the lesson taught was the principal matter, the main point compared with which all others were quite subservient'.[3]

In that case does it matter seriously whether the story as it is told here reproduces actual words spoken by the Buddha? The attitudes and values represented here are the attitudes and values of the Buddhist (and other) critics of the costly Vedic sacrificial system in ancient India. These attitudes and values in time permeated Indian culture to such an extent that, together with other developments, they had the effect of bringing about the virtual abandonment of the Vedic system of large-scale animal sacrifice and the forced labour which was necessary to its performance.

As it stands in the received text, the Kutadanta Dialogue is related within the context of an actual historical occasion, and the words are represented as those of *the* Buddha himself (*Gotama/Shakyamuni*). It is questionable whether, from a Buddhist point of view, exactly which historical human 'person' or even which Buddha (of all those whom Buddhists recognize) actually spoke these words is very important. In the end *the brahman was convinced of the cogency of the critics' arguments*. Once he is convinced, it is the brahman, as so often in Indian history, who becomes the bearer of the new ideas.

1   Malalasekera, *DPPN*, I, 158.
2   Rhys Davids, *Dialogues*, I, 161.
3   ibid., p. 162.

Thus have I heard:

1. When the Master was going on a tour through Magadha, with a large number of the brethren, about five hundred altogether, he came to a brahman village in Magadha called Khanumata. And there at Khanumata he stayed in the Ambal-atthika park.

At that time the brahman Kutadanta was living at Khanu-mata, a place teeming with life, having much grassland, and woodland, and water, and corn. A royal domain had been presented to him by Seniya Bimbisara, the raja of Magadha, as a royal possession, and he had power over it as though he were a raja.

Just then a great sacrifice was being got ready on behalf of Kutadanta the brahman. A hundred bulls, and a hundred steers, and a hundred heifers, and a hundred goats, and a hundred rams had been brought to the post for the sacrifice.

2. When the brahmans and householders of Khanumata heard the news of the arrival of Samanna Gotama, they began to leave Khanumata in companies and in bands to go to the Am-balatthika park.

3. Just then Kutadanta the brahman had gone to the upper terrace of his house for his siesta; and seeing the people going by, he asked his doorkeeper the reason. The doorkeeper told him.

4. Whereupon Kutadanta thought: 'I have heard that Samanna Gotama understands about the successful perform-ance of a sacrifice, the three methods and the sixteen accessory instruments. Now I don't know all this, and yet I want to carry out a sacrifice. Perhaps I should go to Samanna Gotama, and ask him about it.'

So he sent his doorkeeper to the brahmans and householders of Khanumata, to ask them to wait until he could go with them to call upon the Master.

5–8. But there were at that time a number of brahmans staying at Khanumata to take part in the great sacrifice. And when they heard this they went to Kutadanta, and tried to persuade him, on the same grounds as the brahmans had laid before Sonadanda, not to go. But he answered them in the same terms as Sonadanda had used to those brahmans. [Paragraphs 6 to 8 of the text set out the same arguments as those used in the *Sonadanta Sutta*, paragraphs 3 to 7 inclusive.] Then they were satisfied, and went with him to call upon the Master.

9. When he was seated there Kutadanta the brahman told the Master what he had heard concerning him, that he understood about the successful performance of a sacrifice, with the three methods and the sixteen accessory instruments. And he requested the Master to tell him about success in performing a sacrifice.

'Well then, brahman, pay attention and listen carefully and I will tell you.'

'Very good, sir,' said Kutadanta; and the Master told him the following story:

10. 'Long ago, brahman, there was a raja by name Wide-realm [*Maha Vijita*], mighty, with great wealth and much property; with stores of silver and gold, and various luxuries, with goods and corn; and with his treasure-houses and his garners full. Now, one day Wide-realm was sitting alone, thinking, and he became anxious at the thought: "Although I have in abundance all the good things a mortal can enjoy, and although the whole wide circle of the earth is mine by conquest to possess, nevertheless it would be as well if I were to offer a great sacrifice, to ensure my comfort and welfare for many days to come."

'So he had the brahman, his chaplain, called; and telling him all that he had thought, he said: "So, brahman, I think I should offer a great sacrifice – if the venerable one will instruct me how – for my comfort and welfare for many days to come."

11. 'The brahman who was chaplain then said to the raja: "Your majesty's country, sir, is harassed and harried. There are dacoits about who pillage the villages and townships, and who make the roads unsafe. So long as that is so, your majesty would be acting wrongly to levy a fresh tax. But perhaps your majesty

might think: 'I'll soon put a stop to these scoundrels' game by punishment and deportation and fines and imprisonment and death!' But their dacoity cannot be satisfactorily put down in that manner. The remnant who were left unpunished would still go on harassing the realm. Now there is one method to adopt to put a thorough end to this disorder. Whoever there may be in this royal realm who devote themselves to keeping cattle and cultivating the soil, to them let his majesty give food and seed-corn. Whoever there may be in this royal realm who devote themselves to trade, to them let his majesty give capital. Whoever there may be in this realm who devote themselves to government service, to them let his majesty give wages and food. Then those men, each following his own business, will no longer harass the realm; his majesty's revenue will go up; the country will be quiet and at peace; and the people will be pleased and happy, and with their children in their arms will dwell with open doors."

'Then, brahman, Wide-realm the raja accepted what his chaplain had advised and did as he had said. And those men, each following his business, harassed the realm no more. The revenue went up, and the country became quiet and at peace. The populace, pleased and happy, their children in their arms, dwelt with open doors.

12. 'So Wide-realm had his chaplain called, and said: "The disorder is at an end. The country is at peace. I want now to offer that great sacrifice – if the venerable one will instruct me how – for my comfort and welfare for many days to come."

' "Then let his majesty send invitations to whomsoever there may be in his realm who are landed gentry [*kshatriyas*], vassals of his, either in the country or the towns, or who are ministers and officials of his, either in the country or the towns; or who are brahmans of superior position, either in the country or the towns; or who are householders of substance, either in the country or the towns, and say to them: 'I intend to offer a great sacrifice. Let the venerable ones give their sanction to what will be, to me, for comfort and welfare for many days to come.' "

'Then, brahman, Wide-realm the raja again accepted the advice of his chaplain, and did as he had said. And these four – kshatriyas and officials and brahmans and householders – alike made reply: "Let his majesty celebrate the sacrifice. This is the right time to do it, your majesty, before you are too old."

'Thus did these four, as colleagues by consent, become supporters of that sacrifice.

13. 'Now King Wide-realm was endowed with eight personal qualities.

'He was well born on both sides, on the mother's side and on the father's, of pure descent back through seven generations, and so no slur was cast upon him, and no reproach, in respect of birth;

'He was handsome, pleasant in appearance, inspiring trust, gifted with great beauty of complexion, fair in colour, fine in presence, stately to behold;

'He was mighty, with great wealth, and large property, with stores of silver and gold, and various luxuries, stores of goods and corn, and with his treasure-houses and his garners full;

'He was powerful, he had command of an army, loyal and disciplined, in four divisions [of elephants, cavalry, chariots and bowmen], burning up his enemies by his very glory –

'He was a believer, and generous, a noble giver, keeping open house, a great source of benevolence whence samannas and brahmans, the poor and the wayfarers, beggars and petitioners might draw, a doer of good deeds;

'He was learned in all kinds of knowledge;

'He knew the meaning of what had been said, and could explain: "This saying has such and such a meaning, and that has such and such";

'Finally, he was intelligent, expert and wise, and able to think out things present or past or future;

'These eight gifts of his also contributed to that sacrifice.

14. 'The brahman his chaplain was endowed in the following four ways:

'He was well born on both sides, on the mother's and on the father's, of pure descent back through seven generations, and no slur was cast upon him, and no reproach in respect of birth;

'He was a student who knew the mystic verses by heart, was master of the three Vedic samhitas and similar scholarly subjects, as well as legends, idioms, grammar, nature-lore and the thirty marks on the body of a great man –

'He was virtuous, very virtuous, most exceedingly virtuous;

'He was so intelligent, so expert, and so wise! And he was absolutely first-class (or nearly so) at handling the sacrificial ladle!

'So these four gifts of his also contributed to that sacrifice.

15. 'Further, brahman, this chaplain, before the sacrifice began, explained to Wide-realm three forms of conceit which were to be avoided: "Should his majesty *before* or *during* the great sacrifice, feel any such regret as: 'Great, alas, will be the portion of my wealth used up in this way'", let him not harbour such regret. Should his majesty when the great sacrifice *has been* offered, feel any such regret as: 'Great, alas, has been the portion of my wealth used up in this way', let him not harbour such regret."

'This was the way, brahman, before the sacrifice began, the chaplain explained to Wide-Realm the "three modes".

16. 'What is more, brahman, the chaplain, before the sacrifice began, in order to prevent any compunction that might afterwards, in ten ways, be felt by those who had taken part in it, said: "There may come to your sacrifice, sir, men who destroy the life of living things, and men who refrain from doing so; there may come men who take what has not been given, and men who refrain from doing so; men who act wrongly in sexual matters, and men who refrain from doing so; men who speak lies, men who slander, men who speak rudely, men who speak foolishly, and men who refrain from all such speech; men who covet, men who harbour ill-will, men whose views are wrong, and men whose views are right. In each of these cases leave those who do wrong to their wrongdoing, and those who do well, let them have the opportunity to take part in the rites; let your majesty encourage them, and be glad of them."

17. 'Further, brahman, the chaplain, while the raja was carrying out the sacrifice, instructed him and gladdened his heart in sixteen ways: "Should there be people who should say of his majesty, as he is offering the sacrifice: 'Wide-realm is offering a sacrifice without having invited the four classes of his subjects, without himself having the eight personal gifts, without the assistance of a brahman who has the four personal gifts'; then what they said would be untrue. For the consent of the four

95

classes has been obtained, his majesty has the eight, and his brahman has the four, personal gifts. With regard to each and every one of these sixteen conditions his majesty may rest assured that it has been fulfilled. He can sacrifice, and do it with a good heart, and be glad.

18. 'And further, brahman, at that sacrifice no oxen were slain, nor goats, nor fowls, nor fatted pigs, nor were any kinds of living creatures put to death. No trees were cut down to be used as posts, no dabbha grasses were mown to strew around the altar. The slaves and messengers and workmen there employed were not driven by big sticks and fear, nor did they carry out their work weeping, with tears running down their faces. Whoever chose to help, he worked; whoever chose not to help, did not. What each chose to do, he did; what they chose not to do wasn't done. With ghee, and oil, and butter, and milk, and honey, and sugar only was that sacrifice offered.

19. 'And what is more, brahman, the kshatriyas, and the officials, and the brahmans of superior position, and the householders of substance, whether of the country or of the towns, all went to Wide-realm, taking with them large funds of money and said: "This great fund of money, sir, we have brought here for his majesty to accept at our hands and use."

' "My friends, I have ample funds available – all obtained honestly from revenue. Please keep your funds – and let me offer you some more!"

'Their generous offer having been declined they went aside, and discussed the matter: "It would not be proper to take all this money home again, so, while Wide-realm is offering a great sacrifice, let us arrange to make an after-sacrifice!"

20. 'So the kshatriyas established a charity to the east of the sacrificial area, and the officials established one to the south, and the brahmans established another to the west, and the householders yet another to the north. The things given, and the way they were given to the people was in all respects in keeping with the manner of the royal sacrifice of Wide-realm himself.

'Thus, brahman, there was a *fourfold* charity, and Wide-realm was endowed with *eight* personal qualities, and his officiating brahman with another four; and three "modes" of the offering of that sacrifice.[1] This, O brahman, is the proper celebration of a sacrifice in its threefold mode and with its sixteen different kinds of "furnishings" .'[2]

21. And when he had thus spoken, those brahmans lifted up their voices in tumult, and said: 'How glorious the sacrifice, how pure its accomplishment!' But Kutadanta the brahman sat there in silence.

Then those brahmans said to Kutadanta: 'Why do you not approve the good words of Samanna Gotama as well said?'

'I do not fail to approve: for he who approves not as well said that which has been well spoken by Samanna Gotama, verily his head would split in twain. But I was considering that Samanna Gotama does not say: "Thus have I heard", nor "Thus behoves it to be", but says only "Thus it was then", or "It was like that then." So I thought: "For a certainty Samanna Gotama himself must at that time have been King Wide-realm, or the brahman who officiated for him at that sacrifice." Does the venerable Gotama admit that he who celebrates such a sacrifice, or causes it to be celebrated, is reborn at the dissolution of the body, after death, into some state of happiness in heaven?'

'Yes, O brahman, that I admit. And at that time I was the brahman who, as chaplain, had that sacrifice performed.'

22. 'Is there, O Gotama, any other sacrifice less difficult and less troublesome, with more fruit and more advantage still than this?'

'Yes, O brahman, there is.'

'And what, O Gotama, may that be?'

'The perpetual gifts kept up in a family where they are given specifically to virtuous recluses.'

23. 'But what is the reason, O Gotama, and what the cause, why such perpetual givings specifically to virtuous recluses, and kept up in a family, are less difficult and troublesome, of greater fruit and greater advantage than that other sacrifice with its three modes and its accessories of sixteen kinds?'

'To the latter sort of sacrifice, O brahman, neither will the arahats go, nor such as have entered on the arahat way. And why not? Because at it beating with sticks takes place, and seizing by the throat.[3] But they will go to the former, where such things are not. And therefore are such perpetual gifts above the other sort of sacrifice.'

24. 'And is there, O Gotama, any other sacrifice less difficult and less troublesome, of greater fruit and of greater advantage than either of these?'

'Yes, O brahman, there is.'

'And what, O Gotama, may that be?'

'The putting up of a dwelling place [*vihara*] on behalf of the Community in all the four directions.'

25. 'And is there, O Gotama, any other sacrifice less difficult and less troublesome, of greater fruit and of greater advantage than each and all of these three?'

'Yes, O brahman, there is.'

'And what, O Gotama, may that be?'

'He who with trusting heart takes a Buddha as his guide, and the Doctrine, and the Community – that is a sacrifice better than open largesse, better than perpetual alms, better than the gift of a dwelling place.'

26. 'And is there, O Gotama, any other sacrifice less difficult and less troublesome, of greater fruit and of greater advantage than all these four?'

'When a man with trusting heart takes upon himself the precepts – abstinence from destroying life; abstinence from taking what has not been given; abstinence from evil conduct in respect of lusts; abstinence from lying words; abstinence from strong, intoxicating, maddening drinks, the root of carelessness – that is a sacrifice better than open largesse, better than perpetual alms, better than the gift of dwelling places, better than accepting guidance.'

27. 'And is there, Gotama, any other sacrifice less difficult and less troublesome, of greater fruit and of greater advantage than all these five?'

'Yes, brahman, there is.'

'And what, Gotama, may that be?'

[The answer which was given is the long passage from the *Samanna-phala Sutta* (see above), paragraphs 40 to 75, which should be read at this point.]

'This, brahman, is a sacrifice less difficult and less troublesome, of greater fruit and greater advantage than the previous sacrifices.'

[The text then repeats what is said in the *Samanna-phala*

Sutta, paragraphs 77 to 84, and 97 to 98, regarding the second, third and fourth stages of meditation and the destruction of the Influxes.]

'And there is no sacrifice man can celebrate, brahman, higher and sweeter than this.'

28. When he had said this, Kutadanta the brahman said to the Master: 'Most excellent, Gotama, are the words you speak, most excellent! It is just as if a man were to set up what has been thrown down, or were to reveal what has been hidden away, or were to point out the right road to someone who had gone astray, or were to bring a light into the darkness so that one could discern the shapes of things – exactly so has the Truth been made known to me in many ways by the venerable Gotama. I take myself to the venerable Gotama as my guide, to the Doctrine and to the Community. May the Venerable One accept me as a disciple, as one who, from this day forth, as long as life endures, has taken him as his guide. And I myself, Gotama, will have the seven hundred bulls, and the seven hundred steers, and the seven hundred heifers, and the seven hundred goats, and the seven hundred rams set free. To them I grant their life. Let them eat green grass and drink fresh water, and may cool breezes blow around them.'

29. Then the Master talked with Kutadanta the brahman, taking everything in its proper order, that is to say, he spake to him of generosity, of right conduct, of heaven, of the danger, the vanity, and the defilement of lusts, of the advantages of renunciation. When the Master became aware that Kutadanta the brahman was receptive, unprejudiced, edified, and single-minded, then he expounded the doctrine the Buddhas alone have won; that is to say, the doctrine of suffering, of its origin, of its cessation, and of the Path. Just as a clean cloth, with all stains in it washed away, will readily take the dye, exactly so Kutadanta the brahman, even while seated there, obtained the pure perception of the Truth and came to know: 'Whatever has a beginning, has inherent in it also the necessity of dissolution.'

30. Then the brahman Kutadanta, as one who had perceived the Truth, mastered it, understood it, gone deep down into it, and had passed beyond doubt, and put away perplexity, and gained full confidence; who had become dependent on no other

for his knowledge of the teaching of the Master, addressed the Master and said: 'May the venerable Gotama grant me the favour of taking his meal with me tomorrow, and the members of the Community with him also.'

The Master signified, by silence, his consent. Then the brahman Kutadanta, seeing that the Master had accepted, got up from his seat, and keeping his right side towards him as he passed, went away.

At daybreak he had delicious food, both curry and sweet-meats, made ready at the place prepared for his sacrifice, and had the time announced to the Master: 'It is time, Gotama; and the meal is ready.' And the Master, who had dressed early in the morning, put on his robe, and taking his bowl with him, went with the brethren to Kutadanta's place of sacrifice, and sat down there on the seat prepared for him. And Kutadanta the brahman himself served the brethren, with the Buddha at their head, with delicious food, both curry and sweetmeats, until they could accept no more. When the Master had finished his meal, and cleansed the bowl and his hands, Kutadanta the brahman took a low seat and sat beside him. When he was thus seated the Master instructed, and stimulated, and gladdened Kutadanta the brahman with his philosophy, and then got up from his seat and went away.

Here ends the Kutadanta Sutta

1 That is, the three 'forms of conceit' to be avoided. See paragraph 15.

2 These *sixteen*, the four charity-offerings, the eight personal qualities of the raja, and the four qualities of the officiant, together with the three 'modes' of avoiding conceit about the offering, are here substituted for the conventional Brahmanical three 'modes', and sixteen kinds of furnishing for the altar.

3 The attendants at such a general largesse, says Buddhaghosa the commentator, push the recipients about, make them stand in a queue, and use violence in doing so.

A Book of Genesis
(*Agganna Sutta*)

To the east of the city of Savatthi there was a large and splendid monastery which had been built for the Buddha and his disciples by Visakha, the mother of Migara. Visakha is said to have been the chief among the Buddha's female disciples. Her father, Dhananja, was a rich merchant of Savatthi, a contemporary of the Buddha and one of his lay followers. The monastery which Visakha built for the Buddha was so magnificent that it is described as the 'palace', or 'mansion' (*pasada*) of Migara's mother (*Migaramatupasada*). The Buddha spent much of the last twenty years of his life in this monastery, and in the nearby monastery in Jeta's Wood, built by Anathapindika, which was mentioned earlier.[1]

We are here introduced to two disciples, named Vasettha and Bharadvaja; both were brahmans and belonged to wealthy families; the former is said to have been an expert in Vedic lore, and to have renounced great wealth when he became a Buddhist bhikkhu. The Dialogue between them and the Buddha which is presented here shows how, during their probationary period, they were being weaned away from the social prejudices of the brahman class (paragraphs 3 to 7); such as, for example, the idea that they were supernaturally born. It offers also a view of the authority by which kings rule which is rather different from the brahman view. Of particular interest here is the account which is given of the historical evolution of life on the earth (paragraphs 10ff.) It is this central theme of the Dialogue which has earned for it the description of a 'Buddhist Book of Genesis'. Beyond the process of physical evolution the Dialogue goes on to deal with the evolution of government (paragraph 19ff.)

In this case the word 'dhamma' is used in the sense of 'universal law', that which comes about by virtue of the nature of the universe, that which is 'natural' and proper. This sense has to be distinguished from 'Dhamma' in the specifically Buddhist sense of the Buddha's teaching or doctrine. I have here also left it untranslated, but the reader is asked to remember that in *this* Dialogue the untranslated term has a sense distinct from that which occurs elsewhere.

1   See *Potthappada Sutta*, Introduction.

Thus have I heard:

1. The Master was once staying near Savatthi, in the East Park, at the mansion of the mother of Migara. Now at that time Vasettha and Bharadvaja were passing their probation among the brethren, in order to become bhikkhus. In the evening, the Master, having arisen from his meditation, came down from the house, and was walking to and fro in the open air, in the shade of the house.

2. On seeing this, Vasettha told Bharadvaja, adding: 'Let us go and approach the Master and perhaps we shall have the good fortune to hear from the Master a talk on matters of doctrine.'

Bharadvaja agreed, and the two went and approached the Master, and having respectfully greeted him, they walked after him as he walked to and fro.

3. Then the Master said to Vasettha: 'You, Vasettha, brahman by birth and family, have gone forth from a brahman family and from your home, to the homeless life. Do the brahmans blame you, and speak badly of you for this?'

'Yes, indeed, sir, they do, with characteristic abuse, full and unstinted.'

'What do they say, Vasettha?'

'They say: "The brahman class is the best." '

'Yes, Vasettha, but how do the brahmans blame you in this respect?'

'They say, sir, that only a brahman is of high social rank; all others are low. Only a brahman is of a fair complexion; other complexions are swarthy. Only brahmans are of pure blood; not so the non-brahmans. Only brahmans are genuine children of Brahma, born of his mouth, offspring of Brahma, created by Brahma, heirs of Brahma. As for you (they say to us), you have renounced high rank, and have become low class, – together with shaven-headed ascetics, the dark-skinned, and the low-born. Such behaviour is not good; it is not proper that you, having forsaken your proper class, should associate with inferiors such as these shavelings and black-skinned menials, the off-scouring of our kinsmen's heels. This is how the brahmans revile us, sir, with unstinted abuse.'

4. 'Well, Vasettha, the brahmans have certainly forgotten the past when they say that sort of thing. Brahman women, like others, are known to be fertile, and are seen to be with child; they give birth and they nurse their children. And yet it is these very womb-born brahmans who say that brahmans are genuine children of Brahma, born from his mouth; his offspring, his creation and his heirs! In saying this they make a travesty of the nature of Brahma. What they say is untrue, and they thereby earn much demerit.

5. 'There are four social classes, Vasettha: nobles, brahmans, tradespeople and work-people.[1] Occasionally a noble deprives a living being of life, or is a thief, or unchaste, speaks lies, slanders, uses rough words, is a gossip, or greedy, or malevolent, or holds wrong views. Thus we see that qualities which are immoral, and are considered to be so, which are blame-worthy, and are considered to be so, which ought not to be followed and are so considered, which are unworthy of an Aryan and are so considered, sinister qualities, discountenanced by the wise, are to be found occasionally in a nobleman. We may say as much concerning brahmans, tradesfolk and work-people.

6. Again, occasionally a noble abstains from murder, theft, inchastity, lying, slandering, gossiping, greed, malevolence and false opinions. Thus we see that qualities which are moral, inoffensive, unexceptional, truly Aryan, benign and of benign effect, commended by the wise, are to be found occasionally in a noble. And we may say as much concerning each of the others – brahmans, tradespeople and work-people.

7. 'Now seeing, Vasettha, that both bad and good qualities,

blamed and praised respectively by the wise, are thus distributed among each of the four classes, the wise cannot admit those claims which the brahmans put forward, because whoever among all these four classes becomes a bhikkhu, an arahat, one who has destroyed the deadly taints, who has lived the life, has done that which was to be done, has laid down the burden, has attained his own salvation, has destroyed the fetter of rebirth, and has become free because he has perfected knowledge – he is declared chief among them, and that in virtue of Dhamma.

8. 'The following, Vasettha, is an illustration of how Dhamma holds the highest place both in this life and in the next. King Pasenadi of Kosala is aware that the ascetic Gotama has gone forth from the neighbouring clan of the Shakyas. The Shakyas are now the vassals of King Pasenadi, and render to him homage and respectful salutation, they rise and do him obeisance, and treat him with ceremony. Now, just as the Shakyans treat King Pasenadi of Kosala, so does the king treat the Tathagata, Gotama. For he thinks: "Is not the ascetic Gotama well born? Then compared with him, I am not. Samanna Gotama is strong, I am weak. He is attractive, I am not; the ascetic Gotama has great influence, I have but little." Now it is because the king honours, reveres and does homage to the Dhamma that he renders homage and respectful salutation to the Tathagata, rising and doing him obeisance, and treating him with due ceremony. By this it may be understood how Dhamma holds the highest place, both in this life and in the next.

9. 'You all, Vasettha, who differ in birth, in name, in clan and family, have gone forth from home into the homeless life, may be asked: "Who are you?"

'Then you should reply: "We are ascetics who follow him who is of the Shakya clan." He, Vasettha, whose faith in the Tathagata is steady, established and firm, a faith not to be destroyed by any recluse or brahman, by any heavenly being, or Mara[2] or Brahma, or anyone in the world, can say: "I am a true son of the Master, born from *his* mouth, born of the Dhamma, created by the Dhamma, heir of the Dhamma."

'How so? Because, Vasettha, these are names tantamount to Tathagata: "The Dhamma-Body" and, "Of the highest", and "Of the same nature as Dhamma", and "Of the same nature as the Highest".

10. 'There comes a time, Vasettha, when, sooner or later, after the lapse of a long, long period, this world passes away. When this happens, beings have mostly been reborn in the World of Radiance; and there they dwell, made of mind, feeding on rapture, self-luminous, traversing the air, continuing in glory; and thus they remain for a long, long period of time. There comes also a time when, sooner or later, this world begins to re-evolve. When this happens, beings who had deceased from the World of Radiance usually comes to life as humans. And they become made of mind, feeding on rapture, self-luminous, traversing the air, continuing in glory, and remain thus for a long, long period of time.

11. 'Now at that time, all had become one world of water, dark, dark as total blindness. No moon nor sun appeared, no stars were seen, nor constellations, neither was night manifest nor day, neither months nor half-months, neither years nor seasons, neither female nor male. Beings were reckoned just as beings only. And to those beings, Vasettha, sooner or later, after a long time, earth with its savour was spread out in the waters. Even as a scum forms on the surface of boiled milky rice that is cooling, so did the earth appear. It became endowed with colour, with odour and with taste. Even as well-made ghee or pure butter, so was its colour; even as the flawless honey of the bee, so sweet was it.

12. 'Then, Vasettha, a being of greedy[3] disposition, said: "Now! what have we here?" and tasted the savoury earth with his finger. Tasting, he became filled with the savour, and craving entered into him. Other beings, following his example, tasted the savoury earth with their fingers. Tasting, they too became filled with the savour, and craving entered into them. Then those beings began to feast on the savoury earth, breaking off lumps of it with their hands. And from doing this the self-luminance of those beings faded away. As their self-luminance faded away, the moon and the sun became manifest. Thereupon star-shapes and constellations became manifest. Thereupon night and day became manifest, months, too, and half-months, the seasons and the years. Thus far, Vasettha, did the world evolve again.

13. 'Now those beings, feasting on the savoury earth, feed-

ing on it, nourished by it, continued in this way for a long, long while. And in measure as they fed, their bodies became solid, and variety of attractiveness became manifest. Some beings were well favoured, some were ill favoured. Those who were well favoured despised those who were ill favoured, thinking: "We are more attractive than they; they are worse favoured than we." And while, through pride in their beauty, they became vain and conceited, the savoury earth disappeared. At the disappearance of the savoury earth, they gathered themselves together and bewailed it: "Alas! the savour has gone! the savour has gone!" In the same way as now, when men have found a good savour, they say: "Ah, the savour of it! ah, the savour of it!" they are repeating a primordial saying, not recognizing the significance of it.

14. 'Then, Vasettha, when the savoury earth had vanished for those beings, shoots appeared in the soil. It was a type of growth like that of the mushroom, it had colour, odour and taste; its colour was well-formed ghee or fine butter, and it was as sweet as honeycomb. Then those beings began to feast on these outgrowths of the soil. They continued feasting on them, finding food and nourishment in them, for a long, long while. In measure as they were fed and nourished, their bodies grew ever more solid, and the differences in their attractiveness more manifest. Some became well favoured, some ill favoured. Then those who were well favoured despised those who were ill favoured, thinking: "We are more attractive than they; they are worse favoured than we." Then as they, through pride in their beauty, became vain and conceited, these outgrowths of the soil disappeared. Then from the soil creepers appeared, looking somewhat like bamboo, and they had colour, odour and taste. Their colour was like that of ghee or fine butter, and they were as sweet as honeycomb.

15. 'Then, Vasettha, those beings began to feast on the creepers. And they continued feasting on them, feeding on them, nourished by them, for a long, long while. In measure as they fed and were nourished their bodies became more solid, and the difference in their attractiveness increased so that, as before, the better favoured despised the worse favoured. While they, through pride in their beauty, became vain and conceited,

the creepers disappeared. When this happened they gathered together and wailed: "Where's our creeper! Our creeper's vanished! Ah, what we have lost!" In the same way as now, when people, being asked what is the matter, say: "Ah, what we have lost!" they are repeating a primordial saying, not recognizing the significance of it.

16. 'Then, Vasettha, when the creepers had vanished rice appeared, ripening in glades of the jungle.

> 'No powder had it, and no husk.
> Pure, fragrant and clean-grained.

'In the place where, in the evening, they gathered and carried it away for supper, there next morning the rice stood ripe and grown again. Where, in the morning, they gathered and carried it away for breakfast, there in the evening it stood ripe and grown again. No break was to be seen where the husks had been broken off from the stalks.

'Then those beings, feasting on this rice in the jungle glades, feeding on it, nourished by it, continued so for a long, long while. And as they thus fed and lived in this way, so their bodies become even more solid, and the differences in their attractiveness became more pronounced. In some appeared the distinctive features of the female, and in others, those of the male. Then women began to be very interested in men, and men in women. As they began to contemplate one another, overmuch passion arose and burning entered their bodies. As a result they followed their desires. And others who saw them doing so threw some, sand, some, ashes, some, cowdung, crying: "Drop dead, you scum! How can a being treat another being so?" So nowadays in certain districts, when a bride is led away, and people throw either sand, or ashes, or cowdung, they are repeating an enduring primordial practice, not recognizing the significance of it.

17. 'That which was reckoned immoral at that time, Vasettha, is now reckoned to be moral. Those beings who at that time followed their desires, were not allowed to enter village or town either for a whole month or even for two months. Inasmuch as those beings at that time quickly incurred blame for immorality, they set to work to make huts, to conceal precisely that immorality.

'Then, Vasettha, this occurred to someone of lazy dispos- ition: "Look! why do I wear myself out fetching rice for supper in the evening, and in the morning for breakfast? Suppose I were to fetch enough rice for supper and breakfast together?" So he gathered at one journey enough rice for the two meals.

'Then some others came to him and said: "Come on, let's go rice-gathering." "That's not necessary," said he, "I have fetched rice for the evening and morning meal." Then the others followed his example and fetched rice for two days at once, saying: "That much, they say, will about do." Then someone else came, and said: "Come on, let's go rice-gathering." Said he: "Don't bother, I have fetched rice enough for two days." So, in this way, they stored up rice enough for four, and then for eight days.

'Now from the time, Vasettha, that those beings began to feed on hoarded rice, powder enveloped the clean grain, and husk enveloped the grain, and the reaped or cut stems did not grow again; a break became obvious where the stalks had been plucked, and the rice-stubble stood in clumps.

18. 'Then those beings, Vasettha, gathered themselves and lamented what had happened; they said: "Evil customs have appeared among us. For in the past we were made of mind, we fed on rapture, self-luminous, we traversed the air in abiding loveliness; long, long was the period we so remained. Then, after a long, long while the savoury earth arose over the waters. Colour it had, and odour and taste. We set to work to make the earth into lumps, and feast on it. As we did so our self-lumin- ance vanished away. When it was gone, moon and sun became manifest, star-shapes and constellations, night and day, the months and half-months, the seasons and the years. Enjoying the savoury earth, feeding on it, nourished by it, we continued so for a long, long while. But since evil and immoral customs became rife among us, the savoury earth disappeared. When it had ceased plant-growths of the soil were seen, clothed with colour, with odour and with taste. We began to enjoy them, and fed and nourished by them, we continued so for a long, long while. But when evil and immoral customs arose among us, these plant growths disappeared. When they had vanished, creepers appeared, clothed with colour, with odour and with

taste. We turned to enjoy them, and fed and nourished by them, we continued so for a long, long while. But since evil and immoral customs became prevalent among us, the creepers also disappeared. When they had ceased, rice appeared, ripening in the glades, without powder, without husk, pure, fragrant and clean-grained. Where we plucked and took away for the evening meal every evening, there next morning it had grown ripe again. Where we plucked and took away for the morning meal, there in the evening it had grown ripe again. There was no break in the rice to be seen. Enjoying this rice, feeding on it, nourished by it, we have continued a long, long while. But from evil and immoral customs becoming manifest among us, powder has enveloped the clean grain, husk, too, has enveloped the clean grain, and where we have reaped is no regrowth; a break has come, and the rice-stubble stands in clumps. Let us divide off the rice fields with boundaries to each field." So they divided off the rice fields and set up boundaries round them.

19. 'Now someone, Vasettha, of greedy disposition, watching over his own plot, stole another plot and made use of it. So they took him and held him fast, and said: "You have done wrong in that, while watching your own plot, you have stolen another plot and made use of it. See that you do not do such a thing again!" "No, sirs," said he. But he did so a second time. And yet a third. So again they took him and admonished him. Some of them smote him with the hand, some with clods, some with sticks. In this way, Vasettha, stealing appeared, and censure, and lying, and punishment became known.

20. 'Those beings, Vasettha, then gathered themselves together, and lamented what had happened; they said: "Our evil deeds have become obvious; stealing, censure, lying, punishment are now known among us. What if we were to select a certain person who should be angry when indignation is called for, who should censure whatever should be censured, and should banish anyone who deserves to be banished? We will give him a certain proportion of the rice in return for these duties."

'Then, Vasettha, they went to the one among them who was the handsomest, the best favoured, the most attractive, the most capable, and said to him: "We wish you to be the one who will be indignant at whatever one should rightly be indignant at, censure whatever should rightly be censured, banish him who deserves to be banished. And we will contribute to you a certain proportion of our rice."

'He consented, and did so, and they gave him a proportion of their rice.

21. ' "Chosen by the whole people", Vasettha; that is what is meant by Maha Sammata;[4] [the Great Elected One]; this was how the name arose. "Lord of the Fields" is what is meant by "kshatriya"; so kshatriya [noble] was the next title to arise. He who charms the others by the dhamma is what is meant by raja; and this was the third title to arise.

'This, Vasettha, was the origin of this social circle of the nobles, according to the meaning of the ancient primordial phrases. Their origin was from among those same beings as themselves, and no others; and it took place according to dhamma, fittingly.

22. 'Now it occurred, Vasettha, to some of them as follows: "Evil deeds have become manifest among us: such as stealing, censure and lying. Punishment and banishment are also common. Let us put away evil and immoral customs." So they put away from them such customs. They put away [bahenti] evil, immoral customs, and that is what the word 'brahman' means; thus it was that 'brahmans' became the earliest title for those who did so.[5] Making leaf huts in woodland spots, they meditated there. No more warm fire for them, vanished the smoke, fallen lie the pestle and mortar. Gathering of an evening for the evening meal, or of a morning for the morning meal, they go down into village and town and royal city, seeking food. When they have received some, back again in their leaf huts they meditate. When men saw this, they said: "These good beings, having made unto themselves leaf huts in the forest, meditate there. For them no more warm fires, smoke is known no more, pestle and mortar have fallen from their hands. They gather of an evening for the evening meal, of a morning for the morning meal, and go down into village and town and royal city seeking food. When they have received some, back again in their leaf-huts they meditate." "They meditate" [jhayanti], Vasettha, is what is meant by the brooding one [jhayaka]. Thus was it that

this was the second phrase that arose.

23. 'Now certain of those beings, Vasettha, being incapable of enduring this meditation in forest leaf-huts, went down and settled on the outskirts of villages and towns, making books. When men saw this, they said: "These good people, being incapable of enduring meditation in forest leaf-huts, have gone down and settled on the outskirts of villages and towns, and there they make books. But they cannot meditate." Now, "They meditate not" [*ajjhayanti*], Vasettha, is what is meant by repeaters [*ajjhayaka*: that is, of the Vedas].

'Thus this third phrase for such people came into use. At that time they were looked upon as the lowest; although now they are thought the best.

'Such then, Vasettha, according to the ancient, primordial, expressions by which they were known, was the origin of this social circle of the brahmans. Their origin was from just those people [above referred to]; [and it took place] according to dhamma [according to what ought to be].

24. 'Now, Vasettha, there were some others of those beings who, adopting the married state, took up various trades. That they, adopting the married state, set on foot various [*vissa*] trades is, Vasettha, the meaning of 'vaisya' [tradesfolk]. So this word came into use as a title for such people. The origin, Vasettha, of the social group called the vaisyas was in accordance with this ancient primordial designation. It was from just those people [above described]. And it took place in accordance with dhamma [according to what ought to be, justly].

25. 'Now, Vasettha, those of them who were left took to hunting. But those who live by hunting, and suchlike pursuits, is what is meant by 'sudra' [the lowest grade of folk]. Thus then, according to the ancient primordial expression, is the origin of this social group called sudras. Their origin was from just those people [above described]; [and it took place] according to dhamma [according to what ought to be.]

26. 'Now there came a time, Vasettha, when some kshatriya, misprising his own dhamma, went from home into the homeless life, saying: "I will become an ascetic." Some brahman did the same; likewise some vaisyas and some sudras, each finding some fault in his particular dhamma. Out of these four

groups the company of the ascetics came into being. Their origin was from just these beings like unto themselves, not different. And it took place according to dhamma, that is, fittingly.

27. 'Now a kshatriya, Vasettha, who has led a bad life, in deed, word and thought, whose views of life are wrong, will, in consequence of his views and deeds, when the body breaks up, be reborn after death in the Waste, the Woeful Way, the Downfall, Purgatory. And a brahman too . . . a vaisya too . . . a sudra too, who has led a bad life, in deed, word and thought, whose views of life are wrong, will, in consequence of his views and deeds, when the body breaks up, be reborn after death in the Waste, the Woeful Way, the Downfall, Purgatory.

28. 'Again, Vasettha, a kshatriya, or a brahman, or a vaisya, or a sudra, who has led a good life, in deed, word and thought, whose views of life are as they should be, will, in consequence of his views and deeds, when the body breaks up, be reborn after death in a happy, bright world.

29. 'Again, Vasettha, any of these who has lived a life both good and bad, in deed, word and thought, whose views of life are mixed, will, in consequence of his mixed views and deeds, when the body breaks up, be reborn after death suffering both happiness and unhappiness.

30. 'Again, Vasettha, any one of these who is self-restrained in deed, word and thought, and has followed after the practice of the seven principles which are the Factors of Wisdom,[6] attains to complete extinction [of evil] in this present life.

31. 'For, Vasettha, whosoever of these four classes becomes, as a bhikkhu, an arahat, who has destroyed the impurities, who has done that which it was proper for him to do, who has laid down the burden, who has won his own salvation, who has wholly destroyed the fetter of re-becoming, who through knowledge made perfect is free – he is declared chief among them, in virtue of dhamma.

32. 'Now this verse, Vasettha, was spoken by Brahma, the ever-youthful:

> The kshatriya is the best among this folk
>   Who put their trust in lineage.
> But one in wisdom and in virtue clothed,
>   Is best of all 'mong spirits and men.

'Now this stanza, Vasettha, was well sung by Brahma the ever-youthful, well said, and full of meaning. And I too, Vasettha, say:

> The kshatriya is the best among this folk
> > Who put their trust in lineage.
> But one in wisdom and in virtue clothed,
> > Is best of all 'mong spirits and men.'

Thus spake the Master. Pleased at heart, Vasettha and Bharadvaja rejoiced in what he had said.

Here ends the Agganna Sutta

1   *Kshatriya, brahmana, vaisya* and *sudra*.
2   The Evil One, in Buddhist mythology.
3   Presumably greedy in a previous life.
4   Name of a famous king, said to have been the first king of the Solar race, and the legendary ancestor of many lines of kings (among others of the kings of the Shakya clan). (RD)
5   The etymologies in this paragraph are purely fanciful; and as a matter of fact the historical order in which the three words are said to have arisen is exactly reversed. *Raja* is the oldest of the three – belonging, as it does, to the oldest Aryan stock of words. *Kshatriya* is the next, and *Maha Sammata* is the youngest of all. But it would show a strange ignorance of history to complain of this. Such plays upon words are common to all ancient literatures. Scientific etymology is a growth of yesterday. The author or authors of this passage (and of all similar ones) were thinking, of course, not of etymology, but of what they regarded as matter of the highest import. (RD)
6   *Bojjhanga*.

War, Wickedness and Wealth
(*Cakkavatti Sihanada Sutta*)

Although Rhys Davids called this Sutta 'a fairy tale', a story about 'personages who ... never existed' and events which never occurred, it is more than that: it is also a prophecy. The prophecy contained in the story follows after the setting out of the Buddhist idea that the observance of dhamma (which here appears to mean moral law) is 'the most important force for the material and moral progress of mankind'.[1]

After certain preliminary details, which may seem slightly baffling to the modern reader, concerning the presence and career in the sky of a 'wheel' (an astronomical sign?), the Universal Monarch's duty to mankind is described (paragraph 5ff). It is interesting to notice (paragraph 6) that the Universal Monarch's code of morality for the defeated rulers who submit to him is, in fact, the Buddhist five-fold code of morality; in other words, Buddhist morality is regarded as of potentially universal application.

This is followed by the main section of the story which seems intended to demonstrate how social disorder follows from the neglect of the ruler to perform his duties fairly and equitably: economic inequality, theft, violence, highway robbery, dishonesty of speech, shortened life-span, malice, sexual immorality, lack of filial piety and lack of regard for holy men and elders; this is the sequence of moral decline and degeneration by which human society marches to its doom, according to the teaching of this Sutta (paragraph 19ff.)

Then the story passes into prophecy: a time will come when promiscuity and mutual slaughter among the inhabitants of the earth will bring all alike to the condition of beasts. Some will then escape to shelters in the wilderness and the mountains, there to subsist on roots and berries until at last the universal slaughter is ended and they can emerge, and greet one another, and determine to establish once again a morally ordered society. Then Metteyya,[2] the coming Buddha, will appear, to usher in the new age. According to Buddhist tradition[3] Metteyya is, during the present age, in the Tusita heaven, awaiting the time for his appearance on earth.

Meanwhile the hearers of the Sutta are reminded that for them the appropriate attitude is to live with the Dhamma as their island, their refuge, and thus to overcome the otherwise irresistible power of Mara, the Evil One.

1 Rhys Davids, *Dialogues*, III, 53.
2 Sanskrit: *Maitreya*.
3 *Mahavamsa*, xxxii, 73.

Thus have I heard:
1. The Master was once staying at Matula, in the land of the Magadhans. There he addressed the company of bhikkhus. 'Bhikkhus!' he said. And they replied: 'Venerable sir!' The Master then said: 'Live as islands unto yourselves, brethren, as refuges unto yourselves, taking no other as refuge; live with the Doctrine[1] as your island, with the Doctrine as refuge, taking no other refuge.

'But, bhikkhus, how does one live as an island unto himself, as a refuge unto himself, taking no other as his refuge? How does he live with the Doctrine as his island, with the Doctrine as refuge, taking no other refuge?

'In our community, bhikkhus, one continually so observes the body, *qua* body, that one remains energetic, conscious and mindful, having disciplined both the desire and the dejection which are common in the world. [And, in the same way as to the body, to sensations, thoughts and mental objects. The first part of the *Maha Satipatthana Sutta* is repeated here.][2]

'Keep to your own pastures, bhikkhus, walk in the ancestral ways. If you walk in them Mara will find no landing-place, no basis of attack. It is precisely by the cultivation of good qualities that this merit grows.

2. 'Long, long ago, bhikkhus, there was a powerful ruler named Strongtyre, a righteous raja ruling in righteousness, lord of the four quarters of the earth, conqueror, the protector of his people, possessor of the seven precious things; that is, the Wheel, the Elephant, the Horse, the Gem, the Woman, the Housefather, the Counsellor. He had also more than a thousand sons: heroes, vigorous of frame, crushers of the hosts of the enemy. He lived in supremacy over this earth to its ocean bounds, having conquered it, not by the scourge, not by the sword, but by righteousness.

3. 'Now after many years, after many hundreds of years, after many thousands of years, Strongtyre commanded a certain man: "If you see that the Celestial Wheel has sunk a little, has slipped down from its place, let me know."

' "Indeed I will, sir," replied the man.

'Now after many years, after many hundreds of years, after many thousands of years, the man saw that the Celestial Wheel had sunk, had slipped down from its place. On seeing this he went to Strongtyre the maharaja and said: "Sir, I have to report the fact that your Celestial Wheel has sunk, has slipped down from its place."

'Then Maharaja Strongtyre had the prince, his eldest son, sent for, and spoke to him, as follows:

' "My dear boy, the Celestial Wheel has sunk a little, has slipped down from its place. Now it has been told me: 'If the Celestial Wheel of a Wheel-turning Monarch[3] shall sink down, shall slip down from its place, that ruler has not much longer to live.' I have had my fill of human pleasures; it is time to think of divine joys. So now, my son, you must take charge of this earth bounded by the ocean. I, shaving my hair and beard, and putting on yellow robes, will go out from home into the homeless state."

'So Maharaja Strongtyre, having in due form established his eldest son on the throne, shaved his hair and beard, put on yellow robes and went out from home into the homeless state. But on the seventh day after the royal hermit had gone forth, the Celestial Wheel disappeared.

4. 'Then a certain man went to the raja, the anointed kshatriya, and told him: "I have to inform your majesty that the

Celestial Wheel has disappeared!"

'Then that raja, the anointed kshatriya, was grieved and was afflicted with sorrow. He went to the royal hermit and told him: "I have come to tell you, sir, that the Celestial Wheel has disappeared."

'When he heard this news, the royal hermit replied: "My son, do not grieve over the fact that the Celestial Wheel has disappeared; this is no cause for sorrow. This is not your heritage, this Celestial Wheel. What you should do, my son, is to act according to the noble ideal of duty set before themselves by the true world-rulers.

' "Then it may well be that if you carry out the noble duty of a Wheel-turning Monarch, and on the feast of the full moon, having ritually bathed your head, you go to keep the feast on the chief upper terrace, the Celestial Wheel will appear again with its thousand spokes, its tyre, hub and all its parts complete."

5. ' "But sir, what is this noble duty of a Wheel-turning Monarch?"

' "It is this, my son, that you, relying on the doctrine of truth and righteousness, honouring, respecting and revering it, doing homage to it, hallowing it, being yourself a banner, a symbol and a servant of this doctrine, should provide the right watch, ward and protection for your own people, for the army, for the nobles, for vassals, for brahmans and householders, for town and country dwellers, for the religious and for beasts and birds. Throughout your kingdom let there be no wrongdoing. And whoever in your kingdom is poor, to him let some help be given.

' "And when in your kingdom men of religious life, renouncing the carelessness arising from the intoxication of the senses, and devoted to forbearance and sympathy, each mastering self, each calming self, each perfecting self, shall come to you from time to time, and question you concerning what is good and what is bad, what is criminal and what is not, what is to be done and what left undone, what line of action will in the long run work for well-being or for suffering, you should hear what they have to say, and should deter them from evil, and tell them to take up what is good. This, my son, is the noble duty of a Universal Monarch."

' "I understand," answered the raja, and in accordance with

117

what had been said, carried out the noble duty of a world-ruler. Having done so, when, on the feast of the full moon, he had gone in due observance to the chief upper terrace, having ritually bathed his head, the Celestial Wheel appeared again, with its thousand spokes, its tyre, its hub and all its parts complete. Seeing this it occurred to the raja: "It has been told me that a king to whom on such an occasion the Celestial Wheel appears completely, becomes a Universal Monarch. May I also become a Universal Monarch."

6. 'Then the raja arose from his seat, and uncovering his robe from one shoulder, took in his left hand a pitcher, and with his right hand sprinkled the Celestial Wheel, saying: "Roll onward, great Wheel! Go forth and overcome, great Wheel!"

'Then the Celestial Wheel rolled onwards towards the region of the East, and after it went the Wheel-turning raja and with him his army, horses and chariots and elephants and men. In whatever place the Wheel stopped, there the raja, the victorious war-lord, took up his abode, and with him his fourfold army. Then all the rival rajas in the region of the East came to the supreme raja, and said: "Come, mighty raja! Welcome, mighty raja! The world is yours, mighty raja. We sit at your feet, mighty raja."

'The raja, the war-lord, then said: "You shall kill no living thing. You shall not take what has not been given. You shall not act wrongly touching bodily desires. You shall speak no lie. You shall drink no maddening drink. Enjoy your possessions in the way you are accustomed to."

'Then all they that were enemy kings in the region of the East became vassals to the king, the Universal Monarch.

7. 'Then, bhikkhus, the Celestial Wheel, plunging down into the Eastern ocean, rose up out again, and rolled onwards to the region of the South. And there everything happened which had happened in the East. And in a similar manner the Celestial Wheel, plunging into the Southern ocean, rose up out again and rolled onward to the region of the West. And there also everything happened which had happened in the South and East. Again in the North, and there too everything happened which had happened in the South and West.

'Then, when the Celestial Wheel had gone abroad conquering over the entire world to its ocean boundary, it returned to the royal city, and stood, so that one might think it fixed, in front of the judgment hall at the entrance to the inner apartments of the raja, the Universal Monarch, lighting up with its glory the façade of his palace.

8. [All this happened many times, throughout the centuries, again and again, to many other rajas; each of them commanded his man to report to him if he saw the Celestial Wheel sink down and slide from its place; in each case it was reported, with the same consequences.]

'Now after many years, after many hundred years, after many thousand years, the man who had been so commanded by his raja saw that the Celestial Wheel had sunk down, had become dislodged from its place. Seeing this, he went to the raja, the war-lord, and told him.

'Then that king did as the others had done. And on the seventh day after the royal hermit had gone away, the Celestial Wheel disappeared.

9. 'Then a certain man went and told this to the king. The king, the anointed kshatriya, was grieved at the disappearance of the Wheel, and afflicted with sorrow. But he did not go to the royal hermit to ask concerning the noble duty of a world-ruler. Instead, he governed his people by his own ideas and they, governed differently from the way they had been, did not prosper as they used to do under former kings who had carried out the noble duty of a world-ruler.

'Then, bhikkhus, the ministers and courtiers, the finance officials, the guards and doorkeepers, and those who lived by sacred verses[4] came to the king, the anointed kshatriya, and said. "Your majesty, your people, whilst you govern them by your own ideas, differently from the way they were used to being governed when former rajas were observing the noble duty, do not prosper. Now there are in your majesty's kingdom ministers and courtiers, finance officers, guards and custodians, and they who live by sacred verses – all of us, and others besides – who preserve the knowledge of the noble duty of a world-ruler. So, your majesty, do ask us about it, and we will relate it to you."

10. 'Then, bhikkhus, the raja, having made the ministers

and all the rest sit down together, asked them about the noble duty of a world-ruler. They declared it to him, and he listened. In response, he provided the due watch and ward and protection; but he provided no help for the poor. Because this was not done, poverty became widespread.[5]

'When poverty had thus become rife, a certain man took what had not been given to him, in other words, committed theft. He was caught and brought before the ruler. "This man", they said, "has taken that which was not given him; he has committed theft." So the raja asked the man: "Is it true that you have taken what was not given you, that you have committed theft?"

' "It is true, your majesty."

' "But why?"

' "Your majesty, I have nothing to keep me alive."

'Then the raja provided him with some money, and said: "Use this, for yourself, and to maintain your parents, your children and wife, and to carry on your business, and to give such alms for holy men as shall be of value in the realms above; gifts which shall result in happiness here and rebirth in the heavenly worlds hereafter."

' "I shall use it as you say, your majesty," replied the man.

11. 'Now another man also took by theft what was not given him. He was caught and brought before the ruler, the anointed kshatriya, with the same accusation saying: "This man, your majesty, has taken by theft what was not given him."

'The ruler spoke to him and provided him also with money as he had done for the first man.

12. 'Thus people came to hear that the ruler was giving money to maintain those who by theft had taken what was not given; and many others began to think: "Let us also commit theft."

'So, a case of theft having again occurred, the man was caught, and being charged before the ruler, he was asked why he had stolen.

' "Because, your majesty, I cannot maintain myself," he replied.

'Then the ruler thought: "If I provide money for everyone who has committed theft there will be an increase of this stealing. Instead, I will put an end to this kind of thing; I will make the punishment fit the crime: I will have his head cut off!"

'So he commanded his men: "Look! you are to bind this man's arms behind him with a strong rope and a tight knot, shave his head bald, lead him around with a harsh-sounding drum, from road to road, from crossways to crossways, take him out by the southern gate, and to the south of the town, and in order to put an end to this you are to inflict on him the final penalty: cut off his head!"

' "Very good, your majesty," answered the men, and did as they had been commanded.

13. 'Now when men heard, brethren, that those who committed theft were thus put to death, they thought: "Let us also now have sharp swords made ready for ourselves, and then, when we commit theft from people, we will ourselves also inflict on them the final penalty and put an end to them by cutting off their heads."

'So they got sharp swords, and started to sack village and town and city, and to commit highway robbery. And those whom they robbed they also finished off, by beheading them.

14. 'Thus, because provision was not made for the poor, poverty became widespread, and from this stealing increased; from the spread of stealing violence grew, and from the growth of violence the destruction of life became common; from the frequency of murder the span of life became shorter and people became coarser; if one generation had a span of life of eighty thousand years, the next would have only forty thousand years.

'Now among humans of the latter span of life, bhikkhus, a certain man committed theft and was accused before the king and questioned if it was true that he had stolen.

' "No, your majesty," he replied, deliberately telling a lie.

15. 'So because provision was not made for the poor, poverty became widespread, and in consequence, stealing; and violence, and murder, and lying became common. As a result of lying becoming common, both the span of life became shorter and people became coarser, so that where one generation had a span of life of forty thousand years, the next lived only twenty thousand years.

'Now among humans of the latter life-span, a certain man

committed theft. Another man reported it to the ruler, the anointed kshatriya. He said, "Your majesty, so and so has taken by theft what was not given him", and spoke evil of the man.

16. 'So, because provision was not made for the poor, poverty became widespread, and as a consequence violence, murder, lying, and evil-speaking increased enormously. As a result of the growth of malicious talk the span of life became shorter and people became coarser, so that the children of those who had lived twenty thousand years themselves lived only ten thousand years.

'Among the latter some were good-looking and some were ugly.

'Those who were ugly, envious of the good-looking ones, committed adultery with their neighbours' wives.

17. 'Thus from provision not being made for the poor, poverty, stealing, violence, murder, lying, evil-speaking and immorality became widespread. From the increase of immorality, both the span of life became shorter and people became coarser, so that the children of those whose life-span was ten thousand years, themselves lived only five thousand years.

'Among the latter, bhikkhus, two things increased, abusive speech and idle talk. From these two things' increasing, the span of life became shorter and people grew coarser, so that, where one generation lived for five thousand years, some of the next generation lived for two-and-a-half thousand years, and some only two thousand.

'Among these, covetousness and ill-will became very common, and as a result the next generation lived only a thousand years. Among them, false opinions grew, and as a result the next generation lived only five hundred years. Among them, incest, wanton greed and perverted lust became widespread, with the result that the next generation lived only five centuries, or even two-and-a-half centuries only. Among that generation there was a great lack of filial piety, lack of regard for holy men and lack of regard for the head of the clan.

18. 'So it came about, bhikkhus, that from provision not being made for the poor, stealing, violence, murder, lying, evil-speaking, adultery, abusive and idle talk, covetousness and ill-will, false opinions, incest, wanton greed and perverted lust,

and finally lack of filial and religious piety and lack of regard for the head of the clan became widespread, and from all this it followed as a consequence that the lifespan of human beings was reduced to a century.

19. 'There will come a time, bhikkhus, when the descendants of those humans will have a life-span of only ten years. Among humans of that kind, girls of five years will be of marriageable age. Among such humans certain kinds of tastes will disappear, such as ghee, butter, oil of tila, sugar and salt, and instead a kind of rye will be the highest and best food available. Just as today, rice and curry is our best food, so will rye be then. Among such humans the ten moral courses of conduct will altogether disappear, the ten immoral courses of action will flourish; there will be no idea of morality among such humans – far less any moral behaviour. And just as today homage and praise are given to the filial-minded, to the pious and to them who respect the heads of their clans, so then it will be those who lack such qualities who will receive homage and praise.

20. 'Among such humans there will be no restraint with regard to intermarriage with one's mother, or mother's sister, or mother's sister-in-law, or teacher's wife, or father's sister-in-law. The world will fall into promiscuity, like goats and sheep, fowls and swine, dogs and jackals.

'Among such humans, keen mutual enmity will become the rule, ill-will, animosity, passionate thoughts of murder will arise, even in a mother towards her child, in a child towards its mother, in a father towards his child and a child towards its father, in brother to brother, in brother to sister, in sister to brother. Just as a hunter feels towards wild animals, they will feel towards one another.

21. 'Among such humans, brethren, there will arise periods of seven days during which they will look on each other as wild beasts; with sharp knives ready to hand they will regard each other as prey, and will slaughter one another.

'Then to some of them the thought will occur: "Let us stop this indiscriminate slaughter! Instead we will make ourselves dens of grass, or dens in the jungle, or holes in trees, or safe places by rivers, or in mountain clefts, and subsist on roots and fruits of the jungle." They will do so for a period, and at the end of that period they will emerge from those dens and fastnesses and mountain clefts; they will embrace each other, and be at peace, comforting one another, saying as they meet: "It's good to meet another human being. How wonderful that you're still alive!"

'Then it will occur to those beings: Now it was because we got into evil ways that this heavy loss of life occurred. Let us change our ways. How should we start? Let us abstain from taking life. That is the first thing that we can do." They will then abstain from slaughter, and will continue well in this way. Because of getting into this good way, they will increase again their span of life and become finer people. Thus, increasing in length and quality of life, their children will live twice as long as the parents.

22. 'Then this, brethren, will occur to those beings: "Because we have taken to good ways of life there is an increase in the length and quality of our life. Let us now improve further. Let us abstain from taking what is not given, let us abstain from adultery, let us abstain from lying, let us abstain from evil-speaking, let us abstain from abuse and from idle talk, let us abstain from covetousness, from ill-will, from false opinions, let us abstain from incest, wanton greed and perverted desires; let us be filial towards our mothers, and our fathers, let us be pious toward holy men, let us respect the heads of clans, yea, let us continue to practise each of these good things."

'So they will practise all these virtues. And because of the good they do they will increase in length of life, and in quality, so that the children of those who lived only twenty years, will come to live forty years. And the children of these will come to live eighty years; their children to one hundred and sixty years; theirs to three hundred and twenty years; and so on, until the generation of those who will come to live eighty thousand years.

23. 'Among humans living eighty thousand years, bhikkhus, young women are marriageable at five hundred years of age. Among such humans there will be only three kinds of disease – appetite, non-assimilation and old age. Among such humans, this India will be mighty and prosperous, the villages, towns and royal cities will be so close that even a cock could fly from each

one to the next. Among such humans this India – one might think it as an ocean at rest – will be thoroughly inhabited. The Benares of our day will be named Ketumati, a royal city, mighty and prosperous, full of people, crowded and well fed. Among such humans in this India there will be eighty-four thousand towns, with Ketumati the royal city at their head.

24. 'Among such humans, brethren, at Ketumati the royal city, there will arise Sankha, a Universal Monarch, righteous and ruling in righteousness, lord of the four quarters, conqueror, protector of his people, possessor of the seven precious things. He will have seven precious things: the Wheel, the Elephant, the Horse, the Gem, the Woman, the Housefather, the Counsellor. He will also have more than a thousand offspring heroes, men of strength, crushers of the hosts of the enemy. He will live in supremacy over this earth to its ocean bounds, having conquered it not by the scourge, nor by the sword, but by righteousness.

25. 'At that period, brethren, there will arise in the world another Master (Buddha) named Metteyya. He will be an arahat, fully awakened, abounding in wisdom and goodness, happy, with knowledge of the worlds, unequalled as a guide to mortals willing to be led, a teacher for gods and men, a Master, a Buddha, even as I am now. He will thoroughly know and see, as it were face to face, this universe, with its worlds of the spirits, its Brahmas and its Maras and its world of ascetics and brahmans, of princes and peoples, even as I now thoroughly know and see them. He will proclaim the Truth, the Dhamma lovely in its origin, lovely in its progress, lovely in its consummation, both in the spirit and in the letter; he will make known in all its fullness and in all its purity, the higher life even as I do now. He will be accompanied by a congregation of some thousands of brethren, even as I am now accompanied by a congregation of some hundreds of brethren.

26. 'Then, brethren, Sankha will raise up again the fairy palace which the King Great Panada had had built. And there he will live. Then, after a time, he will give it away, hand it over as a gift to ascetics and brahmans, to the destitute, to wayfarers and beggars. And he himself, shaving off hair and beard, will put on the yellow robes, and leave his home for the life that is homeless

under Metteyya, the Master, the Arahat, the Buddha. And he, having thus left the world, will remain alone and separate, earnest, zealous, and master of himself. Before long he will attain to that supreme goal for the sake of which clansmen go out from the household life into the homeless state; while he is still in this visible world he will bring himself to the knowledge of that supreme goal, and continue to realize and to know it.

27. 'Live as islands unto yourselves, brethren, as refuges unto yourselves, take no other as your refuge, live with the Dhamma as your island, with the Dhamma as your refuge, take no other as your refuge.

'But how does a brother live as an island to himself, as a refuge unto himself, taking no other as his refuge? How does he live with the Dhamma as his island, with the Dhamma as his refuge, taking no other as his refuge?

'In our community one continually so looks upon the body, feelings, thoughts, and states of mind that one remains energetic, conscious and mindful, so that one may overcome both the desire and the dejection which are common in the world. That is how, bhikkhus, one lives as an island and as a refuge unto oneself, with the Dhamma as an island and as a refuge, having no other refuge.

28. Keep to your own pastures, bhikkhus, walk in the ancestral ways. If you walk in them you shall grow in length of years, you shall grow in quality of life, in well-being, in wealth and in power.

'What is the meaning of length of years to a bhikkhu? Among us a bhikkhu practises the Four Roads to Power, that is, Concentration of Intention, of Energy, of Consciousness and of Investigation. From practising and developing these Four Roads he may, if he so desire, live on for a whole aeon, or the remainder of an aeon. This is the meaning of length of years to a bhikkhu.

'What is the meaning of quality of life to a bhikkhu? It is this, that a brother live in the practice of right conduct, restrained according to the Discipline of the Community, perfect in behaviour and habit; he sees danger in the least of the things he should avoid and, undertaking the precepts himself, he trains himself in them. This is quality of life for a bhikkhu.

'What is the meaning of well-being for a bhikkhu? In our

community, having separated oneself from sensuous appetites and unwholesome ideas, one enters into and dwells in the first stage of meditation, which is accompanied with delight and happiness, and born of seclusion, and in which thought and deliberation are present. Then, allaying thought and deliberation, one enters into and dwells in the second stage of meditation, accompanied with delight and happiness, born of concentration, leading to one-pointedness and inner serenity. And one enters into and dwells in the third stage of meditation. And then into the fourth.[6] This is well-being for a bhikkhu.

'What is the meaning of wealth for a bhikkhu? In our community one continues to let one's mind, filled with love, pervade one quarter of the world, and so, too, the second quarter, and so the third, and so the fourth. Thus the whole wide world, above, below, around, everywhere and altogether, he continues to pervade with love-burdened thought, abounding, sublime and beyond measure, free from hatred and ill-will. Similarly he lets his mind, filled with pity, pervade the world; then filled with sympathy; then filled with equanimity. This is wealth for a brother.

'What is the meaning of power for a bhikkhu? In our community, by destruction of the deadly taints, one enters into and dwells in that untainted emancipation of mind and of insight, which he by himself has both known and realized. This is power for a bhikkhu.

'I consider no power, brethren, so hard to subdue as the power of Mara. But this merit [the merit of these four groups of ethical concepts, beginning at Right Conduct, and culminating in arahatship] expands, bhikkhus, by the appropriating of what is good.'

Thus spoke the Master; the bhikkhus were delighted, rejoicing at what the Master had said.

Here ends the Cakkavatti Sihanada Sutta

1 *Dhamma.*
2 See above, 'Concerning the Application of Mindfulness'.

3 *Cakkavatti* (Universal Monarch).

4 That is, the brahmans.

5 It should be noticed that this king is apparently doing his best – what he thinks is best – and yet that his action leads to long-continued and disastrous results. It is as if a man, doing his best, goes under a tree for protection during a storm, and is struck by lightning attracted by the tree. The cosmic law, the dhamma, acts on in the realm of morals as it does in the realm of physics. The law is inexpugnable, *res inexorabilis*. If the law is not observed, the consequences are inevitable. (RD)

6 For the detailed description of the third and fourth stages, see the *Maha Satipatthana Sutta*, paragraph 21.

The Layman's Social Ethics
(*Sigalavada Sutta*)

The Buddha's doctrine is, in the *Sigalavada Sutta*, given expression in the form of 'domestic and social ethics'.[1] There was a code of ethics for the bhikkhu, the *Vinaya*, which was sufficiently important to constitute one of the three parts into which the entire collection of canonical texts used by the Theravada school was divided. So, too, for the 'householders', the ordinary people, those who had *not* 'gone forth' into the life of the homeless wanderer, there was a code of ethics which the emperor Ashoka described as the householders' Vinaya (*gihivinaya*).[2] This was the code contained in this Sutta, the Sigalavada, by tradition linked with the name of the young householder of Rajgir to whom it was said to have been addressed.

Rhys Davids comments on the fact that no *political* duties are mentioned; nothing is said concerning the 'corporate ideals of citizenship', even though there is enough in some of the other Dialogues to suggest that a discourse on this theme *could* have been uttered.[3] But the tradition includes no such discourse. The reciprocal duties of children and parents, teachers and pupils, husband and wife, friends, workmen and masters, laymen and bhikkhus are dealt with, but not those of citizens and rulers. The extent of Buddhist concern seems to stop short of civil and political affairs.

There is no mention either of any 'obedience' which must be given to the powers that be. Indeed, obedience is not a feature of any of the social ethics outlined here: 'it is most worthy of notice that obedience does not occur in Buddhist ethics . . . it does not occur in any of the clauses of this summary of the ethics of the Buddhist layman, and it does not enter into any one of the divisions of the Eightfold Path . . . Hence no member of the Buddhist Order takes any vow of obedience; and the vows of a

Buddhist layman ignore it'.[4]

It is worth noting also that there is no support for 'punishment' or a penal attitude in Buddhist social ethics – no cutting off of the hand that steals, no capital punishment, no stoning of a woman accused of adultery, no criminal asylums. This lack of support for punitive laws is understandable in view of the Buddhist analysis of the human condition, which entails the idea that the only effective punishment is that which we inflict upon ourselves – sooner or later.

The six sets of social relationships which are depicted in their ideal forms here may in some respects appear to be at variance with modern attitudes and fashions. It has to be remembered (1) that these were formulated in, and reflect the ideal values of a somewhat distant period by modern standards (two and a half thousand years ago), but not so impressively distant by the standards of Indian chronology; and (2) that if they conflict with certain current fashions in the West, it is open to question which of these sets of values is more enduring; late twentieth-century Western modes of conduct are not accepted entirely without question in India even today, any more than were the *mores* of the nineteenth-century British.

1   Rhys Davids, *Dialogues,* III, 168.
2   D. R. Bhandarkar, *Aśoka*, Calcutta, 1955, p. 107ff.
3   loc. cit.
4   Rhys Davids, op. cit., p. 181, note 4.

Thus have I heard:

1. The Master was once staying near Rajagaha in the Bamboo Wood at the Squirrels' Feeding-ground.

Now at this time young Sigala, a householder's son, rising early, went forth from Rajagaha, and with wet hair and wet garments and clasped hands uplifted, paid worship to the several quarters of earth and sky: to the East, the South, the West and the North, to the depths and to the heights.

2. The Master early that morning dressed himself, took bowl and robe, and entered Rajagaha seeking alms. Seeing young Sigala worshipping he spoke to him:

'Young householder, why do you, rising early and leaving Rajagaha, with wet hair and raiment, worship the several quarters of earth and sky?'

'Sir, my father, when he was dying, said to me: "My dear son, you should worship the quarters of earth and sky." So I, sir, honouring my father's word, reverencing, revering and holding it sacred, rise early and, leaving Rajagaha, worship in this way.'

'But in the religion of an Aryan, young householder, the six quarters should not be worshipped like this.'

'How then, sir, in the religion of an Aryan, should the six quarters be worshipped? It would be an excellent thing, sir, if the Master would teach me the doctrine according to which, in the religion of an Aryan, the six quarters should be worshipped.'

'Listen then, young householder, pay attention, and I will tell you.'

'Please do, sir,' responded young Sigala. The Master then said:

3. 'Inasmuch, young householder, as the Aryan disciple has put away the four vices in conduct, inasmuch as he avoids the four evil actions, inasmuch as he does not follow the six ways of dissipating wealth, avoiding evil things, then he is thereby honouring all six quarters; his practice is such as will enable him to overcome both worlds; he has initiated his success both in this world and in the next. At the dissolution of the body, after death, he is reborn to a happy destiny in heaven. What, then, are those four vices of conduct that he has put away? They are: the destruction of life, the taking of what is not given, sexual misconduct and lying speech. These are the four vices that he has put away.'

4. Thus spake the Master. And when he had said those words, the Master recited a verse:

> 'Slaughter of life, theft, lying, adultery:
> To these no word of praise the wise award.

5. 'What four motives lead to evil deeds? Evil deeds are done from motives of partiality, enmity, stupidity and fear. Inasmuch as the Aryan disciple is not led away by these motives, he does no evil deed,' said the Master.

6. And when the Master had said this he recited another verse:

> 'Whoso from partiality or hate
> Or fear or dullness evil deeds commits,
> His name and reputation surely fade,
> As in the ebbing month the waning moon,
> Who ne'er from partiality or hate
> Or fear or dullness evil deeds commits,
> Perfect and full his reputation and his name,
> As in the brighter half the waxing moon.

7. 'And which are the six channels for dissipating wealth? Being addicted to intoxicating liquors, frequenting the streets at unseemly hours, haunting fairs, being infatuated by gambling, associating with evil companions, and habitual idleness.

8. 'There are, young householder, these six dangers connected with being addicted to intoxicating liquors. They are: actual loss of wealth, increase of quarrels, susceptibility to disease, loss of good character, indecent exposure, impaired intelligence.

9. 'And there are six perils from frequenting the streets at unseemly hours: the one who does so is without guard or protection and so also are his wife and children; so also is his property; moreover, he becomes suspected of crimes, false rumours fix on him, and many are the troubles he begins to encounter.

10. 'There are six perils from the haunting of fairs. He is ever thinking, "Where is there dancing? Where is there singing? Where is there music? Where is recitation? Where are the cymbals? Where are the tablas?"

11. 'There are six perils for him who is infatuated with gambling: as winner he attracts hatred; as loser he mourns his lost wealth; his actual substance is wasted; his word has no weight in a court of law; he is despised by friends and officials; he is not considered by those who would give or take in mar-

riage, for they will say that a man who is a gambler cannot afford to keep a wife.

12. 'There are six perils from associating with evil companions: any gambler, any libertine, any tippler, any cheat, any swindler, any man of violence is his friend and companion.

13. 'There are six perils associated with the habit of idleness: he says, "It is too cold", and does no work. He says, "It is too hot", and does no work. He ways, "It is too early", and does no work. He says, "It is too late", and does no work. He says, "I am too hungry", and does no work. He says, "I am too full", and does no work. And while all that he should do remains undone, he has no income, and such wealth as he has dwindles away.'

14. When the Master said this, he recited some more verses:

'Some friends are bottle-comrades; some are they
Who to your face "dear friend! dear friend!" will say.
Who proves a comrade in your hour of need,
Him may you rightly call a friend indeed.

'Sleeping when sun has risen, adultery,
Entanglement in strife, and doing harm,
Friendship with wicked men, hardness of heart
Six causes these, which ruin any man.

'He who, comrade and friend of evil men,
Content in evil ways to spend his life,
Will fall from this world and the world to come,
And plunge in woeful ruin to his fate.

'Dicing and women, drink, the dance and song,
To sleep by day, and prowl around at night,
Friendship with wicked men, hardness of heart:
These causes six to ruin bring a man.

'Playing with dice, drinking strong drink, he goes
To women dear as life to other men,
Following the baser, not th' enlightened minds,
He wanes as in the darker half the moon.

'The tippler of strong drink, poor, and destitute,
Athirst while drinking, haunter of the bar,
As stone in water so he sinks in debt;
Swift will he make his folk without a name.

'One who by habit in the day sleeps on,
Who looks upon the night as time to rise,
One who is ever wanton, filled with wine,
He is not fit to live a household life.

'Too cold! too hot! too late! such is the cry.
And so for those whose work remains undone
The opportunities for good pass by.
But he who reckons cold and heat as less
Than straws, and does his duties as a man,
He nowise falls away from happiness.

15. 'There are four kinds of people should be reckoned as foes in the likeness of friends. They are: a rapacious person, the man of words not deeds, the flatterer and the fellow-waster.

16. Of these the first is on four grounds to be reckoned as a foe in the likeness of a friend. He is rapacious; he gives little and asks much; he does his duty out of fear; he pursues his own interests.

17. 'On four grounds the man of words, not deeds, is to be reckoned as a foe in the likeness of a friend. He professes how friendly his intentions were in the past; he professes how friendly they will be in the future; he tries to gain your favour by empty sayings; when the occasion arises that you ask for his help he excuses his inability to give it.

18. 'On four grounds the flatterer is to be reckoned as a foe in the likeness of a friend. He consents with you to do wrong; he dissents from doing right; he praises you to your face; he speaks ill of you to others.

19. 'On four grounds the fellow-waster companion is to be reckoned as a foe in the likeness of a friend. He is your companion when you indulge in strong drink; he is your companion when you frequent the streets at untimely hours; he is your companion when you haunt shows and fairs; he is your companion when you are infatuated with gambling.'

20. When the Master had said this, he recited another verse:

'The friend who's ever seeking what to take,
The friend whose words are other than his deeds,
The friend who flatters, pleasing you withal,
The boon companion in all evil ways,
These four are foes. Thus having recognized,

The wise man will avoid them from afar;
Walking with them's indeed a path to dread.

21. 'There are four friends who should be reckoned as good-hearted. The helper; the friend who is the same in happiness and adversity; the friend of good counsel; the friend who sympathizes.

22. 'On four grounds the friend who is a helper is to be reckoned as good-hearted. He guards you when you are off your guard; he guards your property when you are off your guard; he is a refuge to you when you are afraid; when you have tasks to perform he provides a double supply of what you may need.

23. 'On four grounds the friend who is the same in happiness and adversity is to be reckoned as good-hearted. He tells you his secrets; he keeps secret your secrets; in your troubles he does not forsake you; he lays down even his life for your sake.

24. 'On four grounds the friend who declares what you need to do is to be reckoned as good-hearted. He restrains you from doing wrong; he encourages you to do what is right; he informs you of what you had not heard before; he reveals to you the way to heaven.

25. 'On four grounds the friend who sympathizes is to be reckoned as good-hearted. He does not rejoice over your misfortunes; he rejoices over your prosperity; he restrains anyone who is speaking ill of you; he commends anyone who is praising you.'

26. When the Master had said this he recited another verse:

'The friend who is a helpmate, and the friend
Of bright days and of dark, and he who shows
What 'tis you need, and he who throbs for you
With sympathy: these four the wise should know
As friends, and should devote himself to them
As mother to her own, her bosom's child.

Whoso is virtuous and intelligent,
Shines like a fire that blazes on the hill.
To him amassing wealth, like roving bee
Its honey gathering and hurting naught,
Riches mount up as ant-heap growing high.

When the good layman wealth has so amassed
Able is he to benefit his clan.
In portions four let him divide that wealth.
So binds he to himself life's friendly things.

One portion let him spend and taste the fruit.
His business to conduct let him take two.
And portion four let him reserve and hoard;
So there'll be wherewithal in times of need.

27. 'Now, young householder, how does the Aryan disciple protect the six quarters? The following should be looked upon as the six quarters: parents as the East,[1] teachers as the South, wife and children as the West, friends and companions as the North, servants and work-people as the nadir, religious teachers and brahmans as the zenith.

28. 'In five ways a child should minister to his parents as the eastern quarter: "Once supported by them I will now be their support; I will perform duties incumbent on them; I will keep up the lineage and tradition of my family; I will make myself worthy of my heritage."

'In five ways parents thus ministered to, as the eastern quarter, by their child, show their love for him: they restrain him from vice, they exhort him to virtue, they train him to a profession, they contract a suitable marriage for him, and in due time they hand over his inheritance.

'Thus is this eastern quarter protected by him and made safe and secure.

29. 'In five ways should pupils minister to their teachers as the southern quarter: by rising [from their seat, in salutation], by waiting upon them, by eagerness to learn, by personal service, and by attention when receiving their teaching.

'And in five ways do teachers, thus ministered to as the southern quarter by their pupils, love their pupil: they train him in that wherein he has been well trained; they make him hold fast that which is well held; they thoroughly instruct him in the lore of every art; they speak well of him among his friends and companions. They provide for his safety in every quarter.

'Thus is this southern quarter protected by him and made safe and secure.

30. 'In five ways should a wife as western quarter be ministered to by her husband: by respect, by courtesy, by faithfulness, by handing over authority to her, by providing her with adornment.

'In these five ways does the wife, ministered to by her husband as the western quarter, love him: her duties are well performed, by hospitality to the kin of both, by faithfulness, by watching over the goods he brings, and by skill and industry in discharging all her business.

'Thus is this western quarter protected by him and made safe and secure.

31. 'In five ways should one minister to one's friends and familiars as the northern quarter: by generosity, courtesy and benevolence, by treating them as one treats oneself, and by being as good as one's word.

'In these five ways thus ministered to as the northern quarter, one's friends and familiars do likewise: they protect one, and on occasions guard one's property; they become a refuge in danger, they do not forsake one in times of trouble, and they show consideration for one's family.

'Thus is the northern quarter by him protected and made safe and secure.

32. 'In five ways does a noble master minister to his servants and employees as the nadir: by assigning them work according to their strength; by supplying them with food and wages; by tending them in sickness; by sharing with them unusual delicacies; by granting leave at all appropriate times.

'In these ways ministered to by their master, servants and employees love their master in five ways: they rise before him, they lie down to rest after him; they are content with what is given to them; they do their work well; and they carry about his praise and good fame.

'Thus is the nadir by him protected and made safe and secure.

33. 'In five ways should the householder minister to recluses and brahmans as the zenith: by affection in act and speech and mind; by keeping open house to them, by supplying their temporal needs.

'Thus ministered to as the zenith, recluses and brahmans

show their love for the householder in six ways: they restrain
him from evil, they exhort him to good, they love him with
kindly thoughts; they teach him what he has not heard, they
correct and purify what he has heard, they reveal to him the way
to heaven.

'Thus by him is the zenith protected and made safe and
secure.'

When the Master had said this, he recited yet again:

> 'Mother and father are the Eastern view,
> And teachers are the quarters of the South.
> And wife and children are the Western view,
> And friends and kin the quarter to the North;
> Servants and working folk the nadir are,
> And overhead the brahman and recluse,
> These quarters should be worshipped by the man
> Who fitly ranks as member of his clan.
>
> He that is wise, expert in virtue's ways,
> Gentle and in this worship eloquent,
> Humble and docile, he may honour win.
> Active in rising, foe to laziness,
> Unshaken in adversities, his life
> Flawless, sagacious, he may honour win.
> If he has winning ways, and making friends,
> Will welcome them with kind and generous heart,
> And can he give sage counsel and advice,
> And guide his fellows, he will honour win.
>
> The giving hand, the kindly speech, the life
> Of service, impartiality to one
> As to another, as the case demands:
> These are the things that make the world go round
> As lynchpin serves the rolling of the car.
> And if these things be not, no mother reaps
> The honour and respect her child should pay,
> Nor doth the father win them through the child.
> And since the wise rightly appraise these things,
> They win to eminence and earn men's praise.'

When the Master had spoken these words, Sigala the young
householder said: 'Beautiful, lord, beautiful! It is as though
someone had set up again that which had been thrown down or
had revealed what had been hidden, or had pointed out the right

road to someone who had gone astray, or had brought a light into the darkness, to enable those who have eyes to see! Just so has the Truth been made known to me by the Master in many ways. And I, even I, take myself to him as my refuge, and to the Doctrine and to the Community. May the Master accept me as his lay-disciple; as one who from this day, as long as life shall last, has taken him for guide.

Here ends the Sigalavada Sutta

1   The symbolism is deliberately chosen: as the day begins in the East, so also life begins with parents' care; teachers' fees and the South are the same word (*dakkhina*); domestic cares follow when the youth becomes man, as the West holds the later daylight; North (*uttara*) means also 'beyond', so by help of friends, etc., he gets *beyond* troubles. (RD)

PART III
The Last Days

Towards Parinibbana
(*Maha Parinibbana Sutta*)

The early Buddhist texts do not provide a complete life of the Buddha told as a continuous narrative. A number of such accounts are to be found in later, Sanskrit, Buddhist literature but in the canon of the Theravada school, with which we are here concerned, the longest continuous narrative is the Sutta which tells the story of the last weeks of the Buddha's life, his passing into complete nibbana (parinibbana) and the subsequent cremation ceremonies. This, 'The Great Sutta of the Parinibbana' (*Maha Parinibbana Sutta*) is presented last in the present collection. Not only is there an obvious, chronological appropriateness in placing it in this final position,[1] but it is appropriate also from another point of view. For this short book, as it could be considered, contains an important summary of the teaching of the Buddha, much of which is scattered elsewhere in the Pali canon.[2]

The events of these last weeks are, briefly, as follows. The Buddha begins his last journey from Rajgir, the capital of the Magadha state. In company with his disciples he travels north-west, through Nalanda, towards the Ganges, reaching the southern shore of the great river at a point where there was a village called Patali-gama. Here he crosses miraculously to the northern shore and then, rejoined by his disciples, continues in a north-westerly directly to Vesali, the capital of the Vajji republic, staying for a short while at various villages on the way. It is at Vesali that he calls together all the disciples and delivers to them a summary of the essential points of his teaching. After some time in Vesali, where he seems particularly to have delighted in the beauty of the shrines with their sacred trees, he continues in company with his disciples north-westwards. It is interesting to notice that the route they were following would, if continued, have led almost certainly to

143

Lumbini, in the Himalayan foothills, the place of his birth. But, almost symbolically, there is no completion of this journey. There is no rebirth for the Buddha. He reaches the little town of Kusinara, and here his last journey ends; here the Parinibbana will take place.

Each of the four major places in this narrative has its own special significance. Rajgir was the capital of Magadha at that time, where was the palace of Ajatasattu, the raja; the nearby forest was the place where Ajatasattu had met the Buddha (as recounted in the first Dialogue in the present collection). Once again the narrative concerning Rajgir initially concerns the raja. In preparation for a contemplated attack on one of the surviving federal republics, the Vajji (whose territory was separated from his own by the Ganges), Ajatasattu sends one of his ministers to ask for the Buddha's comments on his plan. The answer, which affirms the invulnerability of the Vajji to external attack, *provided* that they continue, as they do now, to meet regularly in concord, and maintain their republican institutions with care, has another significance for the Buddha's disciples: provided *they* continue to meet as a Sangha, and maintain their traditions and rule of life, their community also will prosper. By the time this Sutta was being recited and transmitted from generation to generation of bhikkhus the fate of the Vajji republic was well known. The Vajji did *not* survive; intrigue from without and the sowing of dissension from within had brought about their conquest and ruin. The implication was clear: in the Buddhist Sangha was to be seen the continuation of the old republican tradition, but now in a new and different form.

From Rajgir then, to Pataligama. This was already, apparently, in the time of the Buddha, a walled place, for the narrative mentions that the Buddha left Pataligama through the gate known (later) as 'Gautama's Gate'. It is not certain when the place was called 'Patali-village' but it seems likely from other names by which it was known, such as Kusuma-pura and Pushpa-pura (Blossom-town) that it had a special connection with flowers, possibly the 'trumpet-flower' tree. (A part of Patna city which now occupies this position is called Phulwari, from *phul*, a flower).[3] But our narrative tells how fortifications were already being built there by the Magadhan state officials, and in this connection there is mention of the Buddha's being able to see (with supra-normal vision) the thousands of local deities or earth-spirits who were haunting the place. In this stratum of the literature (which is among the earliest) the Buddha is not represented as quite the modern rationalist that he has since been made out to have been by some writers. Following this is a prophecy that Pataligama would one day become a great city, the chief city of India, and this indeed, as Pataliputra, Ashoka's capital, it subsequently became. The Buddha's additional prophecy, that it would always be open to three dangers: fire, water, and dissension among friends found fulfilment in various ways, including the dissension between different schools of the Buddhist Sangha which occurred there. It has been suggested by a modern Buddhist scholar that in the period soon after the Buddha's lifetime his followers 'may perhaps be suspected of slightly embroidering this part of the narrative to connect their Master with the new and prosperous capital'.[4] The narrative records a miraculous crossing of the Ganges by the Buddha at the end of his stay in Pataligama, and adds a verse which is intended to bring out the symbolism, comparing the Buddha's swift passage from one shore to the other with the unsuccessful efforts of those who try to cross in 'basket-rafts'; the crossing to 'the further shore' is a frequent figure in Buddhism for the passage through mortal existence to nibbana. The first stage of Buddhist achievement is that of the 'stream-enterer' (*sota-panna*).

In connection with Vesali the narrative includes a summary of the teaching which is basic to all Buddhist schools.[5] The Buddha sets out the doctrines which he himself has discovered, which he has taught to his disciples and which they should learn, and practise. These are delivered to the assembled disciples once it is clear that the Buddha has now irrevocably fixed the time of the termination of his life. According to the narrative this moment of decision was confirmed by the occurrence of an earthquake. The doctrines are mentioned each by name (paragraph 50), but are not repeated or reviewed at this point. The words which follow are: first, a reminder to the disciples that these are the cardinal doctrines which have been made known 'for the good and the happiness of the great multitude', and then the exhortation: 'Decay is inherent in all conditioned things. Strive diligently!'

The next morning, after gazing on Vesali for the last time, the Buddha sets out on the last stage, to Kusinara. The approaching Parinibbana now dominates the narrative. When Kusinara is reached Ananda, the Buddha's close disciple and attendant, remonstrates that this 'wattle-and-daub-town' is no fit place for the Parinibbana. In reply the Buddha appears to be suggesting that the matter is of no importance; once upon a time Kusinara was a famous and very extensive city, prosperous and mighty; now, if it is a 'branch township', what does that suggest but the relentless process of change which is inherent in all things?

The disciples who have accompanied the Buddha, together with those in Kusinara, are filled with grief at the news of the approaching death of the Buddha. Various supernatural phenomena are associated with the event, and when the final moment comes (Chapter 6, paragraph 9) there is a great earthquake accompanied by thunder, after which the gods Brahma Sahampati and Sakka sing in honour of the unequalled wisdom and insight of the Buddha. In accordance with the instructions which he had given, the Buddha's body was cremated, the ashes divided among worthy recipients and a stupa erected over each portion of the ashes, as places where honour would continue to be done to his memory. Thus Kusinara became one of the four places to which Buddhist pilgrims go from all over the world, the other three being the birth place at Lumbini; the place of the Enlightenment at Bodh-Gaya; and the place of the first teaching of the Dhamma at Sarnath, near Benares. The great teacher of wisdom was already becoming the object of a popular cult. It might seem that the major honour and respect had already begun to shift from the teaching to the teacher. But the honour which Buddhists pay when they recite the words, '*Namo tassa bhagavato arahato samasambuddhassa*'[6] is not to Shakyamuni Buddha, the Master, but to a *parinibbuta* Buddha, to one who has ceased to exist as a teacher.[7] Honour and respect is given to *Buddhahood,* which according to Buddhists continually appears from age to age; it is given to *bodhi*, the principle of enlightenment, of which all the historical Buddhas are examples. At this point we pass into the doctrine of the three 'bodies' of Buddhahood, of which *nirmana-kaya*, the 'historical body' is only one; we pass also into another sphere of discourse, that of the history of the development of Buddhist thought in India, and beyond the scope of this book.

1   It does not have this position in the canon.
2   For a table of the parallel passages see Rhys Davids, *Dialogues*, II, 72.
3   M. S. Pandey, *Historical Geography and Topography of Bihar*, 1963, p. 135ff.
4   A. K. Warder, *Indian Buddhism*, p. 70.
5   For references, see A. K. Warder, op. cit., p. 81.
6   'Honour to him, Master and Arahat, Supremely Enlightened.'
7   It is significant that in early Buddhist art there is no Buddha-figure, but only a bodhi tree with an empty seat beneath it.

Chapter 1: Rajgir to the Ganges

Thus have I heard:

1. The Master was staying in Rajgir, at Vulture's Peak. At that time Ajatasattu, the raja of Magadha, who was son of the princess of Videha, had made up his mind to attack the Vajjians; and he said to himself, 'I will strike at these Vajjians, mighty and powerful though they are, I will uproot these Vajjians; I will destroy them, I will bring them to utter ruin!'

2. So he said to the brahman Vassakara, prime minister of Magadha: 'Now, brahman, you are to go to the Master, and bow down at his feet on my behalf, and inquire in my name whether he is free from illness and suffering, and in the enjoyment of ease and comfort and vigorous health. Then tell him that Ajatasattu, the raja of Magadha, son of the princess of Videha, is eager to attack the Vajjians and has resolved that he

will strike the Vajjians, mighty and powerful though they are, he will uproot them and destroy them, and bring them to utter ruin! Bear carefully in mind whatever the Master may predict, and repeat it to me. For the Buddhas speak nothing untrue!'

3. The brahman Vassakara, noting what the raja had said, replied, 'As you say, your majesty.' Ordering a number of state carriages to be made ready, he got into one of them, and set off from Rajgir in procession, to go to the hill called Vulture's Peak, riding as far as the ground was passable for carriages and then alighting and proceeding on foot to the place where the Master was.[1] When he reached the place he exchanged with the Master the greetings and compliments of politeness and courtesy, sat down respectfully by his side and delivered the message which the raja had entrusted to him.

4. Now at that time the venerable Ananda was standing behind the Master and fanning him. The Master said to him, 'Have you heard, Ananda, that the Vajjians come together often to attend the public meetings of their clan?'

'Lord, I have heard so,' replied he.

'Well, Ananda,' the Master continued, 'as long as the Vajjians gather often, and attend the public meetings of their clan, so long they may be expected not to decline, but to prosper.'

In a similar manner questioning Ananda, and receiving a similar reply, the Master declared the other conditions which would ensure the welfare of the Vajjian confederacy.[2]

'As long, Ananda, as the Vajjians meet together in concord, and rise in concord, and carry out their undertakings in concord; as long as they enact nothing not already established, abrogate nothing that has been already enacted, and act in accordance with the ancient institutions of the Vajjians, established in former days; as long as they honour and esteem, and revere, and support the Vajjian elders, and hold it a point of duty to hearken to their words; as long as no women or girls belonging to their clans are detained among them by force or abduction; as long as they honour, and esteem, and revere, and support the Vajjian shrines in town or country, and do not allow the proper offerings and rites, as formerly given and performed, to fall into disuse; as long as the rightful protection, defence, and support shall be fully provided for the arahats among them, so that arahats from a distance may enter the realm, and the arahats there may live at ease: so long may the Vajjians be expected not to decline, but to prosper.'

5. Then the Master addressed Vassakara the brahman: 'When I was once staying, brahman, at Vesali at the Sarandada Shrine, I taught the Vajjians these conditions of welfare; and as long as these conditions are maintained among the Vajjians, as long as the Vajjians shall be well instructed in those conditions, so long may we expect them not to decline, but to prosper.'

'We may expect then,' answered the brahman, 'the welfare and not the decline of the Vajjians when they are possessed of any one of these conditions of welfare; how much more so when they are possessed of all the seven. So, Gotama, the Vajjians cannot be overcome by the raja of Magadha; that is, not in battle, without diplomacy or breaking up their alliance. Well now, Gotama, we must go; we are busy and have much to do.'

'Whatever you think most fitting, brahman,' was the reply. So the brahman Vassakara, the Rainmaker, delighted and pleased with the words of the Master stood up from his seat, and went away.

6. Now soon after he had gone the Master addressed the venerable Ananda. 'Go now, Ananda,' he said, 'and assemble in the Service Hall all the bhikkhus who live in the neighbourhood of Rajgir.'

Ananda did so; and came back to the Master and told him, 'The company of bhikkhus is assembled, sir; everything is ready for whatever the Master wishes to do.'

The Master stood up, and went to the Service Hall. Having taken his seat there he addressed the bhikkhus:

'Bhikkhus, I will teach you seven conditions of the welfare of a community. Listen, and pay careful attention, and I will explain to you.'

'We are listening, sir,' said the bhikkhus, and the Master spoke as follows:

'As long as the bhikkhus gather together frequently, and attend the meetings of the Order, and as long as they meet together in a spirit of unity and rise in a spirit of unity and carry out the duties of the Order in a spirit of unity, as long as the bhikkhus shall establish nothing that has not been already prescribed, and abrogate nothing that has been already established, and act in accordance with the rules of the Order as now laid down; as long as the bhikkhus honour and esteem and revere and support the elders of experience and long standing, the fathers and leaders of the Order, and hold it a point of duty to listen to their words; as long as the bhikkhus do not fall under the influence of that craving which, springing up within them, would give rise to renewed existence; as long as the bhikkhus delight in a life of solitude; as long as the bhikkhus train their minds in self-possession so that good men among their fellow-disciples shall come to them, and those who have come shall dwell at ease; so long may the bhikkhus be expected, not to decline, but to prosper. As long as these seven conditions shall continue to exist among the bhikkhus and so long as they are well instructed in these conditions, so long may the bhikkhus be expected not to decline, but to prosper.

7. 'Now I will teach you seven other conditions of welfare, brethren. Listen, and pay careful attention, and I will explain them to you.'

'We are listening, sir,' they said. And he spoke as follows:

'As long as the bhikkhus shall not engage in, or be fond of, or be connected with business; as long as the bhikkhus shall not be in the habit of, or be fond of, or be partakers in idle talk; as long as the brethren shall not be addicted to, or be fond of, or indulge in slothfulness; as long as the bhikkhus shall not frequent, or be fond of, or indulge in society; as long as the bhikkhus shall neither have, nor fall under the influence of evil desires; as long as the bhikkhus shall not become the friends, companions or intimates of evil-doers; as long as the brethren shall not come to a stop in their attainment [of the true goal] because they have attained some trifling thing instead, so long may the brethren be expected not to decline, but to prosper.

'As long as these conditions continue to exist among the bhikkhus, and as long as they are instructed in these conditions, so long may the bhikkhus be expected not to decline, but to prosper.

8. 'Now I will teach you seven further conditions of welfare, bhikkhus. Listen and pay careful attention and I will tell you them.'

Again they expressed their assent and he spoke:

'As long as the bhikkhus are full of faith, modest in heart, scrupulous, full of learning, strong in energy, cultivate mindfulness and possess much wisdom; so long may the bhikkhus be expected not to decline, but to prosper.

'As long as these conditions continue to exist among the bhikkhus; as long as they are instructed in these conditions, so long may the bhikkhus be expected not to decline, but to prosper.

9. 'There are seven further conditions of welfare I will teach you, brethren. Listen and pay careful attention and I will tell you them.'

Again they expressed their assent, and he spoke:

'So long as the bhikkhus exercise themselves in the Seven Factors of Enlightenment that is to say, in mindfulness, search after truth, energy, joy, serenity, concentration, and one-pointedness of mind – so long may the bhikkhus be expected not to decline, but to prosper.

'As long as these conditions continue to exist among the bhikkhus – as long as they are instructed in these conditions – so long may the bhikkhus be expected not to decline, but to prosper.

10. Another seven conditions of welfare I will teach you, bhikkhus. Listen and pay careful attention [as before]:

'As long as the bhikkhus exercise themselves in the perception of: impermanence in all things; the non-existence of a permanent ego; ugliness; disadvantage; renunciation; dispassionateness; and cessation; so long may the bhikkhus be expected not to decline, but to prosper.

'So long as these conditions continue to exist among the bhikkhus – so long as they are instructed in these conditions – so long may the bhikkhus be expected not to decline but to prosper.

11. 'Now I will teach you six conditions of welfare. Listen, and pay careful attention and I will tell you them:

'As long as the bhikkhus continue in kindness of action, speech and thought towards their fellow-disciples, both in public and in private – as long as they divide without partiality, and share all things in common with their fellows, all such things as they receive in accordance with the just provisions of the Order, down even to the mere contents of a begging-bowl – as long as the bhikkhus live the religious life in the practice, both in public and in private, of those virtues which are productive of freedom, and praised by the wise; which are untarnished and which are conducive to concentration of heart – as long as the brethren live the religious life, cherishing, both in public and in private, that noble and saving insight which leads to release and to the complete destruction of suffering, so long may the bhikkhus be expected not to decline, but to prosper.

'As long as these six conditions continue to exist among the bhikkhus, as long as they are instructed in these six conditions, so long may the bhikkhus be expected not to decline, but to prosper.'

12. Now while the Master was staying there at Rajgir on the Vulture's Peak he delivered to the bhikkhus that [well-known] discourse: 'Concerning morality, meditation and wisdom'. 'Great becomes the fruit, great the advantage of meditation, when it is set round with morality. Great becomes the fruit, great the advantage of wisdom when it is set round with medit-ation. The mind set round with wisdom is set quite free from the Intoxications, that is to say, from the Intoxication of sensual desire, from the Intoxication of existence, from the Intoxication of opinions, from the Intoxication of ignorance.'

13. Now when the Master had stayed at Rajgir as long as he thought fit, he said to the venerable Ananda, 'Come, Ananda, let us go to Ambalatthika.'

'As you say, lord!' said Ananda, and the Master went with a large company of the bhikkhus to Ambalatthika.

14. While they were there, the Master stayed in the raja's house [and delivered again the same discourse, 'Concerning morality, meditation and wisdom'. The text repeats the dis-course: 'Great becomes the fruit', etc.]

15. Now when the Master had stayed at Ambalatthika as long as he thought fit, he said to the venerable Ananda, 'Come, Ananda, let us go on to Nalanda.'[3]

'As you say, lord!' said Ananda, and the Master, with a great company of bhikkhus, went to Nalanda. There, at Nalanda, the Master stayed in the Pavarika mango grove.

16. Then the venerable Sariputta arrived there, and having greeted the Master, took his seat respectfully at his side, and said: 'Lord! I have such faith in the Master that I believe there never has been, nor will there be, nor is there now any other, whether an ascetic or brahman, who is greater and wiser than the Master, that is to say, as regards the higher wisdom.'

'You speak grandly and boldly, Sariputta. Indeed, quite a paean of ecstasy! So you must have known all the Masters of the past, who were arahats and Buddhas, and you must be able to comprehend their minds and know their actions, their wisdom, their way of life, and the great release to which they attained!'

'Indeed, no, sir,'

'And you must have perceived also all the Masters of the future, who shall be arahats and Buddhas, and be able to comprehend their minds and actions, their wisdom and way of life, and the great release they shall attain.'

'Indeed, no, sir.'

'Well at least then, Sariputta, you know me as the arahat, the present Buddha, and have comprehended my mind, actions, wisdom, way of life and release in the way I have mentioned.'

'Not even that, sir'

'You see then, Sariputta, you do not know the hearts of the arahats, of Buddhas, of the past and of the future. Why then do you speak so grandly, so boldly? Why burst forth into such a paean of ecstasy?'

17. 'Sir! I do not know the hearts of the Buddhas that have been and are to come, and now are. I only know the Dhamma-principle.

'It is, sir, as though a king might have a border city, strong in its foundations, strong in its ramparts and towers, and with only one gate; and the king might have a watchman there, clever, expert and wise, to stop all strangers and admit only men well known. And he, on patrolling in his sentry-walks over the approaches all round the city, might not actually so observe *all* the joints and crevices in the ramparts of that city as to know where even a cat could get out. He might simply be satisfied to know that all living things of larger size that entered or left the city, would have to do so by that gate. In the same way, sir, I know one thing – the Dhamma-principle.

'I know that the Buddhas of the past, putting away all hankering after the world, ill-will, sloth, worry and perplexity – those Five Hindrances, those mental impurities which make the understanding weak – and training their minds in the Four Applications of Mindfulness; thoroughly exercising themselves in the Seven Factors of Enlightenment, realized supreme Enlightenment. And I know that the Buddhas of the times to come will do the same. And I know that the Exalted One, the Able Awakened One of today, has done so now.'[4]

18. There, too, at Nalanda in the Pavarika mango grove the Master [delivered again the discourse, 'Concerning morality, meditation and wisdom'. See paragraph 12.]

19. Now when the Master had stayed as long as he thought fit at Nalanda, he said to the venerable Ananda, 'Come, Ananda, let us go on to Pataligama.'

'As you say, lord!' said Ananda, and the Master, with a great company of the brethren, went to Pataligama.

20. When the disciples at Pataligama heard of his arrival they went to the place where he was, took their seats respectfully beside him, and invited him to their village rest-house. The Master signified, by silence, his consent.

21. Then the Pataligama disciples, seeing that he had accepted the invitation, rose from their seats and went away to the rest-house, bowing to the Master and keeping him on their right as they passed him. Arriving there they strewed all the rest-house with fresh sand, placed seats in it, set up a water-pot, and made ready an oil lamp. Then they returned to the Master, and saluting him they stood beside him, and told him what they had done and said: 'It is all ready for whatever you have in mind.'

22. So the Master dressed and took his bowl and other things, and went with the bhikkhus to the rest-house, washed his feet, entered the hall, and took his seat against the centre pillar, with his face towards the East. The brethren also, after washing their feet, entered the hall, and took their seats round the Master, against the western wall, and facing the East. And the Pataligama disciples too, after washing their feet, entered the hall, and took their seats opposite the Master against the eastern wall, and facing towards the West.

23. Then the Master addressed the Pataligama disciples: 'Householders, there are five kinds of loss suffered by anyone who offends against the moral law. In the first place the offender, lacking morality, falls into great poverty through indolence; in the next place, he becomes known as a bad character; third, whatever society he enters – whether of nobles, brahmans, heads of houses, or men of a religious order, he enters shyly and confused; fourth, he is full of anxiety when his time comes to die; and lastly, on the dissolution of the body, after death, he is reborn into some unhappy state of suffering or woe.[5] These, householders, are the five kinds of loss suffered by one who offends against the moral law.

24. The gain of one who observes the moral law through a good life, householders, is of five kinds. In the first place the well-doer, strong in morality, gets much wealth through his industriousness. In the next place he gets a good reputation. Third, whatever society he enters – whether of nobles, brahmans, heads of houses, or members of a religious order – he enters confident and self-possessed. Fourth, when his time comes, he dies without anxiety. Lastly, on the dissolution of the body, after death, he is reborn into some happy state in heaven. These, householders, are the five kinds of gain enjoyed by one who observes the moral law.'

25. After the Master had in this way taught the lay disciples at Pataligama, and exhorted them, gladdened them, and delighted them, far into the night, he dismissed them. 'It is very late, householders,' he said. 'It is time for you to go.'

'As you say, lord!' answered the disciples of Pataligama. They rose from their seats, and bowing to the Master, and keeping him on their right hand as they passed him, they went away.

And the Master, not long after the disciples of Pataligama had gone away, went to his own room.

26. At that time Sunidha and Vassakara, the chief ministers of Magadha, were building a fortress at Pataligama against the Vajjians, and there were a number of local deities who in thousands haunted the ground there. Now, wherever ground is

so occupied by powerful deities, they influence even the most powerful rajas and ministers to build dwelling-places there. Deities of middling and inferior power influence in a similar way middling or inferior rajas and ministers.

27. The Master, with his great and clear and supra-normal vision, saw thousands of these deities haunting Pataligama. He arose very early in the morning, and said to Ananda, 'Who is it then, Ananda, who is building a fortress at Pataligama?'

'It is Sunidha and Vassakara, lord, chief ministers of Magadha. They are building a fortress there against the Vajjians.'

28. 'They act, Ananda, as if they had consulted with the deities of the Tavatimsa heaven.' He told Ananda what he himself had seen, and then added: 'As far, Ananda, as the Aryan people extend their settlements, as far as merchants travel, this will become the chief city, Pataliputra,[6] a centre for all kinds of trade. But three dangers will hang over Pataliputra; that of fire, that of water, and that of dissension among friends.'

29. Sunidha and Vassakara, the chief ministers of Magadha, then came to the place where the Master was. When they arrived, they exchanged greetings and paid the Master the compliments of politeness and courtesy, and stood there respectfully on one side. So standing, Sunidha and Vassakara, the two chief ministers of Magadha, then said to him: 'Will the venerable Gotama, together with the bhikkhus, do us the honour of taking his meal at our house today?' And the Master signified, by silence, his consent.

30. When Sunidha and Vassakara, the chief ministers of Magadha, understood that he had given his consent, they returned home, and prepared sweet dishes of boiled rice, and cakes. Then they sent a message to the Master: 'It is time to eat, Gotama, and everything is ready.'

The Master dressed early, took his bowl with him, and went with the brethren to the house of Sunidha and Vassakara, and sat down on the seat prepared for him. With their own hands they served the sweet rice and the cakes to the brethren, with the Buddha at their head, and waited on them until they had had enough. When the Master had finished his meal, the ministers brought a low seat, and sat down respectfully at his side.

31. When they were thus seated the Master expressed his

thanks in verse, as follows:

> 'Wheresoe'er the prudent man shall take up his abode
> Let him support the brethren there, good men of self-control,
> And give the merit of his gifts to deities who haunt the spot.
> Revered, they will revere him: honoured, they honour him again;
> Are gracious to him as a mother to her own, her only son.
> And the man who has the grace of the gods, good fortune he beholds.'

32. When he had thanked the ministers in this verse he rose from his seat, and went out. And they followed him as he went, saying, 'The gate Samanna Gotama goes out by today shall be called Gotama's gate, and the ferry at which he crosses the river shall be called Gotama's ferry.' Therefore that gate by which he went out was called 'Gotama's gate'.

33. When the Master arrived at the river, he found that the river Ganges was brimful and overflowing. People who wished to cross to the opposite bank were beginning to seek for boats, some for rafts of wood, whilst some made rafts of basket-work. Then the Master, as suddenly as a strong man would stretch out his arm, or draw it back again when he had stretched it out, vanished from this side of the river, and stood on the further bank with the company of the bhikkhus.

34. As the Master watched the people who wished to cross to the opposite bank looking for boats or for rafts of wood, or for rafts of basket-work, he sang in lyric style:

> 'They who have crossed the ocean drear
> Making a path across the pools –
> While the vain world ties basket rafts –
> These are the wise, the saved indeed.'[7]

End of the First Portion for Recitation

Chapter 2: From the Ganges to Vesali

1. The Master said to the venerable Ananda: 'Come, Ananda, let us move on to Kotigama.'

'As you say, lord!' replied Ananda.

So the Master went with a great company of the bhikkhus to Kotigama. There he stayed in the village itself.

2. There the Master addressed the bhikkhus. He said: 'It is through not understanding and grasping the Four Noble Truths, that we have had to continue so long; to wander so long in this weary path of transmigration, you and I!

'And what are these four?

'The Noble Truth about suffering; the Noble Truth about the cause of suffering; the Noble Truth about the cessation of suffering; and the Noble Truth about the path that leads to that cessation. When these four Noble Truths are grasped and known, the craving for future life is rooted out, that which leads to renewed becoming is destroyed, and then there is no more birth!'

3. These were the words of the Master. When he had said this, he recited the following verse:

'By not seeing the Noble Truths as they really are,
Long is the path that is traversed through many a birth;
When these are grasped, the cause of rebirth is removed,
The root of suffering is destroyed, and then there is no more birth.'

4. There too, while staying at Kotigama, the Master [repeated the discourse, 'Concerning morality, meditation and wisdom'. See Chapter 1, paragraph 12].

5. Now when the Master had stayed as long as he thought fit at Kotigama, he said to the venerable Ananda: 'Come, Ananda, let us move on to the Nadikas.'

'As you say, lord!' Ananda replied.

So the Master went to the Nadikas with a great company of the bhikkhus, and there the Master stayed in the Brick Hall.[8]

6. The venerable Ananda went to the Master, paid him reverence and took his seat beside him. When he was seated, he said to the Master: 'The brother named Salha has died at

Nadika, lord. Where has he been reborn, and what is his destiny? The sister named Nanda has died, lord, at Nadika. Where is she reborn, and what is her destiny?' In the same terms he inquired concerning the lay disciple Sudatta, and the devout lady Sugata, the lay disciples, Kakudha, and Kalinga, and Nikata, and Katissabha, and Tuttha, and Santuttha, and Bhadda, and Subhadda.

7. 'The brother named Salha, Ananda, by the destruction of the intoxicants of the mind, has by himself, and in this world, known and realized and attained to arahatship, to emancipation of heart and to emancipation of mind. The sister named Nanda, Ananda, by the complete destruction of the five fetters that bind people to the lower worlds, has spontaneously gained complete release, never to return. The devout Sudatta, Ananda, by the complete destruction of the three fetters and by the reduction to a minimum of greed, hate and delusion, has become a 'once-returner' who, after one more return to this world, will make an end of suffering. The devout Sugata, Ananda, by the complete destruction of the three fetters, has become converted, is no longer liable to be reborn in a state of suffering, and is assured after this of attaining to the enlightenment of arahatship. The devout Kakudha, Ananda, by the complete destruction of the five fetters that bind people to the lower worlds, has spontaneously gained complete release, never to return. [The same of Kalinga, Nikata, Katissabha, Tuttha, Santuttha, Bhadda and Subhadda, and with more than fifty devout men in Nadika.] More than ninety devout men in Nadika, who have died, Ananda, have by the complete destruction of the three fetters, and by the reduction of greed, hate and delusion, become 'once-returners' who, after one more return to this world will make an end of suffering. More than five hundred devout men of Nadika who have died, Ananda, have by the complete destruction of the three fetters become converted, are no longer liable to be reborn in a state of suffering, and are assured after this of attaining the enlightenment of arahatship.'

8. 'There is nothing strange in this, Ananda, that a human being should die; but what is wearisome is that as each one does so, you should come to me and inquire about them in this

manner. I will, therefore, teach you what is called the Mirror of Truth. If a disciple of the noble ones possesses that he may, if he wishes, discern of himself: "Hell is destroyed for me, and so is rebirth as an animal, or a ghost, or in any place of misery. I am a sotapanna,[9] no longer liable to be reborn in a state of suffering, and am assured after this of attaining to the enlightenment of arahatship."

9. 'What then, Ananda, is this Mirror of Truth, this ordering of the Doctrine in such a way that the disciple of the noble ones is possessed of faith in the Buddha, fully confident that the Master is the arahat, the Fully Enlightened One, perfect in knowledge and in conduct, happy, knowing all worlds, un-equalled as a guide to self-mastery, teacher of celestial and human beings, fully enlightened Master. The disciple possesses faith in the Truth – believing the Truth to have been proclaimed by the Master, visible to all, eternal, open to all, giving access to that which can be attained by the wise, each for himself.

The disciple possesses confidence in the Community, be-lieving that disciples of the Master (that is, the four pairs of humans and the eight human types) are walking in the right path, the proper path; believing that the Community of the Master is worthy of offerings, of hospitality, of gifts, of rever-ence; he believes it to be the supreme source of merit for the world, possessing the virtues beloved by the good, virtues which are complete, intact, unblemished, virtues which make men truly free, virtues which are praised by the wise, untarnished and conducive to meditation.

'This, Ananda, is the Way, the Mirror of Truth, the ordering of the Doctrine by means of which a disciple of the noble ones may, if he should so desire, predict of himself: "Hell is destroyed for me; and so is rebirth as an animal, or a ghost, or in any place of misery. I am a sotapanna, no longer liable to be reborn in a state of suffering, and am assured after this of finally attaining to the enlightenment of arahatship."

10. There also, at the Brick Hall at Nadika, the Master [repeated the discourse, 'Concerning morality, meditation, and wisdom'. See Chapter 1, paragraph 12].

11. Now when the Master had stayed as long as he wished at Nadika, he said to Ananda: 'Come, Ananda, let us move on to Vesali.'

'As you say, lord!' Ananda replied.

Then the Master went to Vesali with a great company of bhikkhus; and there at Vesali he stayed at Ambapali's grove.

12. There the Master addressed the brethren, 'A bhikkhu should be mindful and self-possessed; this is our instruction to you.

'Now how does a bhikkhu become mindful?

'In our community, bhikkhus, one continually so observes the body, *qua* body, that one remains energetic, conscious and mindful, having disciplined both the desire and the dejection which are common in the world. [In the same way with regard to sensations, thoughts and states of mind, he continually so observes each] that he remains energetic, conscious, and mindful, having overcome both the desire and the dejection common in the world.

13. 'Now how does a bhikkhu become conscious? In whatever he may do, in going out or coming in, in looking forward or in looking round, in bending in his arm or in stretching it out, in wearing his robes or in carrying his bowl, in eating or drinking, in chewing or swallowing, in obeying the calls of nature, in walking or standing or sitting, in sleeping or waking, in talking and in being silent.

'In this way, bhikkhus, one should be mindful and conscious; this is our instruction to you.'[10]

14. Now the courtesan Ambapali heard that the Master had arrived at Vesali, and was staying there at her mango grove. Ordering a number of state vehicles to be made ready, she got into one of them, and went, with the others accompanying her, towards her garden. She went in the carriage as far as the ground was passable for carriages, and there she got out and she went on foot the rest of the way to where the Master was. She took her seat respectfully on one side. Then the Master talked to her about Dhamma, instructing, exhorting, gladdening and delighting her.

Then she—instructed, exhorted, gladdened and delighted by what he had said, responded by asking: 'Will the Master do me the honour of taking his meal at my house tomorrow, and the members of the Community with him?'

The Master, by silence, gave his consent. Then, when Ambapali the courtesan saw that the Master had consented, she rose from her seat, bowed to him, and keeping him on her right hand as she passed him, she went away.

15. Now the Licchavis of Vesali heard that the Master had arrived at Vesali, and was staying at Ambapali's grove. Ordering a number of state carriages to be made ready, they each got into one of them and drove in procession out of the town. Some of them were dark in colour, and wearing dark clothes and ornaments; some of them were fair in colour, and wearing light clothes and ornaments; some were ruddy in colour, and wearing red clothes and ornaments; some were pale in colour, and wearing white clothes and ornaments.

16. Then Ambapali drove up. She came alongside the young Licchavis, axle to axle, wheel to wheel and yoke to yoke, and the Licchavis said to Ambapali the courtesan: 'Ambapali, why do you drive alongside us?'

'My lords, I have just invited the Master and the bhikkhus for a meal tomorrow,' said she.

'Ambapali! give it up! We'll pay you a hundred thousand,' they said.

'My lords, if you offered me all Vesali with its subject territory, I would not give up so honourable a feast!'

Then the Licchavis threw up their hands, and cried: 'We have been outdone by this mango woman! We have been outclassed by this mango woman!' and they went on to Ambapali's grove.

17. When the Master saw the Licchavis approaching in the distance, he said to the bhikkhus: "Anyone who has never seen the Tavatimsa gods, just look at this company of the Licchavis, behold this company of the Licchavis, take a long look at them, and compare them, for they are just like a company of Tavatimsa gods.'[11]

18. When they had ridden as far as the ground was passable for carriages, the Licchavis got down, and from there went on foot to the place where the Master was. They took their seats respectfully by his side. Then the Master talked to them about Dhamma, instructing, exhorting, gladdening and delighting them.

Then they – instructed, exhorted, gladdened and delighted

by what he had said, responded by asking:

'Will the Exalted One do us the honour of taking his meal at our house tomorrow, together with the members of the Community?'

'Licchavis, I have promised to dine tomorrow with Ambapali the courtesan,' was the reply.

Then the Licchavis threw up their hands, and cried: 'We are outdone by this mango girl! We have been outclassed by this mango girl!' So expressing their thanks, and their approval of what the Master had taught them, they rose from their seats, bowed to the Master, and keeping him on their right hand as they passed him, they went away.

19. At the end of the night Ambapali the courtesan had sweet rice and cakes prepared at her mansion, and sent a message to the Master: 'It is time, lord; the food is all ready.'

The Master, having dressed himself early in the morning, took his bowl, and his robe, and went with the bhikkhus to the place where Ambapali's mansion was. When he arrived he sat down on the seat prepared for him. And Ambapali the courtesan served the sweet rice and cakes to all the bhikkhus with the Buddha at their head, and waited upon them until they had had enough.

When the Master had quite finished his meal, and had cleaned the bowl and his hands, the courtesan had a low stool brought, and sat down at his side, and said to him: 'Lord, I present this park[12] to the community of bhikkhus of which the Buddha is the chief.' The Master accepted the gift; and after he had talked to her about Dhamma, instructing, exhorting, gladdening and delighting her, he rose from his seat, and left.

20. At Ambapali's mango grove the Master [repeated the discourse, 'Concerning morality, meditation, and wisdom'. See Chapter 1, paragraph 12].

21. When the Master had stayed as long as he wished at Ambapali's grove, he said to Ananda: 'Come, Ananda, let us move on to Beluva.'

'As you say, lord,' Ananda replied.

Then the Master went to Beluva, with a great company of bhikkhus, and there he stayed in the village itself.

22. The Master then addressed the bhikkhus. 'For the rainy

season retreat,' he said, 'you should stay round about Vesali, each according to where he has friends, acquaintances and intimates living. I shall enter upon the rainy season here at Beluva.'

'As you say, lord!' those bhikkhus replied. So they entered upon the rainy season round about Vesali, each according to the place where his friends, acquaintances and intimates lived: while the Master stayed at Beluva.

23. Now when the Master had thus entered upon the rainy season, he became very ill; he had sharp pains, as though he were about to die. But the Master, mindful and aware, bore them without complaint.

Then a thought occurred to the Master: 'It would not be right for me to pass away without addressing the disciples, without taking leave of the Community. I must make a strong effort of the will, and overcome this illness, and keep my hold on life until the allotted time has come.'

So the Master, by a strong effort of the will, overcame his illness, and kept his hold on life until such time as he had decided upon. And the illness subsided.

24. Very soon after that the Master began to recover. When he was quite recovered, he came out from his lodging, and sat down in the shade where a seat had been placed. The venerable Ananda went to where the Master was, and saluted him, and took a seat respectfully on one side, and spoke to the Master: 'I have observed, lord, how you were in good health, and then you became ill. And although at the sight of your illness my own body felt very weak, and the horizon became blurred, and my faculties became confused; nevertheless I took some comfort from the thought that the Master would not pass away until at least he had left instructions concerning the Community.'

25. 'What, then, Ananda? Does the Community expect that of me? I have proclaimed the Dhamma, with no distinction between exoteric and esoteric doctrine; for in respect of these things, Ananda, the Tathagata has no such thing as the closed fist of the teacher, who keeps something back. Surely, Ananda, if there is any one who harbours the thought, "It is I who will lead the bhikkhus", or "The Community is dependent upon me", it is he who should lay down instructions on any question

concerning the Order. The Tathagata, Ananda, does not consider whether it is he who should lead the bhikkhus, or whether the Community is dependent upon him. Why then should he leave instructions on any question concerning the Community? I, too, Ananda, am now grown old, and full of years, my journey is drawing to its close, I have reached my sum of days, I am turning eighty years of age; and just as a worn-out carriage, Ananda, can be kept going only with the help of bits of rope, so I think, the body of the Tathagata can only be kept going by bandaging it up. Only when the Tathagata, by ceasing to attend to any outward thing, and by the cessation of any separate sensation, becomes plunged into that concentration of heart which is concerned with no material object, only then is the body of the Tathagata at ease.

26. 'Therefore, Ananda, you are to be lamps unto yourselves. Be a refuge to yourselves. Take yourselves to no external refuge. Hold fast to the Dhamma as a lamp. Hold fast as a refuge to the Dhamma. Do not look for refuge to any one besides yourselves. And how, Ananda, is a bhikkhu to be a lamp unto himself, a refuge to himself, taking himself to no external refuge, holding fast to the Dhamma as a lamp, holding fast as a refuge to the Dhamma, not looking for refuge to any one besides himself?

'In our community, bhikkhus, one continually so observes the body, *qua* body, that one remains energetic, conscious and mindful, having disciplined both the desire and the dejection common in the world. In the same way with regard to sensations, and thoughts, and states of mind; he continually so observes each that he remains energetic, conscious and mindful, having overcome both the desire and the dejection common in the world.

'Whoever, Ananda, either now or after I am dead, shall be a lamp unto themselves, and a refuge unto themselves, and shall take themselves to no external refuge, but holding fast to the Dhamma as a lamp, holding fast to the Dhamma as their refuge, shall look not for refuge to any one besides themselves – it is they, Ananda, among my bhikkhus, who shall transcend the darkness; but they must be anxious to learn.'[13]

End of the Second Portion for Recitation

Chapter 3: At Vesali

1. One morning the Master robed himself early and taking his bowl, went into Vesali for alms. When he had returned from the round for alms, and had finished eating he said to the venerable Ananda: 'Take up the mat, Ananda; I will go and spend the day at the Chapala Shrine.'

'As you say, lord!' replied the venerable Ananda. Taking up the mat he followed step by step behind the Master.

2. So the Master went to the Chapala Shrine, and when he had come there he sat down on the mat which had been spread out for him, and the venerable Ananda took his seat respectfully beside him. Then the Master said to the venerable Ananda: 'How delightful a spot, Ananda, is Vesali, and how charming the Udena Shrine, and the Gotamaka Shrine, and the Shrine of the Seven Mangoes, and the Shrine of Many Sons, and the Sarandada Shrine, and the Chapala Shrine.[14]

3. 'Ananda, whosoever has developed, practised, dwelt on, expanded and ascended to the very heights of the Four Roads to Iddhi,[15] and so mastered them as to be able to use them as a vehicle, and as a basis, he could, if he so desired, remain in the same birth for an aeon, or for that portion of the aeon which had yet to run. Now the Tathagata has thoroughly practised and developed them in all respects as just more fully described, and he could, therefore, should he desire it, live on yet for an aeon, or for that portion of the aeon which has yet to run.'

4. But even though a suggestion so evident and a hint so clear were given by the Master, the venerable Ananda was incapable of comprehending them; and so he failed to ask the Master: 'Please, lord, remain during the aeon! Live on through the aeon, Happy One! for the good and the happiness of the great multitudes, out of pity for the world, for the good, and the gain, and the welfare of celestial beings and men!' For his mind was possessed by Mara the Evil One.

5. A second and a third time the Master said the same thing, and a second and a third time Ananda's mind was possessed by Mara, and he failed to ask.

6. Then the Master said to the venerable Ananda: 'You may

leave me for a while, Ananda, and do whatever you may have in mind.'

'As you say, lord!' replied the venerable Ananda. Passing the Master on the right he sat down at the foot of a tree not far away.

7. Not long after the venerable Ananda had gone, Mara, the Evil One, approached the Master and stood beside him. So standing there, he addressed the Master: 'Pass away now, lord; let the Master now die. Now is the time for the Master to pass away, in fulfilment of the prediction the Master made when he said:[16] "I shall not die, Evil One! until the brethren and sisters of the Community, and the lay-disciples of both sexes shall have become true hearers, wise and well trained, ready and learned, knowing my teachings by heart, and knowing by heart also the lesser corollaries that follow from the larger Doctrine, correct in life, walking according to the precepts, and until they, having themselves learned the Doctrine, shall be able to tell others of it, expound it, make it known, establish it, open it, minutely explain it and make it clear – until they, when others promulgate doctrines which can easily be refuted by the Truth, shall be competent to refute such doctrines and to spread the wonder-working Truth abroad!"

8. 'And now, lord, the brethren and sisters of the Community and the lay-disciples of both sexes have become all that you required, and are competent. Pass away now therefore, lord; let the Master now die! The time has come for the Master to pass away, in fulfilment of the prediction made when he said, "I shall not die, Evil One! until this pure practice of mine shall have become successful, prosperous, widespread and popular in all its full extent – until, in a word, it shall have been well proclaimed among men." Now, lord, this pure practice of yours has become all this. Pass away now therefore, lord; let the Master now die! The time has come for the Master to pass away!'

9. When Mara had said this, the Master addressed him: 'Evil One! You can relax! The death of the Tathagata will take place before long. At the end of three months from this time the Tathagata will pass away.'

10. Thus the Master, while he was at the Shrine of Chapala, deliberately and consciously rejected the rest of his natural term

of life.[17] On his so rejecting it there arose a mighty earthquake, awful and terrible, and thunder overhead. When the Master perceived this, he broke out into an exultant song:

> 'His sum of life the sage renounced,
> The cause of life immeasurable or small;
> With inward joy and calm, he broke,
> Like coat of mail, his life's own cause!'[18]

11. The following thought then occurred to the venerable Ananda:[19] 'It is indeed wonderful and marvellous that this mighty earthquake should arise, awful and terrible, and that thunder should sound overhead. What may be the immediate cause of this earthquake and thunder, and what the remote cause of it?'

12. Then the venerable Ananda went up to the place where the Master was, and did obeisance to him, and sat down respectfully at one side, and said: 'It is indeed wonderful and marvellous that this mighty earthquake should arise, awful and terrible, and that the thunder should sound overhead! What may be the immediate cause of it? And what the remote cause of it?'

13. 'Eight are the immediate, eight the remote causes, Ananda, for the occurrence of a mighty earthquake. What are the eight? This great earth, Ananda, is established on water, the water on wind, and the wind rests upon space. At such a time, Ananda, as the mighty winds blow, the waters are shaken by the mighty winds as they blow, and by the moving water the earth is shaken. These are the first causes, immediate and remote, of the appearance of a mighty earthquake.

14. 'Again, Ananda, an ascetic or a brahman of great intellectual power, and who has the feelings of his heart well under his control; or a god, or a local deity [*devata*][20] of great might and power, who, by intense meditation on the idea of the minutest portion of earth and on the idea of the widest expanse of water, has succeeded in realizing the comparative value of things, can make this earth move and tremble and be shaken violently. These are the second causes, immediate and remote, of the appearance of a mighty earthquake.

15. 'Again, Ananda, when a Bodhisatta consciously and

deliberately leaves his temporary form in the heaven of delight and descends into his mother's womb, then is this earth made to quake and tremble and is shaken violently. These events constitute the third cause, immediate and remote, of the appearance of a mighty earthquake.

16. 'Again, Ananda, when a Bodhisatta deliberately and consciously quits his mother's womb, then the earth quakes and trembles and is shaken violently. This is the fourth cause, immediate and remote, of the appearance of a mighty earthquake.

17. 'Again, Ananda, when a Tathagata arrives at supreme and perfect enlightenment, then this earth quakes and trembles and is shaken violently. This is the fifth cause, immediate and remote, of the appearance of a mighty earthquake.

18. 'Again, Ananda, when a Tathagata founds the sublime kingdom of righteousness, then this earth quakes and trembles and is shaken violently. This is the sixth cause, immediate and remote, of the appearance of a mighty earthquake.

19. 'Again, Ananda, when a Tathagata consciously and deliberately rejects the remainder of his life, then this earth quakes and trembles and is shaken violently. This is the seventh cause, immediate and remote, of the appearance of a mighty earthquake.

20. 'Again, Ananda, when a Tathagata passes entirely away in that utter passing away in which nothing whatever is left behind, then this earth quakes and trembles and is shaken violently. This is the eighth cause, immediate and remote, of the appearance of a mighty earthquake.

21. 'Now Ananda, there are eight kinds of assemblies. What are the eight? Assemblies of nobles, brahmans, householders and wanderers, and of the angel hosts of the Guardian Kings, of the Great Thirty-Three, of the Maras and of the Brahmas.

22. 'Now I call to mind, Ananda, how when I used to enter into an assembly of many hundred nobles, before I had seated myself there or talked to them or started a conversation with them, I used to become like them in colour, and in voice. Then with religious discourse I used to instruct, and exhort, and liven them, and fill them with gladness. But they did not know me when I spoke, and they would say: "Who can this be who speaks in such a way – a man or a god?" Then having instructed,

exhorted, livened and gladdened them with religious discourse, I would vanish. But they did not know me even when I vanished, and would say: "Who can this be who has just vanished away? a man or a god?" '

23. In the same words the Master spoke of how he had been used to enter into assemblies of each of the other of the eight kinds, and of how he had not been made known to them either in speaking or in vanishing. 'Now these, Ananda, are the eight assemblies.

24. 'Now, Ananda, there are the eight positions of mastery over the delusion arising from the apparent permanence of external things.[21] What are the eight?

25. 'When a man having subjectively the idea of form sees forms external to himself which are finite, and pleasant or unpleasant to the sight, and having mastered them, is conscious that he knows and sees – this is the first position of mastery.

26. 'When a man having subjectively the idea of form sees externally forms which are boundless, and pleasant or unpleasant to the sight, and having mastered them, is conscious that he knows and sees – this is the second position of mastery.

27. 'When a man without the subjective idea of form sees forms external to himself which are finite, and pleasant or unpleasant to the sight, and having mastered them, is conscious that he knows and sees – this is the third position of mastery.

28. 'When a man without the subjective idea of form sees externally forms external to himself which are boundless, and pleasant or unpleasant to the sight, and having mastered them, is conscious that he knows and sees – this is the fourth position of mastery.

29. 'When a man without the subjective idea of form sees externally forms external to himself that are blue, blue in colour, blue in appearance, and reflecting blue – just, for instance, as the flax blossom is blue in colour, blue in appearance, and reflecting blue; or, again, as that fine muslin of Benares, of delicate finish on both sides, is blue in colour, blue in appearance, and reflecting blue – when a man without the subjective idea of form sees externally forms which, just in that way, are blue, blue in colour, blue in appearance, and reflecting blue, and having mastered them, is conscious that he knows and

sees – that is the fifth position of mastery.

30–2. [The sixth, seventh and eighth positions of mastery are then explained in words identical with those used to explain the fifth; save that yellow, red and white are respectively substituted throughout for blue; and the kanikara flower, the bandhu-givaka flower, and the morning star are respectively substituted for the flax blossom, as the first of the two objects given as examples.]

33. 'Now these stages of deliverance, Ananda, [from the hindrance to thought arising from the sensations and ideas due to external forms] are eight in number. What are the eight?

'A man possessed of form sees forms – this is the first stage of deliverance.

'Unaware of his own form, he sees forms external to himself – this is the second stage of deliverance.

'With the thought "it is well", he becomes intent – this is the third stage of deliverance.

'By passing quite beyond all idea of form, by putting an end to all ideas of sensory impact, by paying no attention to the idea of multiformity, he, thinking "it is all infinite space", reaches [mentally] and remains in the state of mind in which the idea of the infinity of space is the only idea that is present – this is the fourth stage of deliverance.

'By passing quite beyond all idea of space being the infinite basis, he, thinking "it is all infinite reason", reaches [mentally] and remains in the state of mind to which the infinity of reason is alone present – this is the fifth stage of deliverance.

'By passing quite beyond the consciousness of the infinity of reason, he, thinking "nothing at all exists", reaches mentally and remains in the state of mind to which nothing at all is specially present – this is the sixth stage of deliverance.

'By passing quite beyond all idea of nothingness he reaches mentally and remains in the state of mind to which neither ideas nor the absence of ideas are specially present – this is the seventh stage of deliverance.

'By passing quite beyond the state of "neither ideas nor the absence of ideas" he reaches mentally and remains in the state of mind in which both sensations and ideas have ceased to be – this is the eighth stage of deliverance.

'Now these, Ananda, are the eight stages of deliverance.

34. 'On one occasion, Ananda, I was resting under the goatherd's nigrodha tree on the bank of the river Neranjara, immediately after having reached the Great Enlightenment. Then Mara, the Evil One, came to the place where I was, and standing beside me said to me: "Pass away now, lord, from existence! Let the Master now die! Now is the time for the Master to pass away!"

35. 'And when he had said this, Ananda, I replied to Mara, the Evil One, and said: "I shall not pass away, Evil One! until not only the brethren and sisters of the Community, but also the lay-disciples of both sexes shall have become true hearers, wise and well trained, ready and learned, knowing my teachings by heart, and knowing by heart also the lesser corollaries that follow from the larger Doctrine, correct in life, walking according to the precepts and until they, having themselves learned the Doctrine, shall be able to tell others of it, expound it, make it known, establish it, open it, minutely explain it and make it clear, and until they, when others promulgate vain doctrine which can easily be refuted by the Truth, shall be competent to refute such doctrines and to spread the wonder-working Truth abroad! I shall not die until this pure practice of mine shall have become successful, prosperous, widespread and popular in all its full extent – until, in a word, it shall have been well proclaimed among men!"

36. 'And now again today, Ananda, at Chapala's Shrine, Mara, the Evil One, came to the place where I was, and standing beside me [said again what he had said then].

37. 'And when he had spoken, Ananda, I answered him: "You can relax! The passing away of the Tathagata shall take place before long. At the end of three months from this time the Tathagata will pass away!"

'And now again, Ananda, the Tathagata has today at Chapala's Shrine consciously and deliberately rejected the rest of his allotted term of life.'

38. When he had said this the venerable Ananda replied: 'Deign lord, to remain during the aeon: live on through the kalpa, Master, for the good and the happiness of the great multitudes, out of pity for the world, for the good, and the gain,

and the welfare of celestial beings and of men!'

'Enough, Ananda! No more entreaties! The time for making such a request is past.'

39. But again, the second time, the venerable Ananda pleaded with the Master in the same words. And he received the same reply.

Again, the third time, the venerable Ananda pleaded with the Master in the same words.

'Do you have faith, Ananda, in the wisdom of the Tathagata?'

'Indeed, lord!'

'Why, then, Ananda, do you trouble the Tathagata even for a third time?'

40. 'From his own mouth I have heard from the Master, from his own mouth I have these words: "Whoever has developed, practised, dwelt on, expanded, and ascended to the very heights of the Four Roads to Iddhi, and so mastered them as to be able to use them as a vehicle, and as a basis, he could, if he so desired remain in the same birth for an aeon, or for that portion of the aeon which had yet to run." Now the Tathagata has thoroughly practised and developed them [in all respects as just now fully described,] and he could, therefore, should he so desire, live on yet for an aeon, or for that portion of the aeon which has yet to run.'

'Have you faith, Ananda?'

'Indeed, lord!'

'Then, Ananda, the wrong action, the offence is yours, in that when a suggestion so evident and a hint so clear were given you by the Tathagata, you were nevertheless incapable of comprehending them, and you did not at that time beseech the Tathagata, and say: "Deign, lord, to continue through this aeon, for the good and the happiness of the great multitudes, out of pity for the world, for the good, and the gain, and the welfare of celestial beings and of men." If you had then so pleaded with the Tathagata, the Tathagata might have rejected the appeal the first time, and possibly even the second time, but the third time he would have granted it. Therefore, Ananda, the wrong action, the offence, is yours!

41. 'On one occasion, Ananda, I was staying at Rajgir, on

the hill called the Vulture's Peak. Now there, Ananda, I said to you: "How pleasant a spot, Ananda, is Rajgir; how pleasant is this Vulture's Peak. Whoever, Ananda, has developed, practised, dwelt on, expanded and ascended to the very heights of the Four Roads to Iddhi, and so mastered them as to be able to use them as a vehicle, and as a basis, he could, if he so desired, remain in the same birth for an aeon, or for that portion of the aeon which had yet to run. Now the Tathagata has thoroughly practised and developed them in all respects as just now fully described, and he could, therefore, should he so desire, live on yet for an aeon, or for that portion of the aeon which has yet to run." But even when a suggestion so evident and a hint so clear was given you by the Tathagata, you were still not able to comprehend them, and you failed to entreat the Tathagata: "Deign, lord, to continue during this aeon. Live on, Master, through this aeon for the good and the happiness of the great multitudes, out of pity for the world, for the good, and the gain, and the welfare of celestial beings and of men." If you then had so pleaded, the Tathagata might have rejected the appeal the first or even perhaps the second time, but the third time he would have granted it. Therefore, Ananda, the wrong action, the offence, is yours!

42. 'On one occasion, Ananda, I was staying at the same place, at Rajgir, in the Banyan Grove, on another occasion at the Robbers' Cliff, on another occasion at Rajgir in the Sattapanni cave on the slope of Mount Vebhara, on another occasion at the Black Rock on the slope of Mount Isigili, and on other similar occasions at the Sitavana Grove, in the mountain cave Sappasondika, at the Tapoda Grove, at the Bamboo Grove in the Squirrels' Feeding-ground, at Jivaka's Mango Grove, and at the Deer Forest at Maddakucchi.

43. 'Now there too, Ananda, I spoke to you, on each occasion, and said, "How pleasant, Ananda, is Rajgir; how pleasant the Vulture's Peak; how pleasant the banyan tree of Gotama; how pleasant the Robbers' Cliff; how pleasant the Sattapanni cave on the slope of Mount Vebhara; how pleasant the Black Rock on the slope of Mount Isigili; how pleasant the mountain cave of the Serpent's Pool in the Sitavana Grove; how pleasant the Tapoda Grove; how pleasant the Squirrels' Feed-

ing-ground in the Bamboo Grove; how pleasant Jivaka's Mango Grove; how pleasant the Deer Forest at Maddakucchi!

44. ' "Whosoever, Ananda, has developed, practised, dwelt on, expanded and ascended to the very heights of the Four Roads to iddhi, and so mastered them as to be able to use them as a vehicle, and as a basis, could, if he so desired, remain in the same birth for an aeon, or for that portion of the aeon which had yet to run. Now the Tathagata has thought out and thoroughly practised them, and might, should he so desire, remain alive for an aeon, or for that portion of an aeon which has yet to run." But even when a suggestion so evident and a hint so clear were thus given you by the Tathagata, you were yet incapable of comprehending them, and you failed to entreat the Tathagata: "Deign, lord, to continue through the aeon. Live on, Master, through the aeon for the good and the happiness of the great multitudes, out of pity for the world, for the good, and the gain, and the welfare of celestial beings and of men. If you had then so pleaded with the Tathagata he might have rejected the appeal once, or possibly twice, but the third time he would have granted it. Therefore, Ananda, the wrong action, the offence is yours!'

45–47. [The same words are repeated for the Udena Shrine, the Gotamaka Shrine, the Shrine of the Seven Mangoes, the Shrine of Many Sons, and the Sarandada Shrine, all in Vesali, concluding in each case with the same, 'Therefore, Ananda, the wrong action, the offence, is yours.']

48. 'Now, Ananda, have I not formerly declared to you that it is in the very nature of all things near and dear unto us that we must separate ourselves from them, leave them and live apart from them? How, then, Ananda, can this be possible? Since anything that is born, brought into being, and conditioned, contains within itself the inherent necessity of dissolution, how can it be that it should not be dissolved? Clearly, it is impossible. And with regard to what has been relinquished, cast away, renounced, rejected and abandoned by the Tathagata [the remaining sum of life surrendered by him] with regard to that the Tathagata has declared: "The passing away of the Tathagata shall take place before long. At the end of three months from this time the Tathagata will die!" That the Tathagata should go

back on what he has thus declared is also impossible.[22]

'Come, Ananda, let us go to Kutagara Hall, to the Great Wood.'

'Indeed, lord!' replied the venerable Ananda.

49. Then the Master, accompanied by Ananda, went to the Great Wood, to Kutagara Hall. When they arrived, he said to the venerable Ananda: 'Bring all the bhikkhus who live in the vicinity of Vesali, and assemble them in the audience-hall.'

'As you say, lord!' replied the venerable Ananda. So when he had assembled them in the vicinity of Vesali, he went to the Master, bowed, and stood beside him. Then he said: 'Lord! the community of bhikkhus is assembled, ready for whatever the Master has in mind.'

50. Then the Master went to the audience-hall, and sat down there on the mat spread out for him. Then he addressed the bhikkhus. He said: 'You to whom the truths I have perceived I have made known, you who have thoroughly made yourselves masters of them, must practise them, meditate upon them and spread them abroad: in order that religious life[23] may endure and be perpetuated, in order that it may continue, for the good and happiness of the great multitudes, out of pity for the world, for the good, and the gain, and the welfare of celestial beings and of men.

'Now, bhikkhus, which are the truths which, when I had perceived them, I made known to you, and which when you have mastered you should practise, meditate upon and spread abroad, in order that religious life may endure and be perpetuated, in order that it may continue, for the good and the happiness of the great multitudes, out of pity for the world, for the good, and the gain, and the welfare of celestial beings and of men? They are these:[24]

The Four Applications of Mindfulness,
The Four Right Efforts,
The Four Roads to Power,
The Five Spiritual Faculties,
The Five Powers,
The Seven Factors of Enlightenment,
The Noble Eightfold Path.

'These, bhikkhus, are the truths, which, when I had perceived them, I made known to you, and which when you have mastered, you should practise, meditate upon and spread abroad, in order that religious life may endure and be perpetuated, in order that it may continue for the good and the happiness of the great multitudes, out of pity for the world, for the good, and the gain, and the welfare of celestial beings and of men.'

51. Then the Master exhorted the bhikkhus: 'Decay is inherent in all conditioned things; strive diligently! The Parinibbana of the Tathagata will not be long now. When three months have passed the Tathagata will become Parinibbana.

'My age is now full ripe, my life draws to its close:
I leave you for the refuge I have made.
Be earnest, therefore, bhikkhus, mindful, pure in life,
With firm resolve, keep watch upon your minds,
Who to the Doctrine and the Discipline holds fast,
No more reborn, shall come to suffering's end.

End of the Third Portion for Recitation

Chapter 4: Vesali to the River Kakuttha

1. The Master, having dressed early in the morning, took his bowl and entered Vesali for alms. When he had passed through Vesali, and had eaten his meal and was returning from his alms-round, he turned in the way an elephant does,[25] and gazed at Vesali. Then he said to the venerable Ananda, 'This will be the last time, Ananda, that the Tathagata will see Vesali. Now, Ananda, let us move on to the village of Bhandagama.'

'As you say, lord!' replied the venerable Ananda.

So the Master went with a great company of the bhikkhus to Bhandagama, and there the Master stayed in the village itself.

2. Then the Master addressed the bhikkhus: 'It is through

not understanding and grasping four principles that we have had to run so long, to wander so long in this weary path of transmigration, both you and I.

'What are these four? The principle of noble Morality; and that of noble Meditation; of noble Wisdom; and noble Liberation. When noble Morality is realized and known, when noble Meditation is realized and known, when noble Wisdom is realized and known, when noble Liberation is realized and known – then is the craving for future life rooted out, that which leads to renewed existence is destroyed, and there is no more birth.'

3. These were the Master's words, and when he had said this, he added the following:

'Righteousness, earnest thought, wisdom, and liberation,
These are the truths of great renown which Gotama has seen.
Knowing them, the Buddha to the bhikkhus then proclaimed:
"Now is all suffering ended; he who saw is seen no more." '[26]

4. There, too, while he was staying at Bhandagama, the Master [delivered to the bhikkhus the discourse, 'Concerning morality, meditation and wisdom'. See Chapter 1, paragraph 12].

5, 6. Now when the Master had stayed at Bhandagama as long as he required, he said to the venerable Ananda, 'Come now, Ananda, let us move on to Hatthigama.'

[Then in similar words to those which refer to Bhandagama, it is related how the Buddha went there; and from there to Ambagama, and then to Jambugama. At each place there was similar discourse. Then he went on to Bhoganagara.]

7. There at Bhoganagara the Master stayed at the Ananda Shrine. There the Master addressed the bhikkhus: 'I will teach you these Four Great Principles.[27] Listen carefully and pay attention, and I will tell you them.'

'As you say, lord!' the brethren replied. The Master then spoke as follows:

8. 'In the first place, a bhikkhu may say: "From the mouth of

the Master himself have I heard, from his own mouth have I received it. This is the Doctrine, this the Discipline, this the Teaching of the Master." The word spoken by that bhikkhu should neither be received with praise nor treated with scorn. Without praise and without scorn every word and syllable should be carefully understood and then put beside the Suttas,[28] and compared with the Vinaya.[29] If, when so compared, they do not harmonize with the Suttas, and do not fit in with the rules of the Community, then you may come to the conclusion: "Certainly, this is not the word of the Master, and has been wrongly grasped by that bhikkhu." Therefore you should reject it. But if they harmonize with the Suttas and fit in with the rules of the Community, then you may come to the conclusion: "Certainly, this is the word of the Master, and has been well grasped by that brother." This, bhikkhus, you should receive as the first Great Principle.

9. 'Again, a bhikkhu may say: 'In such and such a dwelling-place there is a company of the bhikkhus with their elders and leaders. From the mouth of that company have I heard, face to face have I received it. This is the Doctrine, this the Discipline, this the Teaching of the Master." The word spoken, brethren, by that bhikkhu should neither be received with praise nor treated with scorn. Without praise and without scorn every word and syllable should be carefully understood, and then put beside the Suttas and compared with the rules of the Community. If when so compared they do not harmonize with the Suttas, and do not fit in with the rules of the Community, then you may come to the conclusion: "Certainly, this is not the word of the Master, and has been wrongly grasped by that company of the bhikkhus." Therefore, you should reject it. But if they harmonize with the Suttas and fit in with the rules of the Community, then you may come to the conclusion: "This is certainly the word of the Master and has been well grasped by that company of the bhikkhus." This you should receive as the second Great Principle.

10. 'Again, a bhikkhu may say: "In such and such a dwelling-place many elders of the Community are living, deeply read, holding the faith as handed down by tradition, versed in the Doctrine, versed in the regulations of the Community, versed in

the summaries[30] of the doctrines and the law. From the mouth of those elders have I heard, from their mouth have I received it. This is the Doctrine, this the Discipline, this the teaching of the Master." The word spoken by that bhikkhu should neither be received with praise nor treated with scorn. Without praise and without scorn every word and syllable should be carefully understood, and then put beside the Suttas and compared with the rules of the Community. If when so compared they do not harmonize with the Suttas and do not fit in with the rules of the Community then you may come to the conclusion: "This is certainly not the word of the Master, and has been wrongly grasped by those elders." Therefore, brethren, you should reject it. But if they harmonize with the Suttas and fit in with the rules of the Community, then you may come to the conclusion: "This is certainly the word of the Master, and has been well grasped by those elders." This, bhikkhus, you should receive as the third Great Principle.

11. 'Again, a bhikkhu may say: "In such and such a dwelling-place a brother is living who is deeply read, holds the faith as handed down by tradition, is versed in the truths, versed in the regulations of the Community, versed in the summaries of the doctrines and the law. From the mouth of that elder have I heard, from his mouth have I received it. This is the Doctrine, this the Discipline, this the teaching of the Master." The word spoken by that bhikkhu should neither be received with praise nor treated with scorn. Without praise and without scorn every word and syllable should be carefully understood, and then put beside the Suttas and compared with the rules of the Community. If when so compared they do not harmonize with the Suttas, and do not fit in with the rules of the Community, then you may come to the conclusion: "This is certainly not the word of the Master, and has been wrongly grasped by that bhikkhu." Therefore you should reject it. But if they harmonize with the Suttas and fit in with the rules of the Community then you may come to the conclusion: "This is certainly the word of the Master, and has been well grasped by that bhikkhu." This, bhikkhus, you should receive as the fourth Great Principle.

'These, brethren, are the Four Great Principles.'

12. There, too, the Master [delivered to the bhikkhus the

discourse, 'Concerning morality, meditation and wisdom'. See Chapter 1, paragraph 12].

13. Now when the Master had stayed as long as he required at Bhogagama, he said to the venerable Ananda: 'Come, Ananda, let us move on to Pava.'

'As you say, lord!' replied the venerable Ananda. So the Master went with a great company of the bhikkhus to Pava. And there at Pava the Master stayed at the Mango Grove belonging to Chunda, who was by family a smith.

14. Now Chunda, the worker in metals, heard that the Master has come to Pava, and was staying there in his Mango Grove.

So Chunda went to the place where the Master was, and saluting him took his seat respectfully on one side. When he had sat down, the Master instructed, exhorted, gladdened and delighted him with talk about Dhamma.

15. Then he, instructed, exhorted, gladdened and delighted with this talk about Dhamma, said: 'Will the Master do me the honour of taking his meal, together with the bhikkhus, at my house tomorrow?'

And the Master signified, by silence, his consent.

16. Then seeing that the Master had consented, Chunda rose from his seat and bowed to the Master, and keeping him on his right hand as he passed him, went away.

17. Then at dawn Chunda, in his house, began to prepare sweet rice and cakes, and a quantity of tender pork.[31] Then he sent a message to the Master: 'It is time for the meal, lord, and everything is ready.'

18. So the Master, having dressed early in the morning, took his bowl, and went with the bhikkhus to the house of Chunda, the worker in metals. When he arrived he sat down in the place prepared for him. When he was seated he said to Chunda: 'As to the pork you have made ready, serve it to me, Chunda: and as to the other food, the sweet rice and cakes, serve it to the bhikkhus.'

'As you say, lord!' replied Chunda. So the pork which he had prepared he served to the Master, while the other food, the sweet rice and cakes, he served to the members of the Community.

19. Then the Master said to Chunda, the worker in metals, 'Whatever of this pork, Chunda, is left over, bury in a pit. I am aware of no one, Chunda, on earth, nor in Mara's realm, nor in Brahma's realm, no one among ascetics and brahmans, among gods, or men, who could possibly digest that food! Nobody, in fact, but a Tathagata.'

'As you say, lord!' replied Chunda. So the pork that was left over he buried in a pit. Then he went to the place where the Master was, and took his seat respectfully on one side. When he had sat down he was instructed, exhorted, gladdened and delighted by the Master with talk of Dhamma. Then the Master rose from his seat and went away.

20. The Master, having eaten the food prepared by Chunda, the worker in metals, became ill, with acute dysentery, and had acute pain, as though he were about to die. But the Master, mindful and aware, endured it without distress. Then the Master said to the venerable Ananda: 'Come Ananda, let us move on to Kusinara.'

'As you say, lord!' replied the venerable Ananda.

'Thus have I heard: from food that Chunda gave,
Chunda the smith, the Master sickness knew;
Thus gripped with violent pain that spoke of death
He bore the suffering with fortitude.

Having consumed pork as his food,
Dire sickness on the Master quickly came.
Then, being purged, the Master said,
To Kusinara now I go.'

21. Now the Master went aside from the path to the foot of a certain tree; and when he had reached it he said to the venerable Ananda: 'I pray you, Ananda, fold the robe in four; and spread it out for me. I am weary, Ananda, and must rest for a while!'

'As you say, lord!' replied the venerable Ananda, and spread out the robe when he had folded it fourfold.

22. The Master sat down on the seat prepared for him, and then said to the venerable Ananda: 'I pray you, Ananda, fetch some water. I am thirsty, Ananda, and would like a drink.'

When he had said this, the venerable Ananda replied: 'But just now, lord, about five hundred carts have gone over the ford.

The shallow water, stirred up by the wheels, is disturbed and dirty. This river Kakuttha, lord, not far off, is clear and pleasant, cool and transparent, easy to get down into, and delightful. There the Master may both drink the water, and cool his limbs.'

23. But the Master asked Ananda a second time: 'I pray you, Ananda, fetch some water. I am thirsty, Ananda, and would like a drink.'

And a second time the venerable Ananda said to the Master: 'But just now, lord, about five hundred carts have gone over. That water stirred up by the wheels has become disturbed and dirty. The river Kakuttha, lord, not far off, is clear and pleasant, cool and transparent, easy to get down into, and delightful. There the Master may both drink the water, and cool his limbs.'

24. But the Master asked Ananda a third time: 'I pray you, Ananda, fetch some water. I am thirsty, Ananda, and would like a drink.'

'As you say, lord!' replied the venerable Ananda, and taking a bowl he went down to the stream. And the stream which, stirred up by the wheels, had only just before been disturbed and dirty, began, as the venerable Ananda came up to it, to flow clear and bright, and free from all dirt.

25. Then Ananda thought: 'How wonderful, how marvellous is the great might and power of the Tathagata![32] For this stream which, stirred up by the wheels, only just now was disturbed and dirty, now, as I come up to it, is flowing clear and bright and free from all dirt.'

So, taking water in the bowl, he returned to the Master. When he reached the place where the Master was sitting, he said to him: 'How wonderful, how marvellous is the great might and power of the Tathagata! For this stream which, stirred up by the wheels, only just now was disturbed and dirty, now, as I come up to it, is flowing clear and bright, and free from all dirt. Let the Master drink the water! Let the Happy One drink the water!'

Then the Master drank the water.

26. Now at that time a man named Pukkusa, a young Malla, a disciple of Alara Kalama's, was passing along the high road from Kusinara to Pava.

And Pukkusa, the young Malla, saw the Master seated at the foot of a tree. On seeing him, he went towards the place where the Master was, and on his arrival there he saluted the Master, and took his seat respectfully on one side. And when he was seated Pukkusa, the young Malla, said to the Master: 'How wonderful a thing it is, lord! and how marvellous, that those who have gone forth out of the world should pass their time in a state of mind so calm!

27. 'Formerly, lord, Alara Kalama was once walking along the high road; and leaving the road he sat himself down under a certain tree to rest during the heat of the day. Now, lord, five hundred carts passed by one after the other, each close to Alara Kalama. And a certain man, who was following close behind that caravan of carts, went towards the place where Alara Kalama was, and on his arrival there he spoke as follows to Alara Kalama:

' "But, lord, did you see those five hundred carts go by?"

' "No, indeed, I saw them not."

' "But, lord, did you hear the sound of them?"

' "No, indeed, sir, I did not hear their sound."

' "But, lord, were you asleep then?'

' "No, sir, I was not asleep."

' "But, lord, were you conscious then?"

' "I was, sir."

' "So that you, lord, though you were both conscious and awake, neither saw, nor heard the sound of five hundred carts passing by, one after the other, and each close to you. Why, lord, even your robe was sprinkled over with the dust of them!"

' "That is true, sir."

'Then the man thought: "How wonderful a thing this is, and how marvellous, that those who have gone forth out of the world should pass their time in a state of mind so calm! So much so that a man though he is both conscious and awake, neither sees, nor hears the sound of five hundred carts passing by, one after the other, and each close to him."

'And after giving utterance to his deep faith in Alara Kalama, he went away.'

28. 'Now what do you think, Pukkusa: which is the more difficult thing either to do or to meet with, that a man, being conscious and awake, should neither see, nor hear the sound of five hundred carts passing by, one after the other, close to him,

or that a man, being conscious and awake, should neither see, nor hear the sound when the falling rain goes on beating and splashing, and the lightning is flashing forth, and the thunder-bolts are crashing?'

29. 'What in comparison, lord, can these five hundred carts do, or six or seven or eight or nine or ten hundred, yea, even hundreds and thousands of carts? That certainly is more diffi-cult, both to do and to meet with, that a man, being conscious and awake, should neither see, nor hear the sound when the falling rain goes on beating and splashing, and the lightning is flashing forth, and the thunderbolts are crashing.'

30. 'Now on one occasion, Pukkusa, I was dwelling at Atuma, and was at the Threshing-floor. At that time the falling rain began to beat and to splash, and the lightning to flash forth, and the thunderbolts to crash; and two peasants who were brothers, and four oxen were all killed. Then, Pukkusa, a great crowd of people went out from Atuma, and went to the place where the two peasants and the four oxen lay killed.

31. 'Now at that time, Pukkusa, I had gone out from the Threshing-floor, and was walking up and down at the entrance to the Threshing-floor, thinking. A certain man came, Pukkusa, out of that great crowd of people, to the place where I was; and when he came up he saluted me, and took his place respectfully on one side. As he stood there, Pukkusa, I said to this man:

32. ' "Why then, sir, has this great crowd of people come together?"

' "Why? Because the falling rain began to beat and to splash, and the lightning to flash forth, and the thunderbolts to crash; and two peasants who were brothers, were killed, and four oxen. That is why this great crowd of people has come together. But where, lord, were you?"

' "I, sir, have been here all the while."
' "But, lord, did you see it?"
' "I, sir, saw nothing."
' "But, lord, did you hear it?"
' "I, sir, heard nothing."
' "Were you then, lord, asleep?"
' "I, sir, was not asleep."
' "Were you then conscious, lord?"

' "I was, sir."

' "So that you, lord, being conscious and awake, neither saw, nor heard the sound when the falling rain went on beating and splashing, and the lightning was flashing forth, and the thunderbolts were crashing."

' "This is so, sir."

33. 'Then, Pukkusa, the thought occurred to that man: "How wonderful it is, and marvellous, that those who have gone forth out of the world should pass their time in a state of mind so calm! – so that a man, being conscious and awake, neither sees, nor hears the sound thereof when the falling rain is beating and splashing, and the lightning is flashing forth, and the thunderbolts are crashing." And after giving utterance to his deep faith in me, he went away, with the customary demonstrations of respect.'

34. When he had said this, Pukkusa, the young Malla, addressed the Master: 'Now, lord, with regard to the faith that I had in Alara Kalama, I now let it blow away, as in a mighty wind; I let it wash away, as in a swiftly running stream. Most excellent! It is as if someone had set up again what had been thrown down, or had revealed what had been hidden away, or had pointed out the right road to someone who has gone astray, or had brought a light into the darkness, so that those who had eyes could see the shape of things. Just so, lord, has the Truth been made known to me, in many a figure, by the Master. Now I betake myself, lord, to the Master as my guide, to the Doctrine and to the Community. May the Master accept me as a disciple, as one who, from this day forth, as long as life lasts, has taken them as his guide.'[33]

35. Then Pukkusa, the young Malla, said to someone: 'I pray you, fetch me, my good man, a pair of robes of cloth-of-gold, burnished and ready for wear.'

'As you say, sir!' replied the man; and he brought a pair of robes of cloth-of-gold, burnished and ready for wear.

Then the Malla, Pukkusa, presented the pair of robes of cloth-of-gold, burnished and ready for wear, to the Master, and said: 'Lord, these robes of burnished cloth-of-gold are ready for wear. Will the Master do me the honour of accepting them at my hands? '

'In that case, Pukkusa, robe me in one, and Ananda in the other.'

'As you say, lord!' replied Pukkusa, and in one he robed the Master, and in the other, Ananda.

36. Then the Master instructed, and exhorted, and gladdened, and delighted Pukkusa, the young Malla, with talk of Dhamma. And Pukkusa, the young Malla, when he had been instructed, and exhorted, and gladdened, and delighted by the Master with talk of Dhamma, rose from his seat, and bowed to the Master, and keeping him on his right hand as he passed him, went away.

37. Now not long after the Malla Pukkusa had gone, the venerable Ananda placed the pair or robes of cloth-of-gold, burnished and ready for wear, on the body of the Master; and when they were so place on his body they appeared to have lost their splendour.[34]

The venerable Ananda therefore said to the Master: 'How wonderful a thing is it, lord, and how marvellous, that the colour of the skin of the Master should be so clear, so exceedingly bright! For when I placed even this pair of robes of burnished cloth-of-gold, ready for wear, on the body of the Master, suddenly it seemed as if it had lost its splendour!'

'It is so, Ananda. There are two occasions on which the colour of the skin of a Tathagata becomes clear and exceedingly bright. What are these two?

'On the night, Ananda, on which a Tathagata attains to the supreme and perfect Enlightenment and on the night in which he passes finally into complete nibbana, leaving nothing whatever to remain – on these two occasions the colour of the skin of the Tathagata becomes clear and exceedingly bright.

38. 'And now this day, Ananda, at the third watch of the night, in the neighbourhood of Kusinara, in the Sal Grove of the Mallas, between the twin sal trees, the Parinibbana of the Tathagata will take place. Come, Ananda! Let us go to the river Kakuttha.'

'As you say, lord!' replied the venerable Ananda.

The pair of robes of cloth-of-gold,
All burnished, Pukkusa had brought,

The Master, clad in them, shone out
In splendour bright as that of gold![35]

39. Then the Master, with a great company of bhikkhus,
went to the river Kakuttha; and when he arrived there, he went
down into the water, and bathed, and drank. And coming up out
again on the other side he went towards the Mango Grove.

When he reached the Mango Grove he said to the venerable
Chundaka: 'I pray you, Chundaka, to fold a robe in four and
spread it out. I am weary, Chundaka, and wish to lie down.'

'As you say, lord!' replied the venerable Chundaka. And he
folded a robe in four, and spread it out.

40. Then the Master lay down on his right side, with one
foot resting on the other; and mindful and aware he meditated,
intending to rise up again soon. And the venerable Chundaka
seated himself there in front of the Master.

41. The Buddha to Kakuttha's river came
  Whose clear and pleasant waters limpid flow.
He plunged beneath the stream wearied and worn,
The Buddha without equal in the world!
When he had bathed and drunk, the Teacher then
Crossed o'er, the brethren thronging round his steps;
The Blessed Master, preaching the while the Truth,
The Mighty Sage came to the Mango Grove.
There spake he to the brother Chundaka:
'Spread me the fourfold robe out as a couch.'
Urged by the Holy One, he quickly spread
The fourfold robe in order on the ground.
The Master laid him down, wearied and worn;
And there, before him, Chunda took his seat.

42. Then the Master said to the venerable Ananda: 'Now it
may happen, Ananda, that someone should stir up remorse in
Chunda the smith, by saying: 'This is bad for you, Chunda; it is
something to your discredit that the Tathagata ate his last meal
from food provided by you, and then died.'' This kind of
remorse, Ananda, in Chunda the smith should be checked by
saying: "This is good for you, Chunda, and to your credit, that
the Tathagata ate his last meal from food provided by you, and
then died. From the mouth of the Master himself, Chunda, I
have heard; from the Master himself I have received this saying:

'These two offerings of food are of equal fruit, and of equal profit, and of much greater fruit and much greater profit than any other – and which are the two? The offering of food which, when a Tathagata has eaten, he attains to supreme and perfect insight; and the offering of food which, when a Tathagata has eaten, he passes away by that utter passing away in which nothing whatever remains behind – these two offerings of food are of equal fruit and of equal profit, and of much greater fruit and much greater profit than any others. There has been laid up by Chunda the smith karma redounding to length of life, redounding to good birth, redounding to good fortune, redounding to good fame, redounding to the inheritance of heaven, and of supremacy.' " In this way, Ananda, should be checked any remorse in Chunda the smith.'

43. Then the Master, perceiving how the matter stood, uttered on that occasion this hymn of exultation:

'In him who gives, virtue is thus increased;
Where there is self-control, no anger can arise;
The good man casts off evil ways,
And rooting out all greed and hate,
And all illusion, is at peace!'

*End of the Fourth Portion for Recitation,
containing The Episode of Alara*

Chapter 5: At Kusinara

1. Then the Master said to the venerable Ananda: 'Come, Ananda, let us move on to the Sal Grove of the Mallas of Kusinara, known as the Upavattana, on the further side of the river Hiranyavati.'

'As you say, lord!' replied the venerable Ananda.

So the Master went, with a great company of bhikkhus, to the Upavattana, the Sal Grove of the Mallas of Kusinara, on the further side of the river Hiranyavati: and when he arrived there he said to the venerable Ananda: 'I pray you, Ananda, spread the couch for me with its head to the north, between the twin sal trees. I am weary, Ananda, and wish to lie down.'

'As you say, lord!' replied the venerable Ananda. And he spread a covering over the couch with its head to the north, between the twin sal trees. And the Master laid himself down on his right side, with one leg resting on the other; and he was mindful and aware.

2. Now at that time the twin sal trees were all one mass of bloom with flowers out of season; and all over the body of the Tathagata[36] these dropped, and sprinkled, and scattered themselves, out of reverence for the successor of the Buddhas of old. And flowers of the tree of Paradise, too, and heavenly sandalwood powder came falling from the sky, and all over the body of the Tathagata they descended, and sprinkled, and scattered themselves, out of reverence for the successor of the Buddhas of old. And heavenly music was sounded in the sky, out of reverence for the successor of the Buddhas of old. And heavenly songs came wafted from the skies, out of reverence for the successor of the Buddhas of old!

3. Then the Master said to the venerable Ananda: 'The twin sal trees are all one mass of bloom with flowers out of season; all over the body of the Tathagata these drop, and sprinkle, and scatter themselves, out of reverence for the successor of the Buddhas of old. And flowers of the tree of Paradise too, and heavenly sandalwood powder come falling from the sky, and all over the body of the Tathagata they descend, and sprinkle, and scatter themselves, out of reverence for the successor of the Buddhas of old. And heavenly music sounds in the sky, out of reverence for the successor of the Buddhas of old. And heavenly songs come wafted from the skies, out of reverence for the successor of the Buddhas of old!

'Now it is not thus, Ananda, that the Tathagata is rightly honoured, reverenced, venerated, held sacred or revered. But the bhikkhu or the bhikkhuni,[37] the devout man or the devout woman, who continually fulfils all the greater and the lesser duties, who is correct in life, walking according to the precepts, these all honour, reverence, venerate, hold sacred and revere the

Tathagata with the worthiest homage. Therefore, Ananda, be constant in the fulfilment of the greater and of the lesser duties, and be correct in life, walking according to the precepts; and this, Ananda, is what should be taught.'

4. Now at that time the venerable Upavana was standing in front of the Master, fanning him. And the Master was not pleased with Upavana, and he said to him: 'Stand aside, brother, do not stand in front of me!'

Then this thought arose in the mind of the venerable Ananda: 'This venerable Upavana has long been in close personal attendance and service on the Master. And now, at the last moment, the Master is not pleased with Upavana, and has told him to stand aside, and not to stand in front of him. What may be the cause and the reason that the Master is not pleased with Upavana, and speaks to him in this way?'

5. So the venerable Ananda said to the Master: 'This venerable Upavana has long been in close personal attendance and service on the Master. And now, at the last moment, the Master is not pleased with Upavana, and has told him to stand aside, and not to stand in front of him. What may be the cause and the reason that the Master is not pleased with Upavana, and speaks to him in this way?'

'In great numbers, Ananda, are the celestial beings of the ten world-systems assembled together to behold the Tathagata. For twelve leagues, Ananda, around the Sal Grove of the Mallas, the Upavattana of Kusinara, there is no spot in size even as the pricking of the point of the tip of a hair which is not pervaded by celestial powers and beings. And all these, Ananda, are murmuring, and say: "From afar we have come to behold the Tathagata. Few and far between are the Tathagatas, the arahat Buddhas who appear in the world; and now today, in the last watch of the night, the death of a Tathagata will take place; and this eminent brother stands in front of the Tathagata, concealing him, and in his last hour we are prevented from beholding the Tathagata"; this, Ananda, is what the celestial beings are murmuring.'

6. 'But of what kind of beings is the Master thinking?'

'There are deities, Ananda, in the sky, but of worldly mind, who dishevel their hair and weep, who stretch forth their arms and weep, who fall prostrate on the ground, and roll to and fro in anguish at the thought: "Too soon will the Master pass into Parinibbana. Too soon will the Master pass away! Full soon will the Eye of the world vanish away."[38]

'There are deities too, Ananda, on the earth, and of worldly mind, who tear their hair and weep, who stretch forth their arms and weep, who fall prostrate on the ground, and roll to and fro in anguish at the thought: "Too soon will the Master pass into Parinibbana. Too soon will the Happy One pass away! Full soon will the Eye of the world disappear from sight."

'But the deities who are free from passion bear it, calm and self-possessed, mindful of the saying which beings: "Impermanent indeed are all conditioned things. So where is the gain?" '

7. 'In times past, lord, the bhikkhus, when they had spent the rainy season in different districts, used to come to see the Tathagata, and we used to receive those very reverend bhikkhus who had come to wait upon the Master. But, lord, after the Master's decease we shall not be able to receive those very reverend brethren who come to wait upon the Master.'

8. 'There are these four places, Ananda, which the devoted person should visit with feelings of reverence. What are the four?

'The place, Ananda, at which the devoted person can say: "Here the Tathagata was born!" is a spot to be visited with feelings of reverence.

'The place, Ananda, at which the devoted person can say: "Here the Tathagata attained to supreme and highest wisdom!" is a spot to be visited with feelings of reverence.

'The place, Ananda, at which the devoted person can say: "Here the wheel of Dhamma was set in motion by the Tathagata!" is a spot to be visited with feelings of reverence.

'The place, Ananda, at which the devoted person can say: "Here the Tathagata passed finally away in that utter passing away which leaves nothing whatever to remain behind!" is a spot to be visited with feelings of reverence. These are the four places, Ananda, which the devoted person should visit with feelings of reverence.

'And there will come, Ananda, to such spots, devotees,

bhikkhus and bhikkhunis and devout householders, who will say: "Here was the Tathagata born!" or, "Here the Tathagata attained supreme and highest wisdom!" or, "Here was the wheel of Dhamma set in motion by the Tathagata!" or, "Here the Tathagata passed away in that utter passing away which leaves nothing whatever to remain behind!"

'And they, Ananda, who die while, with devout heart, they are journeying on such pilgrimage, shall be reborn after death, when the body dissolves, in the happy realms of heaven.'

9. 'How are we to conduct ourselves, lord, with regard to womankind?'

'As not seeing them, Ananda.'

'But if we should see them, what are we to do?'

'No talking, Ananda.'

'But if they should speak to us, lord, what are we to do?'

'Keep wide awake, Ananda.'

10. 'What are we to do, lord, with the remains of the Tathagata?'

'Do not hinder yourselves, Ananda, by honouring the remains of the Tathagata. Be zealous, I beseech you, Ananda, in your own behalf! Devote yourselves to your own good! Be earnest, be zealous, be intent on your own good! There are wise men, Ananda, among the nobles, among the brahmans, among the heads of houses, who are firm believers in the Tathagata; and they will do due honour to the remains of the Tathagata.'

11. 'But what should be done, lord, with the remains of the Tathagata?'

'As men treat the remains of a Universal Monarch, Ananda, should they treat the remains of a Tathagata.'

'And how, lord, do they treat the remains of a Universal Monarch?'

'They wrap the body of a Universal Monarch in a new cloth. When that is done they wrap it in carded cotton wool. When that is done they wrap it in a new cloth, and so on till they have wrapped the body in five hundred successive layers of both kinds. Then they place the body in an oil vessel of iron, and cover that close up with another oil vessel of iron. They then build a funeral pyre of all kinds of perfume, and burn the body of the Universal Monarch. And then at the four cross-roads they erect a stupa.[39] This, Ananda, is the way in which they treat the remains of a Universal Monarch.

'And as they treat his remains, so, Ananda, should they treat the remains of the Tathagata. At the four cross-roads a stupa should be erected to the Tathagata. And whoever shall place there garlands or perfumes or paint, or make salutation there, or become in its presence calm in heart – that shall long be to them for profit and joy.

12. 'The men, Ananda, worthy of a stupa, are four in number. What are the four?

'A Tathagata, a Supremely Enlightened One, is worthy of a stupa. A 'Silent' Buddha[40] is worthy of a stupa. A true disciple of the Tathagata is worthy of a stupa. A Universal Monarch is worthy of a stupa.

'And on account of what circumstances, Ananda, is a Tathagata, a Supremely Enlightened One, worthy of a stupa?

'At the thought, Ananda: "This is the stupa of the Master, of the Supremely Enlightened One", the hearts of many shall be made calm and happy; and having thus calmed and satisfied their hearts they will be reborn after death, when the body has dissolved, in the happy realms of heaven. It is on account of this circumstance, Ananda, that a Tathagata, a Supremely Enlightened One, is worthy of a stupa.

'And on account of what circumstance, Ananda, is a 'Silent' Buddha worthy of a stupa?

'At the thought, Ananda: "This is the stupa of that Master, that Silent Buddha", the hearts of many shall be made calm and happy; and having thus calmed and satisfied their hearts they will be reborn after death, when the body has dissolved, in the happy realms of heaven. It is on account of this circumstance, Ananda, that a 'Silent' Buddha is worthy of a stupa.

'And on account of what circumstance, Ananda, is a true disciple[41] of the Master, the Worthy One, worthy of a stupa?

'At the thought, Ananda: "This is the stupa of that true disciple of the Master, the Worthy One", the hearts of many shall be made calm and happy; and having thus calmed and satisfied their hearts they will be reborn after death, when the body has dissolved, in the happy realms of heaven. It is on account of this circumstance, Ananda, that a true disciple of the Master, the Worthy One, is worthy of a stupa.

'And on account of what circumstance, Ananda, is a Universal Monarch worthy of a stupa?

'At the thought, Ananda: "This is the stupa of that righteous king who ruled in righteousness", the hearts of many shall be made calm and happy; and having thus calmed and satisfied their hearts they will be reborn after death, when the body has dissolved, in the happy realms of heaven. It is on account of this circumstance, Ananda, that a Universal Monarch is worthy of a stupa.

'These four, Ananda, are the persons worthy of a stupa.'

13. Then the venerable Ananda went into the living quarters, and stood leaning against the lintel of the door, and weeping at the thought: 'Alas! I am still only a learner, one who has yet to work out his own perfection.[42] Who will care for me when the Teacher passes into nibbana?'

Then the Master called the bhikkhus, and asked, 'Where then, brethren, is Ananda?'

'The venerable Ananda, lord, has gone into the living quarters, and is standing against the lintel of the door, and weeping at the thought that he is still only a learner, one who has yet to work out his own perfection, and asking who will care for him when the Teacher passes into nibbana.'

So the Master called a certain bhikkhu, and said: 'Go and call Ananda for me, and say: "Brother Ananda, the Master is calling you." '

'As you say, lord!' replied the bhikkhu. And he went to the place where Ananda was: and when he had come there, he said to the venerable Ananda: 'Brother Ananda, the Master is calling you.'

'Very well, brother,' replied the venerable Ananda. And he came to the place where the Master was, and when he reached the place he bowed to the Master, and took his seat respectfully on one side.

14. Then the Master said to the venerable Ananda, as he sat there by his side: 'Enough, Ananda! Do not grieve so! do not

weep! Have I not already, on previous occasions, told you that it is in the very nature of all things most near and dear to us that we must separate ourselves from them, leave them, part from them? How, then, Ananda, can it be otherwise; anything that is born, brought into being and conditioned, contains within itself the inherent necessity of dissolution, so how is it possible that such a being should not be dissolved? It is not possible. For a long time, Ananda, you have been very near to me by acts of love, kind and good, love that never varies and is beyond all measure. For a long time, Ananda, you have been very near to me by words of love, kind and good, love that never varies and is beyond all measure. For a long time, Ananda, you have been very near to me by thoughts of love, kind and good, love that never varies and is beyond all measure. You have done well, Ananda! Be earnest in effort, and you too shall soon be free from the Intoxicants.'[43]

15. Then the Master addressed the bhikkhus: 'Whoever, brethren, have been Buddhas through the long ages of the past, they also had servitors just as devoted to them as Ananda has been to me.

'He is a wise man, brethren, for he knows when it is the right time for the brethren or for the sisters of the Community, for devout followers, both men and women, for a king, or for a king's ministers, or for other teachers or for their disciples, to come and visit the Tathagata.

16. 'Brethren, there are four wonderful and marvellous qualities in Ananda. What are they?

'If, brethren, a number of the members of the Community should come to visit Ananda, they are filled with joy on beholding him; and if Ananda should then proclaim the Doctrine to them, they are filled with joy at his discourse; whereas the company of brethren is ill at ease, brethren, when Ananda is silent.

'If, brethren, a number of the sisters of the Community, or a number of devout men, or of devout women, should come to visit Ananda, they are filled with joy on beholding him; and if Ananda should then proclaim the Doctrine to them, they are filled with joy at his discourse; whereas they are ill at ease, brethren, when Ananda is silent.

'Brethren, there are these four wonderful and marvellous qualities in a Universal Monarch. What are they?

'If, brethren, a number of nobles, or brahmans, or heads of houses, or members of a religious order should come to visit a Universal Monarch, they are filled with joy on beholding him; and if he should then speak, they are filled with joy at what is said; whereas they are ill at ease, brethren, when he is silent.

'Just so, brethren, are the four wonderful and marvellous qualities in Ananda.'

17. When he had said this, the venerable Ananda said to the Master: 'Let not the Master die in this little wattle-and-daub town, in this town in the midst of the jungle, in this branch township. For, lord, there are other great cities, such as Champa, Rajgir, Savatthi, Saketa, Kosambi and Benares. Let the Master die in one of them. There, there are many wealthy nobles, and brahmans, and heads of houses, believers in the Tathagata, who will pay due honour to the remains of the Tathagata.'

'Do not say so, Ananda! Do not say that this is but a small wattle-and-daub town, a town in the midst of the jungle, a branch township.

18. 'Long ago, Ananda, there was a raja, by name Maha Sudassana, a Universal Monarch, a righteous man who ruled in righteousness, lord of the four quarters of the earth, conqueror, the protector of his people, possessor of the seven royal treasures. This town of Kusinara was the royal city of Raja Maha Sudassana. It was then called Kusavati, and on the east and on the west it was twelve leagues in length, and on the north and on the south it was seven leagues in breadth.

'That royal city Kusavati, Ananda, was mighty and prosperous and full of people, crowded with them, and provided with all kinds of food. Just as the royal city of the gods, Alakamanda by name, is mighty, prosperous, and full of people, crowded with the gods, and provided with all kinds of food, so, Ananda, was the royal city Kusavati mighty and prosperous, full of people, crowded with them, and provided with all kinds of food.

'Both by day and by night, Ananda, the royal city Kusavati resounded with the ten cries; that is to say, the noise of elephants, and the noise of horses, and the noise of chariots; the sounds of the drum, of the tabor, and of the lute; the sound of singing, and the sounds of the cymbal, and of the gong; and lastly, with the cry: "Eat, drink, and be merry!"

19. 'Now, Ananda, go and enter Kusinara, and tell the Mallas of Kusinara: "In the last watch of the night, the final passing away of the Tathagata will take place. Please take notice of this, Vasetthas, please take notice! So that you do not reproach yourselves afterwards, and have to say: 'In our own village the death of our Tathagata took place, and we did not take the opportunity of visiting the Tathagata in his last hours.' " '

'As you say, lord,' replied the venerable Ananda. He robed himself and taking his bowl, entered Kusinara, attended by another member of the Order.

20. Now at that time the Mallas of Kusinara were assembled in the council hall, on some business. The venerable Ananda went to the council hall of the Mallas of Kusinara; and having arrived there he informed them: 'In the last watch of the night, the final passing away of the Tathagata will take place. Please take notice of this, Vasetthas, please take notice, so that you do not reproach yourselves afterwards, and have to say: "In our own village the death of our Tathagata took place, and we did not take the opportunity of visiting the Tathagata in his last hours." '

21. When they had heard the venerable Ananda's message, all the Mallas, and their wives, and young men, and young women were grieved, and sad, and deeply distressed. Some of them wept, dishevelling their hair, and stretched forth their arms and wept, fell prostrate on the ground, and rolled to and fro in anguish at the thought: 'Too soon the Exalted One will die! Too soon the Happy One will pass away! So soon now the Eye of the world will vanish from us!'

Then they all went to the Sal Grove of the Mallas, to the Upavattana, and to the place where the venerable Ananda was.

22. Then the venerable Ananda thought: 'If I allow the Mallas of Kusinara, one by one, to pay their respects to the Master, the whole of the Mallas of Kusinara will not have been presented to the Master until night brightens into the dawn. Let

me, now, cause the Mallas of Kusinara to stand in groups, each family in a group, and so present them to the Master, saying: "Lord! a Malla of such and such a name, with his children, his wives, his retinue and his friends, humbly bows down at the feet of the Master." '

So the venerable Ananda caused the Mallas of Kusinara to stand in groups, each family in a group, and so presented them to the Master, and said: 'Lord! a Malla of such and such a name, with his children, his wives, his retinue and his friends, humbly bows down at the feet of the Master.'

After this manner the venerable Ananda presented all the Mallas of Kusinara to the Master in the first watch of the night.

23. Now at that time a homeless wanderer named Subhadda, who was not a believer, was dwelling at Kusinara. The wanderer Subhadda heard the news: 'This very day, they say, in the third watch of the night, will take place the final passing away of Samanna Gotama.'

Then the wanderer Subhadda thought: 'I have heard from fellow-wanderers, old and well stricken in years, teachers and disciples, that sometimes, but very seldom, Tathagatas appear in the world, Supremely Enlightened Ones.' Yet this day, in the last watch of the night, the final passing away of Samanna Gotama will take place. Now a certain feeling of uncertainty has sprung up in my mind. Yet I have this faith in Samanna Gotama, that he, I believe, is able so to present the Truth, that I may get rid of this feeling of uncertainty.'

24. So the wanderer Subhadda went to the Sal Grove of the Mallas, to the Upavattana of Kusinara, to the place where the venerable Ananda was.

When he arrived there he told the venerable Ananda how he had heard from fellow-wanderers, old and well stricken in years, teachers and disciples, that sometimes, but very seldom, Tathagatas appear in the world, Supremely Enlightened Ones, and that he had heard that this night, the final passing away of the Samanna Gotama would take place. 'Now a certain feeling of uncertainty has sprung up in my mind. Yet I have this faith in Samanna Gotama, that he, I believe, is able so to present the Truth that I may get rid of this feeling of uncertainty. I wish that I, even I, might be allowed to see Samanna Gotama!'

When he had said this the venerable Ananda replied: 'Enough! friend Subhadda. Do not trouble the Tathagata. The Master is weary.'

But again the wanderer Subhadda made the same request in the same words, and received the same reply. Again, a third time, the wanderer Subhadda made the same request in the same words, and received the same reply.

25. Now the Master overheard this conversation of the venerable Ananda with the wanderer Subhadda. And he called the venerable Ananda, and said: 'It is enough, Ananda! Do not keep out Subhadda. Subhadda may be allowed to see the Tathagata. Whatever Subhadda may ask of me, he will ask from a desire for knowledge, and not to annoy me. And whatever I may say in answer to his questions, that he will quickly understand.'

Then the venerable Ananda said to Subhadda, the wanderer: 'Enter in, friend Subhadda; for the Master gives you leave.'

26. Then Subhadda, the wanderer, went in to the place where the Master was, and saluted him courteously, and after exchanging with him the compliments of respect and of civility, he took his seat on one side. When he was thus seated, Subhadda, the wanderer, said to the Master: 'Wandering ascetics and brahmans who are heads of companies of disciples and students, teachers of students, well known, renowned, founders of schools of doctrine, esteemed as good men by the multitude, such as Purana Kassapa, Makkhali of the cow-pen. Ajit of the hairy blanket, Kakkayana of the pakudha tree, Sanjay the son of the Belatthi slave-girl, and Niganth of the Natha clan, according to what they say, have they thoroughly understood things? Or have they not? Or are there some of them who have understood, and some who have not?'

'Enough, Subhadda! Let this matter rest, whether, according to what they say, they have thoroughly understood things, or whether they have not, or whether some of them have understood and some have not! The Truth, Subhadda, I will teach you. Listen well to that, and pay careful attention to what I shall say!'

'Indeed, lord!' replied the wanderer Subhadda.

27. Then the Master spoke as follows: 'In whatever doctrine and discipline, Subhadda, the Noble Eightfold Path is not

found, neither in it is there found a man of true saintliness of the first, or of the second, or of the third, or of the fourth degree. In whatsoever doctrine and discipline, Subhadda, the Noble Eight-fold Path is found, in it is found the man of true saintliness of the first, and the second, and the third, and the fourth degree. Now in our Doctrine and Discipline, Subhadda, is found the Noble Eightfold Path, and in it too are found, Subhadda, men of true saintliness of all the four grades. The systems of any other teachers are empty of true saints. And in this one, Subhadda, may the brethren live the true life, so that the world shall not be left empty of arahats.

> 'Mere twenty-nine was I when I renounced
> The World, Subhadda, seeking after Good.
> For fifty years and one year more, Subhad,
> Since I went out, a pilgrim have I been,
> The Dhamma-system was my realm entire;
> For therein is the ascetic's only life.

'Ascetics of the four grades are found in no other. Empty are the systems of other teachers, empty of true saints. But in this one, Subhadda, may the brethren live the true life, that the world shall not be left empty of arahats.'

28. When he had said this, Subhadda, the wanderer, replied: 'Most excellent, lord, are your words, most excellent! It is as though someone had set up what had been thrown down, or had revealed what was hidden away, or had pointed out the right road to someone who had got lost, or had brought a light into the darkness, so that those who had eyes could see the shape of things. Just so lord, has the Truth been made known to me, in many a figure, by the Master. And I, even I, take myself, lord, to the Master, as a full member in his Community.'

'Whoever, Subhadda, has formerly been a follower of another doctrine, and thereafter desires to be received into the higher or the lower grade in this doctrine and discipline, he remains on probation for a period of four months; and at the end of the four months, the brethren, exalted in spirit, receive him into the lower or into the higher grade of the Community. Nevertheless in this case I acknowledge the difference in persons.'

29. 'If, lord, whosoever has formerly been a follower of another doctrine, and then desires to be received into the higher or the lower grade in this doctrine and discipline – if, in that case, such a person remains on probation for a period of four months; and at the end of the four months, the brethren, exalted in spirit, receive him into the lower or into the higher grade of the Order – I too, then, will remain on probation for a period of four months; and at the end of the four months let the brethren, exalted in spirit, receive me into the lower or into the higher grade of the Order!'

But the Master called the venerable Ananda, and said to him: 'As things are, Ananda, receive Subhadda into the Order!'

'As you say, lord!' replied the venerable Ananda.

30. And Subhadda, the wanderer, said to the venerable Ananda: 'Great is your gain, friend Ananda, great is your good fortune, in that you all have been consecrated with novice's consecration here, of discipleship in this brotherhood at the hands of and in the presence of the Master.'

So Subhadda, the wanderer, was received into the higher grade of the Community of the Master; and from immediately after his ordination the venerable Subhadda remained alone and separate, earnest, zealous and resolved. Before long he attained to that supreme goal of the higher life, nibbana, for the sake of which the clansmen leave all household gain and comfort to become homeless wanderers: to the knowledge of that supreme goal he, by himself, while yet in this visible world, brought himself, and continued to realize, and to see face to face. He became conscious that birth was at an end, that the higher life had been fulfilled, that all that should be done had been accomplished, and that after this present life there would be no beyond!

So the venerable Subhadda became yet another among the arahats; and he was the last disciple whom the Master himself converted.

End of the Fifth Portion for Recitation

Chapter 6: The Parinibbana

1. The Master addressed the venerable Ananda: 'It may be, Ananda, that in some of you the thought may arise, "The teaching of the Master is ended; no longer have we a teacher." But you should not regard it in this way Ananda. The Doctrine and the Discipline, which I have set forth and laid down for you all, let them, after I am gone, be your Teacher!

2. 'Ananda! when I am gone do not address one another in the way in which the brethren have hitherto addressed each other, with the epithet of "avuso" [friend]. A younger brother may be addressed by an elder with his name, or his family name, or the title "friend". But an elder should be addressed by a younger brother as "sir" or as "venerable sir" [*bhante*].

3. 'When I am gone, Ananda, let the Order, if it should so wish, abolish all the lesser and minor precepts.

4. 'When I am gone, Ananda, let the higher penalty be imposed on brother Channa.'[44]

'But what, lord, is the higher penalty?'

'Let Channa say whatever he may like, Ananda, the brethren should neither speak to him, nor exhort him, nor admonish him.'

5. Then the Master, addressing the brethren, said: 'It may be, bhikkhus, that doubt or misgiving may arise in the mind of some one among you concerning the Buddhas, or the Doctrine, or the Path, or the Method. Inquire freely, now. Do not have to reproach yourselves afterwards with the thought, "Our teacher was face to face with us, and we could not bring ourselves to inquire of the Master when we were face to face with him." '

When he had said this, the bhikkhus were silent.

Again, the second and the third time the Master addressed them, and said: 'It may be, bhikkhus, that there may be doubt or misgiving in the mind of some one among you concerning the Buddha, or the Doctrine, or the Path, or the Method. Inquire freely, now. Do not have to reproach yourselves afterwards with the thought, "Our teacher was face to face with us, and we could not bring ourselves to inquire of the Master when we were face to face with him." '

Even the third time the brethren were silent.

Then the Master addressed the bhikkhus: 'It may be, bhikkhus, that you put no questions out of reverence for the teacher. So speak friend to friend.'

When he had said this the brethren were silent.

6. And the venerable Ananda said to the Master: 'How wonderful a thing is it, lord, and how marvellous! Indeed, I believe that in this whole assembly of bhikkhus there is not one who has any doubt or misgiving as to the Buddha, or the Doctrine, or the Path, or the Method!'

'It is out of confidence that you have spoken, Ananda! But, Ananda, the Tathagata knows for certain that in this whole assembly of bhikkhus there is not one who has any doubt or misgiving as to the Buddha, or the Doctrine, or the Path, or the Method! For even the most backward, Ananda, of all these five hundred bhikkhus has become a stream-enterer [*sotapanna*] and is sure not to be born in a realm of suffering, and is assured of attaining hereafter to final enlightenment.

7. Then the Master, addressing the brethren, said: 'Behold now, brethren, I exhort you, saying: "Decay is inherent in all conditioned things. Strive diligently!" '

This was the last word of the Tathagata!

8. Then the Master entered into the first stage of meditation. Rising out of the first stage he passed into the second. Rising out of the second he passed into the third. Rising out of the third stage he passed into the fourth.[45] And rising out of the fourth stage of meditation he entered into the sphere of the infinity of space.[46]

And passing out of the sphere of the infinity of space he entered into the sphere of the infinity of consciousness. And passing out of the sphere of the infinity of consciousness he entered into the sphere in which nothing exists. And passing out of the sphere of nothingness, he fell into the sphere of 'neither-perception-nor-nonperception'. And passing out of the sphere of 'neither-perception-nor-nonperception' he entered the sphere of the 'cessation-of-perception-experience'.[47]

Then the venerable Ananda said to the venerable Anuruddha: 'My lord, Anuruddha, the Master has entered Parinibbana!'

'No, brother Ananda, the Master has not entered Parinibbana. He has entered the sphere of "cessation-of-perception-experience".'

9. Then the Master, passing out of that sphere, entered the sphere of 'neither-perception-nor-nonperception'. And passing from that sphere, he entered the sphere of nothingness . . . and continued in the reverse order through the spheres and the stages of meditation, to the first stage; from this he passed again to the second stage, then to the third stage, and then to the fourth stage of meditation. From the fourth stage of meditation the Master passed immediately into Parinibbana.

10. When the Master passed into Parinibbana there arose, at the moment of his passing, a mighty earthquake, terrible and awe-inspiring: and the thunders of heaven burst forth.

At the moment of his passing away from existence, Brahma [the supreme deity] uttered this stanza:

'They all, all beings that have life, shall lay
Aside their complex form – that aggregation
Of mental and material qualities,
That gives them, or in heaven or on earth,
Their fleeting individuality!
Just as the Teacher – being such a one,
Unequalled among all the men that are,
Successor of the prophets of old time,
Mighty by wisdom, and in insight clear –
    Hath died!'

When the Master passed into Parinibbana, Sakka, the lord of the heavenly beings, at the moment of his passing away from existence, uttered this stanza:

'They're transient all, each being's parts and powers,
Growth is their very nature, and decay.
They are produced, they are dissolved again:
To bring them all into subjection – that is bliss.'

When the Master passed into Parinibbana, the venerable Anuruddha, at the moment of his passing away from existence, uttered these stanzas:

'When he who from all craving want was free,
Who to nibbana's tranquil state had reached,

When the great sage finished his span of life,
No gasping struggle vexed that steadfast heart!
All resolute, and with unshaken mind,
He calmly triumphed o'er the pain of death.
E'en as a bright flame dies away, so was
The last emancipation of his heart.'

When the Master passed into Parinibbana, the venerable Ananda, at the moment of his passing away from existence, uttered this stanza:

'Then was there terror!
Then stood the hair on end!
When he endowed with every grace,
The supreme Buddha, passed.'[48]

When the Master died, of those of the brethren who were not yet free from the passions, some stretched out their arms and wept, and some fell headlong on the ground, rolling to and fro in anguish at the thought: 'Too soon has the Master died! Too soon has the Happy One passed away! Too soon has the Eye of the world disappeared!'

But those of the brethren who were free from the passions, the arahats, bore their grief collected and composed at the thought: 'Impermanent are all conditioned things! How is it possible that they should not be dissolved?'

11. Then the venerable Anuruddha exhorted the bhikkhus: 'Enough, my friends! Do not weep, and do not lament! Did not the Master previously declare to us, that it is in the very nature of all things near and dear to us, that we must separate ourselves from them, leave them, be parted from them? How then, brethren, can this be possible – that whereas anything whatever born, brought into being, and organized, contains within itself the inherent necessity of dissolution – how then can this be possible, that such a being should not be dissolved? No such condition can exist! Even the spirits, brethren, will reproach us.'

'But of what kind of spirits, sir, is the venerable Anuruddha thinking?'

'There are spirits, brother Ananda, in the sky, but of worldly mind, who dishevel their hair and weep, and stretch forth their arms and weep, fall prostrate on the ground, and roll to and fro in anguish at the thought: "Too soon has the Exalted One died!

Too soon has the Eye of the world disappeared!"

'There are spirits, too, Ananda, on the earth, and of worldly mind, who tear their hair and weep, and stretch forth their arms and weep, fall prostrate on the ground, and roll to and fro in anguish at the thought: "Too soon has the Blessed One died! Too soon has the Happy One passed away! Too soon has the Eye of the world disappeared!"

'But the spirits who are free from passion bear it, calm and self-possessed, mindful of the saying which begins: "Impermanent indeed are all component things. How then is it possible . . . [that such a being should not be dissolved]?" '

12. The venerable Anuruddha and the venerable Ananda spent the rest of that night in talk concerning Dhamma.

Then the venerable Anuruddha said to the venerable Ananda: 'Ananda my friend, go now to Kusinara and inform the Mallas of Kusinara; say: "The Master has passed into Parinibbana. Please do whatever seems to you to be appropriate." '

'As you say, sir,' replied the venerable Ananda. So having robed himself early in the morning, he took his bowl, and with a companion went into Kusinara.

Now at that time the Mallas of Kusinara had assembled in the council hall to consider the matter.

When the venerable Ananda arrived at the council hall of the Mallas of Kusinara he informed them: 'Vasetthas, the Master has passed into Parinibbana. Please do whatever seems to you to be appropriate!'

When they heard what the venerable Ananda said, the Mallas, with their young men, and their maidens, and their wives, were grieved, and sad, and afflicted at heart. And some of them wept, dishevelling their hair, and some stretched forth their arms and wept, and some fell prostrate on the ground, and some reeled to and fro in anguish at the thought: 'Too soon has the Master died! Too soon has the Happy One passed away! Too soon has the Eye of the world disappeared!'

13. Then the Mallas of Kusinara gave orders to their attendants, saying: 'Gather together perfumes and garlands, and all the music in Kusinara!'

And the Mallas of Kusinara took the perfumes and garlands,

and all the musical instruments, and five hundred suits of clothing, and went to the Upavattana, to the Sal Grove of the Mallas, where the body of the Master lay. There they passed the day in paying honour, reverence, respect and homage to the remains of the Master with dancing, and hymns, and music, and with garlands and perfumes; and in making canopies of their garments, and preparing decoration wreaths to hang on these canopies.[49]

Then the Mallas of Kusinara thought: 'It is much too late to burn the body of the Master today. Let us perform the cremation tomorrow.' And in paying honour, reverence, respect and homage to the remains of the Exalted One with dancing, and hymns, and music, and with garlands and perfumes; and in making canopies of their garments, and preparing decoration wreaths to hang on them, they passed the second day too, and then the third day, and the fourth, and the fifth, and the sixth day.

14. On the seventh day the Mallas of Kusinara thought: 'Let us carry the body of the Master, by the south and outside, to a spot on the south, and outside of the city, paying it honour, and reverence, and respect, and homage, with dance, and song, and music, with garlands and perfumes, and there, to the south of the city, let us perform the cremation ceremony!'

So eight chieftains among the Mallas bathed their heads, and clad themselves in new garments with the intention of bearing the body of the Master. But they found they could not lift it up!

Then the Mallas of Kusinara said to the venerable Anuruddha: 'What, sir, can be the reason, what can be the cause, that eight chieftains of the Mallas who have bathed their heads, and clad themselves in new garments with the intention of bearing the body of the Master, are unable to lift it up?'

'It is because, Vasetthas, you have one purpose, and the spirits have another.'

15. 'But what, sir, is the purpose of the spirits?'

'Your purpose, Vasetthas, is this, to carry the body of the Master, by the south and outside, to a spot on the south, and outside of the city, paying it honour, and reverence, and respect, and homage, with dance, and song, and music, with garlands and perfumes, and there, to the south of the city, to perform the cremation ceremony. But the purpose of the spirits, Vasetthas, is this: to carry the body of the Master by the north to the north of the city, and entering the city by the north gate, to bring it through the midst of the city into the midst thereof. And going out again by the eastern gate, paying honour, and reverence, and respect, and homage to the body of the Exalted One, with heavenly dance, and song, and music, and garlands, and perfumes, to carry it to the shrine of the Mallas called Makuta-bandhana, to the east of the city, and there to perform the cremation ceremony.'

'Let it be according to the purpose of the spirits, lord.'

16. Then immediately all Kusinara, even the dustbins and rubbish heaps, became strewn knee-deep with mandarava flowers from heaven, and while both the spirits from the skies, and the Mallas of Kusinara upon earth, paid honour, and reverence, and respect, and homage to the body of the Master, with dance, and song, and music, with garlands, and with perfumes, they carried the body by the north to the north of the city; and entering the city by the north gate they carried it through the midst of the city into the midst thereof; and going out again by the eastern gate they carried it to the shrine of the Mallas, called Makuta-bandhana; and there, to the east of the city, they laid down the body of the Master.[50]

17. Then the Mallas of Kusinara said to the venerable Ananda: 'What should be done, lord, with the remains of the Tathagata?'

'As men treat the remains of a Universal Monarch, so, Vasetthas, should they treat the remains of a Tathagata.'

'And how, lord, do they treat the remains of a Universal Monarch?'

'They wrap his body, Vasetthas, in a new cloth. When that is done they wrap it in carded cotton wool. When that is done they wrap it in a new cloth, and so on till they have wrapped the body in five hundred successive layers of both kinds. Then they place the body in an oil vessel of iron, and cover that close up with another oil vessel of iron. They then build a funeral pyre of all kinds of perfumes, and burn the body. Then at the four cross-roads they erect a stupa to him. This, Vasetthas, is the way in which they treat the remains of a Universal Monarch.

'So, Vasetthas, should they treat the remains of the Tathagata. At the four cross-roads a stupa should be erected to the Tathagata. And whoever shall place garlands or perfumes or paint there, or make salutation there, or become in its presence calm in heart, that shall long be to them for a profit and a joy.'

18. So the Mallas gave orders to their attendants, saying: 'Gather together all our carded cotton wool!'

Then the Mallas of Kusinara wrapped the body of the Master in a new cloth. When that was done, they wrapped it in carded cotton wool. And when that was done, they wrapped it in a new cloth, and so on till they had wrapped the body of the Master in five hundred layers of both kinds. Then they placed the body in an oil vessel of iron, and covered that close up with another oil vessel of iron. And then they built a funeral pyre of all kinds of perfumes, and upon it they placed the body of the Master.

19. Now at that time the venerable Maha Kassapa was journeying along the high road from Pava to Kusinara with a great company of the brethren, about five hundred. And the venerable Maha Kassapa left the high road, and sat himself down at the foot of a certain tree.

Just at that time an Ajivaka,[51] who had picked up a flower of the coral tree in Kusinara, was coming along the high road to Pava.

Now the venerable Maha Kassapa saw the naked ascetic coming in the distance; and he said to the Ajivaka: 'Friend! surely you know our Master?'

'Yes, friend! I know him. This day Samanna Gotama has been dead a week! That is how I obtained this flower.'

On that, of those of the brethren who were not yet free from the passions, some stretched out their arms and wept, and some fell headlong on the ground, and some reeled to and fro in anguish at the thought: 'Too soon has the Master died! Too soon has the Happy One passed away! Too soon has the Eye disappeared from the world!'

But those of the brethren who were free from the passions, the arahats, bore their grief self-possessed and composed at the thought: 'Impermanent are all conditioned things! How is it possible that they should not be dissolved?'

20. Now at that time a brother named Subhadda, who had been received into the Community in his old age, was sitting among those who were assembled there.

And Subhadda said to the bhikkhus: 'Enough, sirs! Do not weep, and do not lament! Did not the Master previously declare to us that it is in the very nature of all things near and dear to us that we must separate ourselves from them, leave them, be parted from them? How then, brethren, can this be possible — whereas anything whatever born, brought into being and organized, contains within itself the inherent necessity of dissolution — how then can this be possible that such a being should not be dissolved? No such condition can exist!'

21. Now just at that time four chieftains of the Mallas had bathed their heads and clad themselves in new garments with the intention of setting on fire the funeral pyre of the Master. But they were unable to set it alight!

Then the Mallas of Kusinara said to the venerable Anuruddha: 'What, lord, can be the reason, and what the cause of this?'

'The purpose of the spirits, Vasetthas, is different.'

'But what, sir, is the purpose of the spirits?'

'The purpose of the spirits, Vasetthas, is this: The venerable brother Maha Kassapa is now journeying along the way from Pava to Kusinara with a great company of bhikkhus, five hundred altogether. The funeral pyre of the Master will not catch fire until the venerable Maha Kassapa has been able reverently to salute the feet of the Master.'

'According to the purpose of the spirits so, sir, let it be!'

22. Then the venerable Maha Kassapa went on to Makutabandhana of Kusinara, to the shrine of the Mallas, to the place where the funeral pyre of the Master was. When he had reached it, he arranged his robe on one shoulder; and after bowing with clasped hands, he walked reverently round the pyre three times, and then, uncovering the feet, he bowed in reverence at the feet of the Master.

And the five hundred brethren arranged their robes on one shoulder; and bowing with clasped hands, they, too, walked reverently round the pyre three times, and then bowed in reverence at the feet of the Master.

And when the homage of the venerable Maha Kassapa and of those five hundred brethren was ended, the funeral pyre of the Master caught fire of itself!

23. Now as the body of the Master burned itself away, from the skin, and the integument, and the flesh, and the nerves, and the fluid of the joints, neither soot nor ash was seen. Only the bones remained behind. Just as one sees no soot or ash when ghee or oil is burned; so, as the body of the Master burned itself away, from the skin and the integument, and the flesh, and the nerves, and the fluid of the joints, neither soot nor ash was seen. Only the bones remained behind. Of the five hundred pieces of raiment, the very innermost and outermost were both consumed.

When the body of the Master had been burnt up, streams of water came down from the sky and extinguished the funeral pyre of the Master; and streams of water gushed out of the storehouse of the waters beneath the earth, and extinguished the funeral pyre of the Master. The Mallas of Kusinara also brought water scented with all kinds of perfumes, and extinguished the funeral pyre of the Master.

Then the Mallas of Kusinara surrounded the bones of the Master in their council hall with a lattice-work of spears, and with a rampart of bows; and there for seven days they paid honour, and reverence, and respect, and homage to them with dance, and song, and music, and with garlands and perfumes.

24. Now the raja of Magadha, Ajatasattu, son of the princess of Videha, heard the news that the Master had died at Kusinara. He thereupon sent a messenger to the Mallas, saying: 'The Master was a kshatriya and so am I. I am worthy to receive a portion of the relics of the Master. Over the remains of the Master I will put up a sacred stupa, and in their honour I will celebrate a feast!'

The Licchavis of Vesali also heard the news that the Master had died at Kusinara. And they sent a messenger to the Mallas, saying: 'The Master was a kshatriya and so are we. We are worthy to receive a portion of the relics of the Master. Over the remains of the Master we shall put up a sacred stupa, and in their honour we shall celebrate a feast!'

And the Shakyas of Kapilavatthu heard the news that the Master had died at Kusinara. They, too, sent a messenger to the Mallas, saying: 'The Master was our most celebrated kinsman. We are worthy to receive a portion of the relics of the Master. Over his remains we shall put up a sacred stupa, and in their honour we shall celebrate a feast!'

And the Bulis of Allakappa heard the news that the Master had died at Kusinara; they, too, sent a messenger to the Mallas, saying: 'The Master was a kshatriya and so are we. We are worthy to receive a portion of the relics of the Master. Over his remains we shall put up a sacred stupa, and in their honour we shall celebrate a feast!'

The Koliyas of Ramagama also heard the news. And they, too, sent a messenger to [say the same thing, and so also did] the brahman of Vethadipa.

The Mallas of Pava heard the news that the Exalted One had died at Kusinara, and they sent the same message.

25. When they heard these things the Mallas of Kusinara spoke to the assembled crowds: 'The Master died in our village area. We will not give away any part of the remains of the Master!'

When they had said this, then Dona the brahman addressed the crowds:

'Hear gracious sirs, one single word from me.
Forbearance was our Buddha wont to teach.
It is unseemly that dividing up
His body – who was highest among men –
Should quarrels cause, and wounds, and war!
Let us all, sirs, with one accord unite
And with rejoicing hearts eight portions make;
Wide spread let cairns spring up in every land
That multitudes his vision yet may trust!'

'Then it is for you, brahman, to divide the remains of the Master into eight parts, well apportioned.'

'Indeed, sirs!' replied Dona the brahman. And he divided the remains of the Master equally into eight parts, fairly. And he said to them: 'Give me this vessel, sirs, and I will set up over it a sacred stupa, and in its honour will I establish a feast.'

So they gave the vessel to Dona the brahman.

26. The Moriyas of Pipphalivana also heard the news that the Master had died at Kusinara.

Then they sent a messenger to the Mallas, saying: 'The Master was a kshatriya and so are we. We are worthy to receive a portion of the relics of the Master. Over his remains we shall put up a sacred stupa, and in their honour we shall celebrate a feast!'

When they heard the answer: 'There is no portion of the remains of the Master left. The remains of the Master have all been distributed,' then they took away the embers.

27. So the raja of Magadha, Ajatasattu, the son of the princess of Videha, made a stupa in Rajgir over the remains of the Master, and celebrated a feast.

The Licchavis of Vesali make a stupa in Vesali over the remains of the Master, and celebrated a feast.

The Shakyas of Kapilavatthu made a stupa in Kapilavatthu over the remains of the Master, and celebrated a feast.

The Bulis of Allakappa made a stupa in Allakappa over the remains of the Master, and celebrated a feast.

The Koliyas of Ramagama made a stupa in Ramagama over the remains of the Master, and celebrated a feast.

Vethadipaka the brahman made a stupa in Vethadipa over the remains of the Master, and celebrated a feast.

The Mallas of Pava made a stupa in Pava over the remains of the Master, and celebrated a feast.

The Mallas of Kusinara made a stupa in Kusinara over the remains of the Master, and celebrated a feast.

Dona the brahman made a stupa over the vessel in which the remains had been collected, and celebrated a feast.

And the Moriyas of Pipphalivana made a stupa over the embers, and celebrated a feast.

Thus were there eight stupas for the remains, one for the vessel, and one for the embers. This was how it used to be.

Here ends the Maha Parinibbana Sutta

1 The hillside is very steep and even now is accessible only by climbing a steep, rough path, or by funicular.

2 In the text there is a question, answer, and reply with each clause.

3 Afterwards the seat of the famous Buddhist University, for so many centuries a centre of learning in India.

4 The *tertium quid* of the comparison is the completeness of the knowledge. Sariputta acknowledges that he was wrong in jumping to the wide conclusion that his own lord and master was the wisest of all the teachers of the different religious systems that were known to him. So far – after the cross-examination by the Buddha – he admits that his knowledge does not reach. But he maintains that he does know that which is to him, after all, the main thing, namely, that all the Buddhas must have passed through the process here laid down as leading up to the enlightenment of arahatship.

    All the details he gives are details, not of Buddhahood, but of arahatship. He makes no distinction between the two states of attainment. This is most important for the history of Buddhology in after centuries. (RD)

5 Four such states are mentioned: *apaya, duggati, vinipato* and *nirayo*, all of which are temporary states. The first three seem to be synonyms. The last is one of the four divisions into which the first is usually divided, and is often translated 'hell'; but not being an eternal state, and not being dependent or consequent upon any judgment, it cannot be accurately so rendered. (RD)

6 Pataliputra (or Patna, in Bihar) was to become the capital of Magadha, and also the venue for the so-called Third Council of the Buddhists in the time of Ashoka. It was thus the scene of 'dissension among friends', for it was the occasion of a great schism. This saying may be taken by the orthodox Buddhist, therefore, as proof of the Buddha's power of prophecy. On the other hand, Rhys Davids comments: 'To those who conclude that such a passage must have been written after the event that is prophesied (if any), it may be valuable evidence of the age of this *Maha Parinibbana Sutta*'.

7 That is, those who cross the 'ocean drear' of *tanha,* or craving; avoiding by means of the 'dyke' or causeway of the Noble Path, 'pools' or shallows of lust, ignorance and delusion (comp. *Dhammapada*, 91), while the vain world looks for salvation by means of rites, and ceremonies, and gods – 'these are the wise, the saved indeed!' (RD)

8 The 'Brick Hall' was the public resting-place for travellers, and the name is noteworthy as almost all buildings were then of wood. (RD)

9   That is, 'one who has entered the stream', has embarked on the crossing from the world of suffering to nibbana.

10 For a fuller treatment of this subject, see the *Maha Satipatthana Sutta*, above.

11 The *Tavatimsa-deva* are the gods in the heaven of the Great Thirty-Three, the principal deities of the Vedic Pantheon. (RD)

12 *Arama*: literally, 'pleasure'; hence 'pleasure-ground' or park.

13 The last words, 'but they must be anxious to learn', seem to be an afterthought. It is only those who are thoroughly determined to work out their own salvation, without looking for safety to anyone else, even to the Buddha himself, who will, whilst in the world, enter into and experience nibbana. But, of course, let there be no mistake, merely to reject the vain baubles of the current superstitious beliefs is not enough. There is plenty to learn and to acquire, of which enough discourse is elsewhere. (RD)

14 Shrines of pre-Buddhist worship. They were probably trees and barrows; but the point is uncertain.

15 See *Cakkavatti Sihanada Sutta*, paragraph 28.

16 The words here quoted were spoken by the Buddha, after he had been enjoying the first bliss of nibbana, under the goatherd's nigrodha tree (see below, Chapter 3, paragraph 34).

17 He renounced those tendencies, potentialities, which in the ordinary course of things, would otherwise have led to the putting together of, the building up of, more life (that is, of course, in this birth. Any more life in a future birth he had already renounced when, under the Wisdom Tree, he attained nibbana). (RD)

18 This verse is obscure and possibly corrupt. (RD). Windisch (*Mara and Buddha*) holds that instead of the last line, which in the present Pali text reads: '*abhida kavacam iv'atta-sambhavan'ti*', the Sanskrit version of this incident is to be preferred, both for sense and verse: '*abhinat kosam ivandasambhavah*'. But this, too, is capable of various renderings and *doubles-entendres*; in general terms, the figure used is that of the breaking of an egg (possibly the Indian 'cosmic' egg) and the appearance of new life. (TL)

19 The narrative is now interrupted by the insertion of paragraphs which at first sight seem to be quite out of place. But the connection, or want of connection, between them and the main story is very suggestive as to the way in which the Sutta was put together. The whole chapter is an answer to a possible objection, either from outsiders or from weaker members of the fold, that if the Buddha were really so great why did he die at all. The suggested answer is that he could have lived on if he had so wished; but he did not wish because he had certain kinds of power and insight and self-mastery

which prevented him from doing so. For the purpose of this answer these paragraphs, already in existence among the Suttas current in the Community, and dealing with these powers, are here repeated without any such connecting argument as we should find, under similar circumstances, in a modern (written) book of apologetics. (RD)

20 *Devata* is a 'divinity', a divine power, 'devata' and 'divinity' having a common Indo-European usage, and signifying originally a 'shining one'. For this reason, perhaps, Rhys Davids rendered the word 'devata' by the English 'fairy'. But this does not have quite the same connotation as 'devata' in Indian usage, where it indicates something more in the nature of a local deity.

21 This and the next paragraph are based upon the Buddhist belief as to the long-vexed question between the Indian schools who represented more or less closely the European Idealists and Realists. When cleared of the many repetitions inserted for the benefit of the repeaters or reciters, the fundamental idea seems to be that the great necessity is to get rid of the delusion that what one sees and feels is real and permanent. Nothing is real and permanent but character. (RD)

22 I do not understand the connection of ideas between this paragraph and the idea repeated with such tedious iteration in the preceding paragraph. The two seem to be in marked contrast, if not in absolute contradiction. Perhaps we have here the older tradition; and certainly this paragraph is more in accordance with the general impression of the character, and with the other sayings, of Gotama as handed down in the Pali Pitakas. (RD)

23 Or, the celibate life (*brahmacariya*).

24 For other references to these doctrines, see Index and Glossary.

25 The Buddhas were accustomed, says Buddhaghosa, on looking backwards to turn the whole body round as an elephant does; because the bones in the neck were firmly fixed, more so than those of ordinary men! (RD)

26 He is *parinibbuto*, completely *nibbuto*, or 'cooled', or 'well'. See Ling, *The Buddha*, p. 112 (see Bibliography).

27 *Mahapadesa*: that is, following Buddhaghosa and Rhys Davids, *maha-apadesa*. *Apadesa* means 'principle' or 'statement'.

28 The blocks of '*strings*' of teaching which were committed to memory by the bhikkhus; the collection of these is known as the *Sutta Pitaka*. See Introduction, p. xii.

29 The collection of rules for the Community of bhikkhus, which eventually formed one of the three parts of the Tipitaka, the

threefold canon of scripture, is known as the Vinaya Pitaka. The Sutta Pitaka is another of the three.

30 *Matrika*, 'matrixes', the elementary forms of the doctrines contained in the Dialogues and discourses. These *matika* seem to have formed the basis of what eventually became the third collection (*pitaka*) of texts, known as the Abhidhamma Pitaka.

31 Pali: *sukara maddava*. *Sukara* normally means 'pig', and *maddava* has the sense of 'mild' or 'soft'; thus the two words may be rendered 'tender pork'. Another explanation of the words is that they refer not to *sukara* as 'pork', but to a tuber which grows in Bihar, called *Sukara-kanda*, that is, 'pig-tuber', a sort of truffle. (See Rhys Davids, *Dialogues*, II, 137, n.1.) This explanation seems intended to avoid offence to vegetarian readers or hearers. Rhys Davids's statement that Buddhists 'have been mostly vegetarians, and are increasingly so', is difficult to accept.

32 This is a most unusual way of speaking of the Buddha. In the Suttas believers are represented as addressing him as 'bhante', lord, or sir (the same form as that used by junior members of the Order in addressing their seniors); and as speaking of him by the epithet 'Bhagava' (the Master). Unbelievers address him as Gotama, and speak of him as Samanna Gotama.

33 This stock phrase, constituting the final answer of a hitherto unconverted man at the end of one of those argumentative dialogues by which Gotama overcame opposition or expounded the truth, fits in appropriately after a discussion of exalted themes; here and in some other places it is incongruous and strained. (RD)

34 To understand what is here represented to have happened, one must understand the mode in which the Buddhist wanderers wore their robes. There was no tailoring at all. The set of three robes was simply three lengths of cotton cloth about a yard wide. One piece, folded in half, was strapped round the body. Another piece covered the limbs from the waist to the ankles. It was supported by a girdle and went three or four times round. The third piece was put on over this last, went twice round the legs, and then the rest of it was thrown over the left shoulder, and passed under the right arm across the body. Pukkusa had placed the two lengths of cloth, shawl-wise, over the shoulders of the recipients. When he left them Ananda assisted the Buddha to put them on as Nos. 1 and 3 of a set of robes. (RD)

35 We have here the commencement of the legend which afterwards grew into an account of an actual 'transfiguration' of the Buddha. It is very curious that it should have taken place soon after the Buddha had announced to Ananda his approaching death, and

that in the Buddhist Sutta it should be connected so closely with that event; for a similar remark applies also to the Transfiguration mentioned in the Gospels. (RD)

36 We have here the unusual case of the Buddha being called 'Tathagata', not by himself, but by a third person, the compiler of the Sutta. The paragraph is perhaps moulded by inadvertence on the next one. But see paragraph 10. (RD)

37 A member of the Community for women.

38 'Eye' is of course used figuratively of that by the aid of which spiritual truths can be perceived, corresponding exactly to the similar use in Europe of the word 'Light'. The Master is often called 'He with the Eye', 'He of the Spiritual Eye' (see, for instance, the last verses in this book), and here by a bold figure of speech he is called the Eye itself, which was shortly to vanish away from the world, the means of spiritual insight which was no longer to be available for the common use of all men. But this is, it will be noticed, only the lament of the foolish and ignorant. (RD)

39 *Stupa*: a solid mound or tumulus or barrow, in the midst of which the bones and ashes are to be placed. The dome of St Paul's, as seen from the Thames Embankment, gives a very good idea of one of the later of these Buddhist monumental mounds. (RD)

40 *Pacceka-Buddha*: one who is enlightened, but does not teach others.

41 Arahat.

42 Ananda had entered the Noble Path, but had not yet reached the end of it. He had not attained to nibbana. (RD)

43 That is, you too shall become an arahat, shall attain nibbana in this life.

44 Channa, formerly Gotama's charioteer, before the Enlightenment, had subsequently become a bhikkhu, and in a dispute between the nuns (*bhikkhuni*) and the bhikkhus, he had sided with the nuns. This was considered an action perverse enough to merit the penalty here described. See Malalasekera, *DPPN*, I, 924.

45 On the first four stages of meditation (*jhana*) see the *Samanna-Phala Sutta*, paragraphs 75 ff., and the *Maha Satipatthana Sutta*, paragraph 21.

46 See above, Chapter 3, paragraph 33.

47 We have, in this list, a technical, scholastic, attempt to describe the series of ideas involved in what was considered the highest thought. No one, of course, can have known what actually did occur; and the eight boundary lines between the nine states are purely conjectural. (RD)

48 In these four stanzas we seem to have the way in which the death of the Buddha would be regarded, as the early Buddhists thought, by four representative persons – the exalted God of the theologians; the Jupiter of the multitude (allowing in the case of each of these for the change in character resulting from their conversion to Buddhism); the holy, thoughtful arahat; and the loving, childlike disciple. (RD)

49 The dress of the Mallas consisted probably of mere lengths of muslin or cotton cloth; and a suit of apparel consisted of two or, at the outside, of three of these – one to wrap around the loins, one to throw over the shoulders, and one to use as a turban. To make a canopy on occasions of state they would join such pieces together; to make the canopy into a tent they would simply add walls of the same material; and the only decoration, as simple as it is beautiful, would be wreaths of flowers, or single lotuses, hanging from the roof, or stretched along the sides. (RD)

50 The point of this interesting legend is that the inhabitants of an Indian village of that time would have considered it a desecration or pollution to bring a dead body into or through their village. Authorities differ as to the direction in which it should be taken to avoid this. The old custom was to take it to the east or the west. Later priestly books (*Manu*, for instance, V, 92) say to the north. The Mallas wanted to go to the south. The remedy proposed by the spirits, who are shocked at this impropriety, is more shocking still. (RD)

51 A member of another of the ascetic sects of ancient India which survived until the fourteenth century. Like one type of Jains, the Ajivakas went naked.

Bibliography

Bhandarkar, D. R. *Asoka*, Calcutta, 1955.

Chattopadhaya, Sudhukar, *From Bimbisara to Asoka*, Calcutta, 1977.

Chaudhury, B. N., *Buddhist Centres in Ancient India*, Calcutta, 1969.

Conze, E., *Buddhism: Its Essence and Development*, London, 1951. *Buddhist Thought in India*, London, 1962.

Dasgupta, S. N., *A History of Indian Philosophy*, Vol. I, 1922. Reprinted Delhi, 1975.

Dutt, Sukumar, *The Buddha and Five After Centuries*, London, 1957. *Buddhist Monks and Monasteries of India*, London, 1962.

Geiger, W., *Pali Literature and Language*, Calcutta, 1956.

Ghoshal, U. N., *A History of Indian Political Ideas*, Oxford, 1959.

Jayatilleke, K. N., *Early Buddhist Theory of Knowledge*, London, 1963. *The Message of the Buddha*, London, 1975.

Jones, John Garrett, *Tales and Teachings of the Buddha*, London, 1979.

Kalupahana, David, J., *Buddhist Philosophy: A Historical Analysis*, Honolulu, 1976.

Ling, Trevor, *The Buddha*, 1973. *Buddhism and the Mythology of Evil*, London, 1962.

Mahavamsa, The, *The Great Chronicle of Ceylon*, trs. W. Geiger, London, 1964.

Malalasekera, G. P., *Dictionary of Pali Proper Names*: 2 vols., London, 1960.

Marasinghe, M. M. J., *Gods in Early Buddhism*, Vidyalankara, 1974.

Murti, T. R. V., *The Central Philosophy of Buddhism*, London, 1955.

Nyanatiloka, Mahathera, *Buddhist Dictionary* (2nd Revised Edn), Colombo, 1956.

Pande, G. C., *Studies in the Origins of Buddhism*, (2nd Revised Edn), Delhi, 1974.

Pandey, M. S., *Historical Geography and Topography of Bihar*, Delhi, 1963.

Rhys Davids, T. W. and C. A. F., *Dialogues of the Buddha*, Part I, 1899, repr. 1956; Part II, 1910, repr. 1966; Part III, 1921, repr. 1965.

Rhys Davids, T. W., *Buddhist India* (8th Edn) Calcutta, 1959.

Saddhatissa, H., *Buddhist Ethics*, London, 1970.

Silva, Padmasiri de, *An Introduction to Buddhist Psychology*, London, 1979.

Tachibana, S., *The Ethics of Buddhism*, Oxford, 1926; repr. Colombo, 1961, (with a new Preface, by O. H. de A. Wijesekera) and London, 1975 (with a Supplementary Bibliography).

Warder, A. K., *Indian Buddhism*, Delhi, 1970.

Weeraratne, W. H., *Individual and Society in Buddhism*, Colombo, 1977.

Index and Glossary